Veterans Stadium

OTHER BOOKS BY RICH WESTCOTT

The Phillies Encyclopedia
(with Frank Bilovsky)

Diamond Greats

The New Phillies Encyclopedia
(with Frank Bilovsky)

Phillies '93: An Incredible Season

Philadelphia's Old Ballparks

Mike Schmidt

Masters of the Diamond

No-Hitters: The 225 Games, 1893–1999
(with Allen Lewis)

Splendor on the Diamond

Great Home Runs of the 20th Century

A Century of Philadelphia Sports

Winningest Pitchers: Baseball's 300-Game Winners

Tales from the Phillies Dugout

Native Sons: Philadelphia Baseball Players Who Made the Major Leagues

The Phillies Encyclopedia, 3rd Edition
(with Frank Bilovsky)

Mickey Vernon—The Gentleman First Baseman

Veterans Stadium

FIELD OF MEMORIES

Rich Westcott
Foreword by Darren Daulton

Temple University Press
Philadelphia

To all the people who worked and played at Veterans Stadium during its 33 years and who helped to make it such a memorable place.

Rich Westcott is a baseball writer, a historian, and a veteran of more than 40 years as a working journalist. He is a leading authority on the Phillies, and for 14 years was editor and publisher of *Phillies Report*. He is the author of 17 books, including *Philadelphia's Old Ballparks* and (with Frank Bilovsky) *The Phillies Encyclopedia, 3rd Edition*.

Temple University Press
1601 North Broad Street
Philadelphia PA 19122
www.temple.edu/tempress

Copyright © 2005 by Rich Westcott
All rights reserved
Published 2005
Printed in the United States of America
Text design by Christine Cantera

⊗ The paper used in this publication meets the requirements of the American National Standard for Information Sciences—Permanence of Paper for Printed Library Materials, ANSI Z39.48-1992

Library of Congress Cataloging-in-Publication Data

Westcott, Rich.
　　Veterans Stadium : Field of Memories / Rich Westcott.
　　　　p.　cm.
　　Includes index.
　　　　ISBN 1-59213-428-9 (cloth : alk. paper)
　　　　1. Veterans Stadium (Philadelphia, Pa.)—History.　　2. Philadelphia Phillies
　　(Baseball team)—History.　　3. Philadelphia Eagles (Football team)—History.　　I. Title.

　　GV416.P477W47 2005
　　796′.06′80974811—dc22　　　　　　　　　　　　　　　　　　　2005043940

2 4 6 8 9 7 5 3 1

Contents

Foreword

Have you ever been sitting alone reflecting back in life on some of the most memorable moments that are implanted in your soul forever?

Almost always, some of the first recollections are childhood memories. Realizing that I haven't actually grown up yet, some of the most memorable for me were the 14 years of fulfilling a childhood dream at a place called Veterans Stadium.

I recall savoring my first cup of big league coffee back in 1983 with legends such as Mike Schmidt, Steve Carlton, Tony Perez, Joe Morgan, Gary Maddox, and yes, Peter Edward, whose last name is still missing from the archives in Cooperstown.

After 10 years of cultivating, the coffee turned into champagne in 1993. Diehards refuse to forget the long-haired gunslingers led by Jim Fregosi and his band of horse thieves. Yes, Uncle Bill had pulled off one of the all-time capers in assembling a cast of characters that would turn America's pastime into the most watched "reality show" on Earth.

Co-worker and long-time friend Rich Westcott will touch your heart with stories of the Vet from its inception in 1971 to its implosion in 2004. You will have a bird's-eye view from some of the Eagles superstars of what it was like to play on the artificial surface in the dead of a Philadelphia winter as well as what it was like for the "Boys of Summer" to endure 165-degree temperatures in July.

Imagine coming home from a long road trip at 3:30 A.M. and hearing the rats fighting the cats in the dark doldrums below your favorite seat. I honestly believe that over the years the rats grew so big that we swore they decided to share the real estate and started breeding with each other.

I will always remember the curtain calls of various stars who were reluctant to step out into the fickle fog of the Philly faithful, knowing you were an error away from the ever-compromising boobirds that nested in the same seats.

From The Great Wallenda, Kiteman, National League Playoffs, and World Series to Eagles and Army-Navy games to some of your favorite concerts, Rich will pull up "blasts from the past" that will tickle your funny bone as well as draw a memorable tear from the pit that resided right across from the "Broad Street Bullies."

I was born and raised in the land of Oz just south of the border from one of our all-time greats, Whitey Ashburn. He always reminded me that there's no place like home field advantage.

I want to personally thank you, the fans, for sharing with me the experience of Grit, Guts, and Glory—South Philly style. Foremost, I would like to thank Rich for allowing me to write the Foreword to this wonderful read.

So, sit back, put the remote down, pull the cooler over, loosen up your blue collar, and get ready to enjoy 33 years of a place the boys in red and white pinstripes affectionately referred to as "If They Only Knew."

Darren Daulton

Acknowledgments

No book of this kind could possibly be written without the help and cooperation of many people. Accordingly, I wish to express my appreciation to all of those who have taken part in this rather large undertaking. Foremost in that group are the more than 125 people who answered my questions and provided commentary on their experiences and feelings about Veterans Stadium. Without them, this book would never have come to fruition. I also extend a very special thanks to Larry Shenk of the Phillies and Jimmy Gallagher of the Eagles for their limitless help. Thank you Mike Di Muzio; Tina Urban and Art Cassidy of the Phillies; Joel Ralph, the city's director of operations at the Vet; Ray Didinger of NFL Films; Jack Klotz of the NFL Players Alumni Association; the late John McAdams, PA announcer extraordinaire; Bob Moore of the Kansas City Chiefs; Dave Smith of Retrosheet; Al Shrier of Temple University; and Scott Strasemeier of the U.S. Naval Academy. And finally, I want to thank my friend Darren Daulton, whom I have known since he first came to the Phillies in 1983, for his insightful foreword. Thank you one and all.

Photo Credit

The following individuals and organizations generously gave permission to reproduce photographs in this book:

Philadelphia Phillies, 1, 9, 12, 17, 21, 22, 24, 27, 37, 52, 53, 71, 85, 87, 95, 99, 103 (left), 106, 111, 117, 139 (right), 141, 152 (left), 155, 158, 165, 166, 172, 173, 179

Temple University Urban Archives, 5, 11, 31, 55, 57, 58, 74, 135, 147, 188, 189

Alan Kravetz, 46 (right), 63, 102, 103 (right), 113, 139 (left), 145, 153, 161, 163

Edwin J. Mahan, 119, 123, 124, 125, 127, 129, 130, 133

Rosie Rahn, 43, 193

Ralph Bernstein, 171

Merrill Reese, 175

Joel Ralph, 32

Paul Roedig (courtesy of the Phillies), 35, 41, 46 (left), 61, 72, 76, 88, 90, 93, 94, 96, 97, 101, 109, 152 (right)

Rich Westcott, iii, 13, 15, 19, 115 (right), 194, 196, 201, 207

San Francisco Giants, 115 (left)

Temple Sports Media Relations, 185

U.S. Naval Academy, 181

Introduction

It was 4:32 A.M. on March 21, 2004, when I arrived at Veterans Stadium for the last time. As I approached the once-proud structure, it seemed almost human as it stood there in dark, eerie silence. And I couldn't help but think how sad and lonely it looked.

A ghastly pall seemed to cover the old ballpark. Its insides gutted by a demolition crew's scalpel, it waited forlornly on its deathbed as the final hours of its life ticked away. Soon, its old, tired body would be snuffed out in a 62-second implosion.

For me and for many others, it was kind of like going to the funeral of an old friend. And I felt a strong sense of sadness. I had spent thousands of hours in the old stadium's company. I had been with it in the best of times . . . and in the worst of times. I knew it intimately.

I envisioned what an obituary might say: "Veterans Stadium, 33, home of some of the most memorable moments in Philadelphia sports history, died suddenly March 21 at home in South Philadelphia. Cause of death was obsolescence."

The Vet, as everybody called it, had once been considered a state-of-the art facility. One of the last of a group of similarly designed multi-purpose stadiums, it was born in an era when such venues were both fashionable and functional. They could be used for a variety of different sports as well as for all kinds of nonsporting events. And they could accommodate huge crowds.

Indeed, the Vet had been the site of countless great moments. The greatest, of course, was the night in 1980 when the Phillies won the World Series, clinching victory over the Kansas City Royals in the sixth game when Tug McGraw struck out Willie Wilson for the final out.

The Phillies also clinched the 1983 and the 1993 National League pennants at the Vet.

Mike Schmidt hit 286 of his 548 home runs there. Steve Carlton won his 15th straight game and recorded his 3,000th strikeout there. Rick Wise retired 32 straight batters in a game there. Pete Rose got his National League record 3,631st hit there. Terry Mulholland and Kevin Millwood pitched no-hitters there. Jim Thome won the admiration of fans with his down-to-earth manner and his volcanic home runs there.

Two All-Star Games were played at the Vet. The Phillies won a game, 26–7, over the New York Mets. They lost two straight playoff games to the Los Angeles Dodgers, one on a controversial error and one in pouring rain. They bowed to the Toronto Blue Jays in the 1993 World Series, 15–14, one night, then came back to win the next night, 2–0.

Greg Luzinski hit monster home runs. Gregg Jefferies hit for the cycle. Bobby Abreu hit for high average every year. And guys such as Darren Daulton, Garry Maddox, Larry Bowa, Juan Samuel, Lenny Dykstra, Scott Rolen, Gary Matthews, Manny Trillo, John Kruk, Dave Cash, Bob Boone, Von Hayes, Jimmy Rollins, Jim Eisenreich, Glenn Wilson, Rico Brogna, Mickey Morandini, and Mike Lieberthal had sparkling seasons at the Vet, as did pitchers Jim Lonborg, Dick Ruthven, Larry Christenson, Steve Bedrosian, Randy Wolf, John Denny, Al Holland, and Curt Schilling.

The Eagles also had some memorable times. They won the game at the Vet that sent them to the Super Bowl, beating the hated Dallas Cowboys, 20–7, in one of the most celebrated football games ever played in Philadelphia. Who can forget Wilbert Montgomery's 42 yard touchdown in the early minutes of that game?

The Eagles also won two other NFC division titles at the Vet. Ron Jaworski connected with Mike Quick on a 99 yard touchdown pass. Al Nelson raced 101 yards for a touchdown with a missed field goal. Joe Lavender ran back a fumble for a 96 yard TD. Tom Dempsey kicked a 54 yard field goal. Donovan McNabb completed 32 passes in one game. All occurred at the Vet.

Other outstanding Eagles players such as Bill Bergey, Duce Staley, Harold Carmichael, Randall Cunningham, Stan Walters, Randy Logan, Reggie White, Brian Dawkins, Jerry Sizemore, Charley Young, Hugh Douglas, Bill Bradley, Charley Johnson, David Akers, and Troy Vincent played at the Vet.

Army-Navy games, Temple football, and the Stars, Atoms, Fury, and A's all were indelible parts of the Vet's history. So were Bill Giles, the Phillie Phanatic, Karl Wallenda, Dan Baker, Paul Richardson, Harry Kalas, Richie Ashburn, Merrill Reese, Larry Shenk, Jimmy Gallagher, and countless others whose names if listed here would fill the rest of this book. And this is not to overlook the unforgettable contributions of the artificial turf, rowdy 700 level fans, the Zamboni, cats, rats (real or imagined), stuck elevators, overpriced food, sky boxes, Eagles cheerleaders, leaky roofs, cadets, midshipmen, tailgate parties, police dogs and horses, and all the other elements—both good and bad—that were very much parts of the Vet.

Was the Vet unfairly maligned, especially over the last decade? Were the ugly slurs so frequently hurled its way in its later years deserved? Of course, the place had flaws. What doesn't? But the good times outweighed the bad; the good memories trumped the nightmares. The Vet may have had some problems, but it was like a second home for many of us. And at least some of us treated it accordingly.

A few years back, I wrote a book called *Philadelphia's Old Ballparks*. The main subjects of that book were Baker Bowl and Shibe Park/Connie Mack Stadium. Both were particularly appealing ballparks, the former because it was so eccentric, so unusual, in a way so strange, the latter because it was the place where I watched my first game as a kid, covered my first game as an adult, and saw scores of games in between.

My grandfather, who many, many years ago regaled me with stories about games and players he watched at Baker Bowl, and my father, who regarded Shibe Park as though it was some kind of a shrine, would not approve of this view. But at the risk of disturbing their heavenly souls, I must state that as far as I'm concerned, neither ballpark rated nearly as high as the Vet. For me, the Vet was a true field of dreams, a place where I spent much of my professional life, a stadium that would give me a rush virtually every time it came into view as I approached it for a game.

Now, two stadiums have taken the place of the Vet. One houses the Phillies. One houses the Eagles. Both are magnificent stadiums. Both satisfy the needs of teams that have moved into another era in the way games are played and watched. Both will have significant roles in the future years of Philadelphia sports.

Things change. Time marches on. History is pushed aside. The Vet outlived its usefulness. But for just a little longer, let us linger in the past, while we take a close look at the people, the teams, and the games that made the stadium the memorable place that it was. Let us record the comments of well over 100 people who have graciously shared their views and experiences. And let us explore the special parts of the stadium that used to be the centerpiece of Philadelphia sports.

This, then, is the story of that stadium. Veterans Stadium. The Vet. May it rest in peace.

THE LONG TRIP TO COMPLETION

*It took nearly 20 years
to get a new stadium*

When Veterans Stadium opened in 1971, it was the first major outdoor sports facility built in Philadelphia in 45 years. Obviously, such a place was long overdue.

There hadn't been a large stadium built in Philadelphia since the city-owned Sesquicentennial Stadium—later to be renamed Municipal, then Philadelphia, and finally John F. Kennedy Stadium—opened in 1926. Before that, Franklin Field, first constructed in 1895, had been rebuilt in 1903 and

Above: An architectural rendering of Veterans Stadium.

again in 1922. Shibe Park, which later became Connie Mack Stadium, housed its first game in 1909.

Baker Bowl, which was originally called Philadelphia Base Ball Park and Huntingdon Park, first opened in 1887, was partially rebuilt in 1894, and lasted as a major outdoor stadium until 1938. Many other outdoor facilities, most notably Recreation Park, Jefferson Park, Columbia Park, and Penmar Park, had briefly dotted the Philadelphia landscape over the years. But they were all long gone, and the stadiums that did remain had outlived their usefulness.

By the 1960s, the Phillies were stuck at Connie Mack Stadium, which had become not only obsolete but was surrounded by an increasingly undesirable neighborhood. Attendance had declined drastically. The Eagles played at Franklin Field, which, despite huge crowds, also had serious flaws, not the least of which was its antiquated interior, its minimal parking, and the absence of offices for the team. And JFK Stadium, home of the Army-Navy game and assorted other sporting events, had been reduced to being an ancient relic that was virtually dysfunctional as a sports venue.

Clearly, Philadelphia needed a new, first-class outdoor stadium, preferably one that could house the Phillies, the Eagles, the Army-Navy game, and the many other sporting and nonsporting events that would keep it in service throughout much of the year. The time had come to take action.

The idea of building a new stadium in Philadelphia did not arrive suddenly. In the early 1950s, when both the Phillies and Eagles were playing with an ample degree of discontent at Connie Mack Stadium, the vision of a new stadium had crossed the minds of owners of both teams as well as some of the city's political leaders.

Both Phillies president Bob Carpenter and Eagles president Frank McNamee went before the City Planning Commission and pleaded for a new stadium, urging that it be built as soon as possible. If you build it, they will come, Carpenter and McNamee insisted in a far-advanced precursor of a movie that would appear in the future called *Field of Dreams*.

In 1954, Fairmount Park commissioner and millionaire builder John B. Kelly Sr. proposed a new $10-million stadium at 33rd and Oxford Streets, just a few blocks from the site of Columbia Park, first home of the Philadelphia Athletics. But despite the support of Mayor Joseph Clark, Carpenter, and others, the idea was vetoed by the City Planning Commission. Two years later, new Philadelphia mayor Richardson Dilworth, a former attorney for Connie Mack and a man keenly interested in having a new ballpark built, appointed a stadium commission chaired by Kelly. With an appropriation of $35,000, it was asked to study and recommend a site for a new stadium. The commission came up with a handful of possible sites, none of them conclusive.

Two additional study commissions were appointed in the ensuing years. Again, no site was selected, although a leading candidate emerged. It was a site located at 30th and Arch Streets, where the plan would be to build a stadium on stilts that would hover over the tracks of and be built in concert with the Pennsylvania Railroad, with a big contribution from federal urban renewal funds. The idea received little support. Especially strong opposition came from the Philadelphia Chamber of Commerce, which, led by Executive Vice President W. Thatcher Longstreth, argued that a stadium at that location would cause excessive noise and congestion and would attract "unsavory characters."

By 1958, the Eagles had soured sufficiently on Connie Mack Stadium and they bolted to Franklin Field. Soon after, a plan was floated to spruce up Connie Mack Stadium by building an $8 million, multilevel parking garage next door. That deal fell through, as did a plan to build a 45,000-seat stadium near the city-owned Torresdale water filtration plant along the Delaware River in northeast Philadelphia. "If we don't get a stadium soon," Dilworth said, "we'll lose our major league sports and people will think Philadelphia is a creepy city."

By the early 1960s, more than 20 other sites, including ones at 41st Street and Parkside Avenue, Eighth and Race Streets, 11th and Vine Streets, 30th and Walnut Streets, and one on Roosevelt Boulevard, had been proposed. The most appealing site was located at the corner of Broad Street and Pattison Avenue in South Philadelphia. The Chamber of Commerce endorsed a study conducted by a blue-ribbon committee headed by John Wanamaker chairman Richard Bond, that concluded that the site was the best of five possible locations. Although he originally supported the 30th and Arch Streets site, so did Mayor James H. J. Tate, the former City Council president who had replaced Dilworth after he had resigned to run for governor of Pennsylvania.

With calculations that the new stadium would cost $22.7 million, Tate recommended to City Council that it approve a bond issue in that amount and place it before the voters of Philadelphia on the November 6, 1962, ballot. "At that point," Tate said many years later, "I ran into two problems: politics and community opposition, which was also heavily tinged with politics."

Residents of the area near the Broad and Pattison site were vehemently opposed to a stadium in their neighborhood. And they let their political leaders know it in no uncertain terms. City Council members, Democrats and Republicans alike, bickered with the mayor and each other and rejected the loan question. It never went before the voters.

His proposal having been defeated, Tate tried to renew interest in the site at 30th and Arch. Again, heavy opposition materialized. The most outspoken opponent was a powerful local businessman and civic leader named Harry Batten, who was co-chairman of the highly influential Greater Philadelphia Movement. Batten, who had conceived the plan for the nearby University City Science Center, felt that a stadium would be an undesirable neighbor. He not only personally opposed the idea, he also convinced local civic groups to disapprove the plan as well.

Once more, the proposal to build a stadium on stilts was rejected. Shortly afterward, Pennsylvania Railroad announced that it was withdrawing its participation in the project. Once and for all, the plan was dead.

Meanwhile, the frustration mounted. One especially frustrated person was Carpenter. He hired Alexander Ewing & Associates, a local architectural firm, to search for a suitable site for a baseball park and to produce a design for it.

Alexander Ewing was a major figure in that effort. "Bob Carpenter was anxious to build his own ballpark, and when he couldn't persuade the mayor to go along with that, he hired us," Ewing recalled. "We spent several years working with the Phillies."

In 1964, with no action on the part of the city in sight, Carpenter stunned local leaders by purchasing nearly 100 acres of land in Cherry Hill, New Jersey, and threatening to build his own ballpark and move the Phillies there.

"It was really just a ploy to put pressure on the city to get its act together and build a new stadium," remembered Ruly Carpenter, who later succeeded his father as president of the Phillies. "I don't think he would've moved to New Jersey."

Nevertheless, Bob Carpenter was determined to push ahead. He asked Ewing to design a new ballpark. Ewing plunged heavily into the assignment.

"We looked at sites all over the country," Ewing said. "We looked at the Astrodome, we went to Candlestick Park, Chavez Ravine, Shea Stadium. In Los Angeles, we met with Walter O'Malley, owner of the Dodgers, and he strongly advised the Phillies to build their own park. After we came back, we developed a design that could best be described as Connie Mack Stadium without the columns."

Ewing visited a number of City Council members, but he found that there was little interest in a baseball park. "They and the mayor wanted a multi-purpose stadium," he said.

The Carpenters then threw their support behind the site at Broad and Pattison. A survey done by the team showed that a large number of its fans came from New Jersey, Delaware, and Delaware County. "It was accessible to most people, and it had plenty of good parking," Ruly Carpenter said. "It was a very good location for us."

Suddenly, without notice, City Council president Paul D'Ortona jumped into the fray. He said that he, too, favored the South Philadelphia location. Other Democrats dropped their opposition to the plan, as did Republican leaders. And civic leaders, such as Batten and Longstreth, plus the City Planning Commission also endorsed the site.

One body that did not endorse it, however, was a group with the wordy name of the Combined Citizens Committee Opposing the Proposed Stadium Site in South Philadelphia (CCCOPSSSP). It was an extension of the civic group that had fought against a ballpark in its neighborhood two years earlier, but it had vastly increased in numbers.

South Philadelphia residents protested the proposed new stadium.

While the CCCOPSSSP mounted its campaign, City Council approved the South Philadelphia location and voted to place a bond issue—now increased to $25 million—on the November 3, 1964, ballot. Both the Phillies and Eagles were thrilled. "Council did the right thing, and we will be very happy to play in the new stadium," said Eagles owner Jerry Wolman.

The citizens group filed suit to block the question from being placed on the ballot, but it was dismissed by Common Pleas Court Judge Edmund B. Spaeth Jr. The following day, Philadelphia voters approved the loan by a count of 233,247 to 192,424. "We confidently look forward to the stadium opening in 1967," Tate said gleefully.

The stadium, with parking for 12,000 cars, would be built on a 67-acre tract that extended from the northeast corner of Broad Street and Pattison Avenue to 10th Street one way and Packer Avenue the other way. Thirty-eight acres were already owned by the city, which had bought the land in 1957. Another 19 acres on the corner of Broad and Pattison held a drive-in movie theater. The Delaware River Port Authority owned 3.2 acres. The rest of the site consisted of vacant lots that were owned privately by a number of individuals. A man with a pet goat lived in a shack on part of the property.

The city got the ball rolling by awarding contracts to design the stadium to two local architectural companies, Stonorov & Haws and George M. Ewing Company. But major problems soon began to appear.

Lot owners wanted considerably more for their properties than the city, which would condemn them, was willing to pay. A new zoning variance that would allow for the existence of the stadium was met with strong opposition from the neighbors. And fees paid to the architects and engineers and for studies were coming in higher than expected (it cost $73,000 to study the feasibility of putting a dome on the stadium).

The city was also courting the American Football League (AFL) with the hope of bringing a new team to Philadelphia and housing it at the new stadium. AFL expansion committee chairman Lamar Hunt said it was a done deal if the city assured the new team that it would play in the new stadium. "The AFL has definitely decided they want to come into Philadelphia," Hunt told the media.

That, of course, did not sit well with the Eagles. Wolman, who in 1961 had purchased Connie Mack Stadium from the Phillies, ostensibly as an investment, claimed that his team had been granted an exclusive right to play in the new stadium after it was built. He said that if the city failed to live up to that commitment, he would file suit against the city and would play either at Franklin Field or build a new stadium himself. "As long as I own the Eagles, they will not leave Philadelphia unless I'm forced to," Wolman said.

Eventually, a showdown was averted when a blue-ribbon city committee worked out a compromise with the Eagles. Among a variety of terms, the team was given exclusive rights to the stadium for 10 years with renewable clauses for two more 10-year terms. A minimum rent of $150,000 or 10 percent of the gross receipts—whichever was higher—would be paid.

The Phillies, meanwhile, received a 30-year contract that guaranteed the city a minimum rental payment of $160,000 per year. The team would pay an extra 10 percent if its revenue exceeded $1.6 million. Like its deal with the Eagles, the city also got the parking revenue, 50 percent of the concessions, an amusement tax, and percentages of the restaurant, advertising, and seat prices.

On December 3, 1965, the architects unveiled preliminary plans for the stadium at a gala ceremony in the mayor's reception room. Several hundred civic leaders and city officials attended. Not a Phillies or an Eagles representative was in sight, both teams having had practically no participation in the design and sharing a strong distaste for the one that existed.

The plan called for a stadium that would seat 60,750 for baseball and 72,579 for football. But Carpenter said the design favored football, and he wanted just 50,000 seats. Wolman wanted at least 65,000 seats while claiming dissatisfaction on a variety of other counts.

To break the deadlock, still another new commission was appointed to find what was being called an "executive architect" who would redesign and oversee the entire operation. Although he had no previous experience in building stadiums, internationally prominent architect Hugh Stubbins of Cambridge, Massachusetts, got the job for an initial fee of $235,000.

This time, the Phillies and Eagles had more input in the design, while the city had less. And not only were relations between all parties more compatible, but the ultimate design was more satisfactory to both teams.

"Everyone had a significant input in the design," said Ewing, who had been retained by the Phillies as a special consultant. "Upwards of 100 people were involved. The whole process went rather smoothly."

Nearly 1,000 drawings were used before a final design was selected. Ultimately, chief architect Ronald A. Knabb Jr. came up with a design in which the stadium was in the shape of an octorad, "octo" being Latin for the number eight and "rad" a shortened version of the word radius. Although it appeared to be circular, the stadium would actually have eight sides.

Having selected a design, the next step was to launch the actual building process, which was expected to take 22 months to reach completion, with the stadium opening in the spring of 1967. Bids to excavate and build the foundation were solicited. After a public hearing before the municipal development and zoning committee, City Council passed a new ordinance that would change the zoning of the Broad and Pattison area from residential–commercial to a "sports stadium district." And ultimately, the land was fully acquired at a final price of $4.65 million.

Tests at the site, originally begun in late 1964 and performed by the structural engineering company of McCormick, Taylor & Associates, were resumed to determine the best way to build the foundation. Core borings to establish the composition of the land into which columns would be sunk were made by drilling in some locations on the site down to about 110 feet.

"We drove pipes into the ground," recalled Jack Meyer, an engineer working on the job for McCormick, Taylor. "After going through weeds and top soil, the pipes went through old tires, mattresses, and other junk because the site had been a dump. The next level was clay. We went through several different kinds of clay, some which were mixed with rocks and small boulders. Finally, we got down to white sand. It was the whitest sand I've ever seen and as fine as flour." Meyer speculated that the sand remained from a period millions of years ago when it may have been the beach for the ocean that covered much of New Jersey and Pennsylvania.

As the tests progressed, skirmishes continued to erupt. The $25 million cost of the stadium came under repeated criticism. City Controller Alexander Hemphill accused Tate of being "deceitful" for not revealing to the public what he claimed would be a much higher cost to complete the stadium. By September 1966, the city had already spent nearly $5 million without one shovel having been stuck in the ground.

The Phillies wanted seats that would slant toward the baseball diamond; the Eagles wanted no slant in the stands. The debate over whether or not to build a domed stadium continued. A new developer entered the picture with a quickly rejected plan to build a stadium as part of a $100 million riverfront complex near the Ben Franklin Bridge. And it was revealed that architectural fees could reach $2.5 million, including $595,000 to Stubbins, even if the stadium was not built.

Worst of all, Stubbins said that the cost of building the stadium had now risen to $40 million, or $61 million if it had a dome. That news prompted *Evening Bulletin* columnist Hugh Brown to write that the "long-drawn out stadium drama had, in the scheme of civic progress, taken up too much of the stage already," and to question why a far lesser amount couldn't be spent to modernize Connie Mack Stadium and Franklin Field.

With all the hassle, the Eagles were, indeed, interested in remaining at Franklin Field, according to Pete Retzlaff, the team's one-time all-pro tight end who had become its general manager. "We would've been very happy to stay there," Retzlaff said. "Our relationship with Penn was very good, and there was not a better stadium around from which to view a game."

And if the Eagles couldn't stay there, Retzlaff said he proposed having the city renovate JFK Stadium, turning it into a true football stadium while employing a new ballpark strictly for baseball. "But the city said no way it would build a single-occupancy stadium," Retzlaff recalled.

With the projected increased cost in the Broad and Pattison stadium, Tate had no choice but to go back to the voters of Philadelphia and to ask for a new bond issue. After some political maneuvering behind the scenes—which included D'Ortona persuading Stubbins to reduced his estimated cost to $38 million—a $13 million issue was placed on the ballot in the May 16, 1967, spring primary. With a voter turnout of only about 40 percent, the loan was barely approved, 139,733 to 135,022.

Finally, on October 2, 1967—some six months after the stadium was originally supposed to open—a groundbreaking ceremony took place at Broad and Pattison. With Tate, D'Ortona, Carpenter, Ed Snyder representing the Eagles, Bond, and others wielding shovels, the stadium that was first considered 14 years earlier was at long last on its way.

"Today," said Tate, "we, the city officials, are demonstrating that we are prudently spending the $38 million which has been allocated by the voters of Philadelphia to afford them the prestige of having the greatest sports stadium in the nation."

Ironically, right across Pattison Avenue stood the new, privately owned indoor arena called The Spectrum that was built to house the NBA 76ers and the NHL Flyers. Construction on the 14,700-seat arena had started in early 1966. The Flyers played the first regular-season game there October 19, 1967.

It took until mid 1968 before bids that had gone out much earlier for various jobs on the new stadium were finally unsealed. By then, the city had

Dignitaries wielded shovels at the groundbreaking ceremony on October 2, 1967. The diggers included (from left) city council president Paul D'Ortona, mayor James Tate, city managing director Fred Carletto, Ed Snyder of the Eagles, Phillies president Bob Carpenter, and businessman Richard Bond.

spent $252,000 for site excavation and $2.3 million for piling and foundation work, which, along with the money paid for land acquisition, reduced the cost that could be paid for the actual stadium to $28.3 million.

McCloskey & Company was the low bidder for general construction at $19,390,000. Winning bids for other jobs included $1,873,000 for heating, ventilation, and air conditioning, $1,403,799 for seating, and $217,994 for escalators and elevators.

As construction got underway, a new controversy surfaced. What would the stadium be called? Naming the new facility became perhaps the most acrimonious battle of all the stadium's fights.

Nearly everybody had an idea. Independence Stadium, Philadium, William Penn Stadium, Eisenhower Stadium, and Apollo Stadium were among the most popular suggestions. So was Philadelphia Stadium, a name endorsed by some major local businesses. Anti-war activists proposed names such as Peace Park, Love Park, and Dream Park. And in a poll conducted by the *Evening Bulletin*, which attracted some 500 suggestions from 1,650 readers, all of the above names were supported, as were The Pill, Boo-Bird Park, Billy's Penn, Philly's Folly, Quaker Bowl, Raspberry Park, Keystone Stadium, Ye Old Park, Pretzel Stadium, Shocker Field, Bell-Mack Park, and The Playpenn.

The people making the loudest noise about a name were war veterans, especially those affiliated with the American Legion. They wanted the park to be called War Veterans Memorial Stadium as a tribute to the millions of Americans who had served in the military during wars. Except for their proponents, that name was about as popular as the idea of a ballpark beneath the Delaware River.

Naturally, anti-war activists, then embroiled in the social polarization produced by the war in Vietnam, opposed the name. Business leaders did, too, as did most Republican members of City Council.

Republican councilman Longstreth proclaimed: "If we end up with a Veterans Stadium, we will be the laughingstock of the United States."

"It (the name) will do nothing to improve the image of the city," said Councilman John B. Kelly Jr., a Democrat who called it "dull, sedate, and aged. Too many people already think of Philadelphia as a cemetery with lights. The people who will pay for the stadium over the next 30 years don't want that name. It's an unnecessary flashpoint in volatile times."

Twice in 1969, City Council members introduced bills to name the stadium. One bill proposed the name War Veterans Memorial Stadium. City Council Republicans endorsed Gen. Dwight D. Eisenhower Stadium. Both times, the names were referred to committee.

For both teams, it didn't matter what the stadium was called, as long as they could soon play in it. "We don't really care what they call it," said Phillies treasurer George Harrison. "My mind's a blank," added Eagles new owner Leonard Tose. "I haven't been consulted and I haven't thought about it."

Most Democrats on City Council, reacting to heavy pressure put on them by representatives of some 400,000 local war veterans, supported the former name. Finally, after much debate, Council president D'Ortona, under heavy pressure from veterans' groups and seeing an opportunity to make some political hay, proposed a compromise name: Philadelphia Veterans Stadium. Despite accusations that D'Ortona was acting tyrannically, the issue was put to a vote on March 12, 1970.

More than 500 people packed into Council chambers, protesters from both sides, some wearing caps of veterans organizations, others carrying signs with slogans such as "Vets Need Beds in Hospitals, Not Seats in a Stadium."

Democratic councilman George X. Schwartz said he couldn't understand why there were so many objections to the word "veteran." "Why is it so terrible to be patriotic today?" he asked. Councilman David Silver, also a Democrat, called the turnout a "fiasco." Even Republican city controller Tom Gola had his say, making the then-audacious suggestion that the city sell

City Council chambers were packed with veterans groups lobbying for a stadium name that would pay tribute to their members.

the naming rights to the stadium. Claiming that such a tactic might produce revenue of up to $30 million, Gola was virtually laughed off the floor.

When the issue was put to a vote, D'Ortona's proposal carried, 11 to 5. Philadelphia Veterans Stadium was the name of the new facility in South Philadelphia.

But the name that had no stadium was still a long way from having a place to go. And by the time it got a name, the stadium had already been covered with controversy, and more of it was on the way.

After a special investigation, both McCloskey & Company and McCormick, Taylor as well as two individuals had been indicted in 1969 by an October grand jury on charges of false pretense and conspiracy in connection with construction of the new stadium. District Attorney Arlen Specter, using just one witness, based his case on charges that steel that was lighter than specified and other cheaper materials were used in the roof and flooring. The charges were dismissed later by the State Superior Court.

There were other problems. Charged and convicted of trying to solicit a $10,000 bribe from the company that was supplying seats, the city's stadium coordinator Harry Blatstein resigned his $20,000 per year job after serving for two years. Heavy rains caused some 10 feet of water to cover the field before it could be drained. A major snowstorm delayed work for two weeks. Several fires occurred.

To make matters worse, there were two labor strikes, one lasting six weeks. Theft and vandalism were rampant. Graffiti was scrawled throughout the stadium and had to be removed. Worker's tools and equipment and fixtures such as copper tubing were often stolen. So critical was the problem

With the Navy Yard, JFK Stadium, and the Spectrum looming in the background, Veterans Stadium began to take shape.

that fences had to be erected around the site and junk cars used to block gates in an attempt to tighten security.

Financial problems also continued to plague the stadium. It was learned that the city would have to pay at least $500,000 per year to maintain the stadium. A special committee appointed by Tate revealed that architectural fees had again risen. And in several cases, unexpected modifications had to be made. These included removing and rebuilding concrete steps, changing the location of six misplaced fire hydrants, lowering manholes to avoid conflict with drainage lines, and moving construction trailers and temporary offices to a new location.

At least, there was no repeat of the gaff in San Diego. There, during the construction of Jack Murphy Stadium, a builder had been told that there were nine men on a baseball team, and hence had installed nine lockers in the clubhouse.

Of course, all of the alterations at the Philadelphia stadium drove the cost of construction up higher. From $38 million, the estimate went to $43 million. Then it rocketed to $48 million. "Nothing surprises me anymore," said Gola as he claimed that with interest and the continued escalation in costs, the stadium could wind up costing more than $100 million.

Also included in the costs was the $700,000 to reconstruct Broad Street to allow for improved traffic flow—$600,000 being contributed by the State Highway Department and $100,000 by the city. An estimated $1.5 million also was needed to erect a 50-foot-high message tower at 10th and Packer. Added to that was the $600,000 the Phillies would shell out to build 28 luxury boxes that would be rented for $12,000 to $16,000 annually.

One item that would cost zero was the pedestrian walk that the city planned to build over Pattison Avenue for fans who parked their cars in the Spectrum and JFK Stadium lots. That's because the idea was scrapped.

With one delay after another, city officials, still fighting over costs, were now saying that the stadium that was called "The Big Doughnut" by *Evening Bulletin* columnist Sandy Grady wouldn't open until 1970. "The Phillies are counting on playing in the new stadium on May 5," Ruly Carpenter said resolutely. Meanwhile, the Eagles made plans for a 1970 pre-season game at the stadium.

By 1970, all but one (Olympic Stadium in Montreal) of the members of the nation's "Big Doughnut" family were open for business. They were of similar design and shape—circular, concrete, multi-purpose structures that were the trend in that era. The Astrodome in Houston had come to life in 1965. Busch Stadium in St. Louis and Fulton County Stadium in Atlanta had held their first games in 1966. Cincinnati's Riverfront Stadium and Pittsburgh's Three Rivers Stadium opened their gates in 1970.

Phillies general manager John Quinn (left) and future team president Ruly Carpenter inspected progress in the construction of the Vet.

But the Vet, as it was now being called, was still a work in progress. And as costs continued to escalate, the city was forced to take out a $4.7 million loan. At about the same time, the state legislature voted to allow beer and liquor to be sold in the stadium restaurant, the Senate approving the measure unanimously and the House endorsing the bill by a 108-80 vote.

The Phillies, who originally had planned a 1969 special farewell at their last game at Connie Mack Stadium, were now resigned to the idea of playing at the old ballpark again in 1970. The Eagles scheduled one more season at Franklin Field. And Gola, ever the watchdog, withheld payment for an assortment of invoices that he said overcharged the city.

More than 800 workers labored tirelessly to complete construction of the stadium. They toiled through the winter and into the early spring of 1971, using more than 50 pieces of equipment that ranged from bulldozers, front-end loaders, and cherry-pickers to a 250 foot high, 175-ton crane. At long last, the job was completed in time for the Phillies' 1971 season opener. The final cost of the job was $52 million.

It had been an insufferable, anguishing, incredible, nearly two-decade journey packed with virtually every imaginable problem. But Philadelphia finally had its new stadium.

It would become the single most significant facility in Philadelphia's long sports history.

IT'S FINALLY
OPENING DAY

State-of-the-art facility
draws rave reviews

It was a cold, blustery day, with the temperature hovering around 48 degrees and the wind blowing between 20 and 34 miles an hour. It was not a good day for a baseball game. But it was a magnificent day for the city of Philadelphia.

The date was April 10, 1971. On that day, Veterans Stadium was finally opened.

It had been a long time coming. But now, after years of turmoil, the stadium that some said would never be built had become a reality. At long last, the Phillies, as well as the Eagles, had a first-class ballpark.

The new stadium was considered a state-of-the-art facility. Similar in design to some other National League (NL) stadiums—but regarded as being better—it had been preceded in its opening by the Astrodome (1965),

Above: Brand new Veterans Stadium was unveiled in 1971.

Busch Stadium and Fulton County Stadium (both 1966), and Three Rivers and Riverfront Stadiums (each 1970).

Some 55,352 fans—the largest crowd ever to attend a baseball game up to that point in Pennsylvania—crammed into the Vet on that first day. They came to see the Phillies take on the Montreal Expos, the same opponent that had helped the Phils close Connie Mack Stadium the previous fall.

The stands were packed with dignitaries. Most of them found it impossible to contain their enthusiasm for the new multi-purpose edifice that had been built for the then-staggering cost of $52 million.

City Council president Paul D'Ortona called it a "great day for the people of Philadelphia. This is a dream that we've had for a long time," he said.

"It certainly ranks with the finest new stadiums," gushed baseball commissioner Bowie Kuhn, watching the game from owner Bob Carpenter's open super box while not wearing an overcoat. "I'm impressed with the overall attractiveness of the stadium."

Even the Expos' fiesty manager and former Phillies pilot Gene Mauch, a man normally not prone to flattering statements, called it "the best new park in baseball. It looks like they've taken the good things from all the other new parks, added some things of their own, and whipped them into a pretty good place," said Mauch, who like D'Ortona and Kuhn was loudly booed by the fans.

Newspaper headlines and stories were as effusive as the speakers. "It's beautiful," blared the *Evening Bulletin*. *Sports Illustrated* had a similar description. Others called it "A Palace on Pattison Ave.," "Spectacular," "Magnificent." "Veterans Stadium has to be the most gorgeous orbful in Philadelphia," extolled the *Daily News*. "No more bad jokes about Philadelphia," proclaimed the New York *Post*.

The stadium was unlike anything Philadelphians had ever seen before. Its seating capacity (officially 56,371) was the largest in the National League. The Vet could seat 65,000 for football. It had parking spaces for 12,000 cars. There were 60 concessions stands, a picnic area for groups, a stadium club with a 200-foot-long bar and seats for 400 diners, 23 super boxes on the 400 level that held from 20 to 28 people and that rented for between $12,000 and $16,000 per season with five-year leases, and 70 luxury boxes on the front row at field level.

It cost $4.25 for a field box seat and fifty cents to sit in the 700 level of the bleachers. The charge for parking was $1. The stadium had yellow, orange, red, and brown theater-type seats made of heavy plastic, two miles of ramps, eight sets of escalators, and four elevators. There were no steps except those in the stands.

The stadium measured 840 feet in diameter. It rose 135 feet above street level. Instead of being stacked one on top of another, as was the common way to build multi-tiered structures, each floor was like a separate building standing on its own.

Some 87,000 cubic yards of concrete—enough to build two lanes on the Schuylkill Expressway from Vine Street to King of Prussia—were used. There were 7,600 tons of reinforced steel, 1,440 tons of structural steel, and 2,720,000 square feet of form work (the shell that held the concrete in place).

Some 625,000 18-by-18-foot concrete blocks were used to hold up the ramps, rest rooms, and concessions stands. The 146,000-square-foot surface of the field, including even the base paths, was covered with green AstroTurf, and it stood 30 feet below ground level.

The field's dimensions were 330 feet from home plate to both the left and right field fences and 408 feet to straightaway center field. The outfield fences stood eight feet high, although they were increased to 12 feet during the season. It was 60 feet from home plate straight back to the grandstand, and 45 feet from first and third bases to the stands. A 4,000-pound steel model of the Liberty Bell hung from the façade of the 400 level in center field.

Located in the outfield at different places were twin 100-by-25-foot scoreboards that cost $4 million, weighed 66 tons each, and were computerized and fully animated, two 90-by-13-foot auxiliary scoreboards, and an $80,000 "home run spectacular" that burst into action when a Phillies player hit a ball out of the park. An animated character known as Philadelphia Phil

When a Phillies player hit a home run, a cannon fired in center field.

and dressed in Revolutionary War clothes would swing a bat against a huge Liberty Bell replica. When the bat connected, a light would flash from the bell's crack, then a clapper would strike, making a loud noise. Philadelphia Phyllis would then pull a rope hanging from a cannon, setting off a flashing light.

For night games, the stadium utilized 1,500 lamps located around its roof. Each light was aimed at a specific 12-square-inch section on the field. Although they were never on all at once, the lamps could produce 2.1 million watts, enough to light 300 homes. There were 250 miles of cable and 100 miles of raceways used to carry the electrical current. The main substation at the stadium provided 16,000 horsepower, which was fed by two 15,000-volt power lines.

Three huge pumps buried 40 feet underground beyond right field carried water to the city's sewer system. The system had 120,000 feet of pipe. There were 1,100 fixtures in the park including those in 62 rest rooms, 17 water fountains, and 23 electric coolers, plus those in dining areas and elsewhere.

Approaching the stadium, fans were overwhelmed by its enormity. The top was 12 stories high, and the edifice towered over the nearby Spectrum and John F. Kennedy Stadium. Huge vertical columns surrounding the stadium and open walkways at each level punctuated the view.

Closer to the stadium, the most conspicuous feature was the statues. At the Broad and Pattison corner was a statue of Connie Mack waving his familiar scorecard. It had stood at Connie Mack Stadium from the time it was placed in 1957 until it was moved to the Vet. Four other statues—ones of a batter, a base-runner sliding, a punter (which alone was 15-feet high and weighed 6,000 pounds), and a football player being tackled—held spots on the 300 level walkway outside the stadium. They were the work of prominent local sculptor Joe Brown, a professor of sculpture at Princeton University.

The stadium was officially dedicated on April 4 at an open house sponsored by the city. To assure a good attendance, the city distributed 100,000 free tickets. Some 35,000 fans, plus dignitaries and players from the Phillies and Eagles, attended. The fans, who were given an eight-page souvenir booklet and an oversized ticket, cheered the players and booed the politicians.

A good time was had by all. One of the happiest attendees was Phillies owner Bob Carpenter. "This is the best multi-sport facility in the world," he proclaimed. "I'm not speaking as an owner or as a businessman. I'm speaking as a fan of baseball and football."

Eagles owner Leonard Tose was equally pleased. "We've always had the best fans," he said. "Now we have the finest stadium for them to use."

With 250 policemen stationed inside the stadium and 60 more assigned to traffic duty, the festivities began with hardly a hitch. While the Phillies played host to a buffet luncheon for the dignitaries, 100 honor guards

One of four sculptures by Joe Brown depicted a runner sliding into base.

from veterans' organizations and the Cardinal Dougherty High School band entertained the crowd.

Mayor James Tate made the dedicatory address. "Our city regains the distinction of being the sports capital of the nation," he said. "Other new stadiums can't match Veterans Stadium for attractiveness, comfort, convenience, and—most important—for watching sporting events of all kinds."

After the ceremony, the Phillies took the field for a workout. The players were as enthusiastic about their new home as everybody else.

"We knew we were moving into a palace," recalled infielder John Vukovich. "We were all very excited about it."

"To me," remembered second baseman Tony Taylor, "Connie Mack Stadium had the best field you could play on. As a hitter, you had a nice background in center field. And the infield was one of the best in baseball. But the Vet was special because it was brand new. It was a beautiful stadium. You had to make adjustments because it was new, but it was such a big improvement. It had better facilities . . . everything was better."

Even the offices were better. Instead of the isolated, cramped quarters at Connie Mack Stadium, the Phillies had 16,000 square feet of office space on both the second and fourth levels. The 13,000-square-foot Eagles offices were located on the fourth level as well. The team had spent its previous years with offices just off the lobby of the Bulletin Building at 30th and Market Streets.

"When we moved into the Vet, there were no carpets, it was cold, the offices were bare, and we had no windows," recalled Jimmy Gallagher, the Eagles public relations director for nearly three decades and a man who worked for the team from 1949 until his retirement in 1995. "But it was terrific. Everybody was very happy. Compared to what we had come from, it was heaven."

Naturally, the clubhouses were a vast improvement, too, over the seedy little rooms that the players used at Connie Mack Stadium.

"It was like day and night," said first baseman Willie Montanez. "Connie Mack Stadium had a clubhouse that was little league. At the Vet, we had a big clubhouse with a rug. When I walked in, it was very exciting. We all said, 'Wow.' "

"The Vet was such a different place, considering where we came from," catcher Tim McCarver remembered. "At first, the transition was not too comfortable. The clubhouse, for instance, was four times the size of the old one. That took some getting used to."

It wasn't easy forgetting about Connie Mack Stadium and acquiring a taste for the Vet. Quite a few Phillies had difficulty getting used to their new surroundings.

"We all hated to leave Connie Mack Stadium," said Dallas Green, former Phillies player and, at the time, the assistant director of the farm system. "I cried when we left. It was a comfortable stadium. The Vet was a huge stadium, but it was brand, spanking new and everybody was enthusiastic about it."

Pitcher Rick Wise also noticed the enthusiasm. "But the place was pretty sterile," he said. "It didn't have the character of Connie Mack Stadium."

"The dugouts were bigger, the clubhouse was bigger, everything was bigger," said manager Frank Lucchesi, who would become the last skipper to win a game at Connie Mack Stadium and the first to win a game at the Vet. "It was a big change for us because everything at Connie Mack Stadium was so small. It was more friendly there. But everything at the Vet was nice because it was new."

Six days after the stadium was dedicated, and four days after the Phillies opened the new season in Pittsburgh, the first game was held at the Vet. It was launched by a pre-game show that would be the first of 33 highly memorable opening day specials.

Fans, many wearing parkas and carrying blankets, began arriving at 10 A.M. for the 2:15 P.M. start. They used special tickets that measured six inches long and two inches wide. By 12:45 P.M., the Vet was one-third full. Conditions outside the stadium were somewhat harried.

"I don't think most people quite knew what to expect," said Charles Hurd, one of the city policemen assigned to the game. "Traffic was kind of chaotic. But everybody was pretty patient. And there were no problems with crowd control. Most people seemed to be in awe when they walked in because the stadium was so big."

"When they opened the gates and people started coming in and then it became a full house, it was just beautiful," Montanez said. "The crowd was very enthusiastic."

Before the game, the Hegeman String Band played. Four F-106 Air Force jets from Dover Air Force Base staged a flyover. There were speeches. Mayor Tate unveiled a plaque, later placed in the outfield, that dedicated the stadium to the city's military veterans. Some 1,000 balloons were released. And Expos general manager Jim Fanning was transported into the park riding on a dog sled.

"I said, well, Montreal is in Canada," recalled then–vice president Bill Giles, who had been spotted after midnight the night before the game washing windows on the entrance to the Phillies' ground-level office. "Can we do something Canadian? So we got a dog sled."

Brian McGinty sang the Canadian national anthem. Television personality Mike Douglas sang the U.S. national anthem. Then came the highlight of the pre-game pageantry. Catcher Mike Ryan caught a ball dropped from a helicopter hovering some 150 feet above the stadium. Ryan, who won

Catcher Mike Ryan caught a ball dropped from a helicopter.

Marine corporal Frank Mastrogiovanni threw out the first ball on opening day.

the job when McCarver demurred, had made one practice catch the previous day.

"It was really difficult," recalled Ryan, who, stationed near second base, bobbed and weaved under the plummeting missile. "It was one of those gray, overcast spring days, and the wind was pretty strong. It was circling through the stadium. I didn't think I had a chance in the world to catch it.

"The chopper was high enough—well above the stadium—that I couldn't see the ball come out of it. All I saw was the arm action of the guy who dropped it. But I caught it on the first try. The ball hit right on the heel of the glove and bounced in the air. I caught it with my bare hand. How did I do it? To this day, I have no idea."

After the catch, Ryan, who repeated the stunt in 1981 and 1991, delivered the ball to Frank Mastrogiovanni, a 20-year-old Marine corporal who had lost his legs in Vietnam. The South Philadelphia resident then tossed the ball to McCarver, who returned it to him. By then, the fully packed stadium was nearly overcome with excitement.

"There was a tremendous amount of excitement," verified Phillies director of public relations, Larry Shenk. "It was electric. And there was a lot of pride because this really made us major league as far as the ballplayers were concerned."

The first pitch ever thrown at Veterans Stadium was delivered at 2:20 P.M. by right-hander Jim Bunning. Expos center fielder Boots Day swung at it and sent a bouncer back to the mound, where Bunning fielded it and threw to Deron Johnson at first for the out. The ball was then taken out of play and readied for a trip to the Baseball Hall of Fame in Cooperstown.

In the bottom of the first inning, shortstop Larry Bowa singled to right field off Expos pitcher Bill Stoneman on a 3–1 count for the stadium's first hit. But neither team managed to score until the sixth inning, when Montreal's Ron Hunt sent a looper down the right field line that bounced into the stands for a ground rule double. He scored on Bob Bailey's checked-swing bloop double over first.

The Expos may have scored the first run at the Vet, but the Phillies came back in the bottom of the sixth with the first home run. Third baseman Don Money did the honors, blasting a 2–2 pitch into the lower left field seats.

"It just so happened that he [Stoneman] threw me a curveball and I hit it," Money said 33 years later. "I was not a big home run hitter. I was just trying to get on base."

Montanez followed with a walk, then went to third on a single by Johnson that got past left fielder Mack Jones. After Johnny Briggs was intentionally walked, Roger Freed singled to left to score Montanez and send Stoneman to the showers. McCarver followed with a sacrifice fly to center to score Johnson.

Having shown their offensive skills, the Phillies turned to defense in the seventh. Briggs made a dazzling, running, one-handed catch while slamming into the wall in left field on a drive by pinch-hitter Jim Fairey. On the next batter, Bowa went behind second to field Day's grounder and throw him out at first.

The Phillies scored their final run in the seventh as Bowa, who had two hits and a stolen base, tripled to deep right-center and scored on Money's sacrifice fly.

Sitting in the stands during the game was a young man whose long years with the Phillies were yet undetermined. "I was just a fan, and I was sitting in section 330," remembered future broadcaster Chris Wheeler. "I was freezing my tail off. But as I sat there, I kept thinking, wow, this is a pretty neat place. I'm really going to enjoy this as a fan. Little did I know that three months later, I'd be an employee of the Phillies."

Another fan with a sports future who was watching the game was a 12-year-old kid who lived a few blocks away. "We snuck in," said Frank Miceli, who many years later would become vice president of minor league operations for Comcast/Spectacor and general manager of three baseball teams and the ice hockey Phantoms. "There was no way we were going to miss this game. It was the most excited I've ever been."

Back down on the field, Bunning was replaced by Joe Hoerner with two on and one out in the eighth. Hoerner, who admitted later that he was so nervous he was shaking, walked Ron Fairly to load the bases. He then struck out Jones and John Bateman.

An inning later, the Phillies walked off with a 4–1 victory. Bunning had allowed six hits, struck out four, and walked three to get the decision—the 220th win of his career. Hoerner got a save. It was Mauch's first opening-day loss in Philadelphia after five wins as manager of the Phillies.

Don Money hit the first home run at Veterans Stadium.

"I was pretty keyed up," the 39-year-old Bunning said after the game. "Getting to pitch the first game here meant a lot to me."

In its first game, the new stadium was not without problems. A 51-year-old fan collapsed and died 45 minutes before game time. The home run spectacular failed to work after Money's homer. Long lines at concession stands made fans angry. Some of the stands ran out of refreshments. Some elevators failed to work. Some restrooms were not open. Someone with the city forgot to order toilet paper, and the Phillies had to send a worker to a nearby supermarket to buy as much as was available (the Phillies deducted the cost from their rent). The toilet in Bob Carpenter's office flooded. And a pipe burst outside of the door of one restroom, creating a 25-foot-wide pool of water.

Nevertheless, most of the day went as well as could be expected for such a large undertaking. There were no major problems with traffic. There was plenty of parking. And fans, with the help of the newly created 36-member Hot Pants Patrol, had little trouble finding their seats.

"The first sight when you walked in was overwhelming," said John Rossi, a professor of history at La Salle University and a long-time baseball fan. "It was overwhelming . . . so big, so green. A lot of people seemed to spend much of the game turning their heads, gawking at the facility and walking around to see different angles."

The stadium would, of course, suffer growing pains as the season progressed. Unforeseen problems occurred, although none was insurmountable.

"There were always problems when we first moved in," said Ruly Carpenter, then the team's secretary and assistant treasurer. "You have them with any new building. There were leaks into the offices. Sometimes beer would leak through the ceiling. The Eagles fans stamped their feet so much that eventually some of the concrete started to fall down."

Despite their gaudy start, the Phillies finished their first season at the Vet buried in last place in the National League's East Division with a 67–95 record. They did, however, draw 1,511,223 fans for the year, surpassing the club's old record of 1,425,891 set in 1964.

During the season, the Vet was the site of several memorable feats. The Pittsburgh Pirates' Willie Stargell hit the longest home run in the history of the Vet, a shot into section 601 of right field off Bunning. Johnson hit four consecutive homers spread over two games. Wise hit two home runs, including a grand slam, his second two-homer game of the season, in a 7–3 victory over the San Francisco Giants. Three weeks later, he retired 32 batters in a row and won his own game with a 12th-inning single in a 4–3 triumph over the Chicago Cubs. Greg Luzinski hit his first major league homer, and Montanez set a Phillies rookie record with his 30th four-bagger.

Singer Dionne Warwick became the first major entertainer to stage a show at the Vet. Heavyweight boxing champion Joe Frazier also appeared as a singer with his group, The Knockouts. Famed softball pitcher Eddie Feigner with The King and His Court five-man team played a squad headed by District Attorney Arlen Specter. And Stan Musial, Joe DiMaggio, Bob Feller, Satchel Paige, Enos Slaughter, Mickey Vernon, Monte Irvin, and Bobby Thomson were among many ex-major league greats who played in an old-timers game.

In its first year, Veterans Stadium was off to a spectacular start. The new stadium had been well worth the wait.

FAIR OR FOUL?

*The Vet had both its supporters
and its detractors*

Over the years, there was seldom any ambivalence about the way Veterans Stadium was perceived. You either liked it or loathed it.

Those views evolved over time. When it was opened in 1971, the stadium was considered a state-of-the-art facility and was extensively applauded. Mostly in the latter part of its life, the Vet was the victim of strong criticism.

To be sure, the Vet developed flaws as it aged. But the place still had plenty of admirers. Among those were many of the men who worked and played there.

Above: All kinds of messages were displayed on Phanavision, which made its debut in 1983.

"The Vet was different from a lot of places," said infielder Dick Allen, who spent his second term with the Phillies playing there. "After playing at Connie Mack Stadium, playing at the Vet was like a breath of fresh air. Everything was first class. Everything was done well. From a players standpoint, all you had to do was play ball and produce."

Pitcher John Denny also was a big admirer of the Vet. "Coming to the stadium was the real meaning of what it was to be in a big league park," he said. "Even when I was with the Cardinals and we came to the Vet, I always wanted to be a Phillie because of the stadium and its environment. Even at the end, it was better than some of the new stadiums. It had a tremendous history, and it was always kept really well. Vet Stadium will always be close to my heart."

Likewise, Larry Bowa, who played shortstop, coached, and managed the Phillies, had a soft spot for the stadium. "I was always impressed with the Vet," he said. "Maybe it was because we were spoiled because of all the winning teams we had, but it was the best park to play in. It was top of the line. I have nothing but good memories. I loved playing there."

The Vet underwent numerous changes over the years. And, contrary to the views of some, huge amounts of money were spent. In 1986, some $20 million of city funds was spent on new facilities that among other things included new scoreboards, 26 new super boxes, and 90 sky boxes—otherwise known as Penthouse Suites—that altogether could seat 1,211 fans, each suite renting for upwards of $200,000 per year. Another $2 million in 1988 was spent to change low-wattage lights in the standards that stood above the stadium roof to high-intensity lights and to make various other improvements.

The seating capacity of the stadium was increased, too. For baseball, it went from its original total of 56,371 to a high of 66,507 in 1983, with several increases in between. Several reductions thereafter put the number at 61,831 in 2003.

"When it was built, some features were compromised," said David Montgomery, who since 1997 has been the Phillies' president and chief executive officer. "The circular nature of the ballpark took some seats away from the action. In theory, a ballpark should have seats that are on top of the action."

In the early 1990s, the Phillies were interested in purchasing the Vet. The Phillies, negotiating with the city, which at the time was running annual budget deficits in the $50- to $60-million range, fully expected to consummate a sale at a price somewhere between $50 and $75 million.

Instead, the team wound up putting about $14 million into jobs such as repairing the concrete and upper deck superstructure, improving the lower stands, renovating restrooms and the visiting dugout, adding padding on the outfield fences, and painting. In 1992 and in each of the succeeding years, additional funds were applied to the ongoing job of repairing, painting, renovating, and making various cosmetic alterations.

Altogether, between the mid-1980s and the close of the Vet, some $50 million went toward fixing and upgrading facilities. In addition, six different artificial playing surfaces were used over the stadium's 33-year life. And in 1995, attractively colored blue seats replaced the yellow, red, and orange ones, which had originally been designed to match the color of a fan's ticket. At the same time, every other aisle in the 500 level was removed, allowing rows to be 18 seats wide instead of eight and overall adding 649 seats, which compensated for the loss of seats when a section for the disabled was installed on the 300 level.

"Once the Phillies and the city put in all that money, it was a solid facility," said Montgomery. "For a multi-purpose facility, it was undeservedly maligned, much more than it should have been. I feel very strongly about this: of the parks of its era, I think it was at the top of the list. At the very end, it was clearly at the top of that list.

"The stories about how the park was in disrepair always bothered me," Montgomery added. "We had a lot of people who worked very hard to make it as nice as it could be. There was a weak point in the 1980s when we had maintenance and other problems. But once the club and the city got involved, I think over the final 10 or 12 years, the Vet was an excellent ballpark."

Several times, a city budget crisis had an effect on the Vet. Necessary jobs weren't done because the city couldn't come up with the money. There were also two major strikes by city workers. At least, though, after the first two years when the city lost about $1.5 million each year, the stadium operated in the black. It helped, of course, that both the Phillies and the Eagles operated with leases that favored the city.

"We didn't exactly have a sweetheart deal with the city," said Ruly Carpenter, the Phillies' president from 1973 to 1981. "It was one of the toughest deals in baseball. And there were times when we had to take a tough posture with the city. After my family sold the team (in 1981), the Phillies renegotiated a better lease."

At about that time, the Eagles also negotiated a new lease. The most critical feature was the city's consent to defer the Eagles' annual $800,000 rent for 10 years so that the sky boxes could be built at the request of owner Leonard Tose, who had threatened to sell the team to an investor who would move it to Phoenix, Arizona. Subsequently, all revenue from the boxes went to the Eagles.

One of the biggest single capital improvements at the Vet was the installation in 1983 of Phanavision, a $4 million scoreboard-like, computerized screen that sat high in the 700 level in center field. It replaced a large, more conventional scoreboard that was located in right-center field.

Operated from a set of consoles located next to the press box on the 400 level, it showed on a 32-by-42-foot screen with 68,400 light bulbs, pictures of the batters, fans, replays, and various other things, plus statistics, out-of-town scores, standings, and numerous other bits of information. It did not show controversial plays, fights, or unruly fans. But it did make a significant contribution to keeping spectators informed.

Before he became a big league catcher, first with the San Diego Padres, then with the Seattle Mariners and Chicago White Sox, Delaware County native Ben Davis was one of those spectators. As a youth, he sat in the stands admiring the ballpark surrounding him.

"We'd come as soon as the gates opened and watched batting practice," he said. "The Phillies were my favorite team, and I followed them from the time I was a little kid. I always dreamed of playing at the Vet, and I finally got the opportunity. It was a tremendous thrill."

Another person who originally saw the Vet from a different vantage point was former umpire Eric Gregg. "It was a great place to work," he said. "But even though I was born and raised in West Philly, I never came to the Vet as a fan because I was always working as an umpire."

His first game at the Vet came at the end of the 1976 season. The New York Mets were in town. Tom Seaver was going for his 22nd win, and Steve Carlton was seeking his 20th win. "I was so nervous," Gregg said. "Two future Hall of Famers pitching. Bill Giles asked how many tickets I got. I said about 30. He said, 'Why don't we just rope off a section and call it the Soul Bowl.' My whole family was there. But I had a good game. It was a great experience."

One current player who sat in the stands as a kid was a guy who grew into becoming one of baseball's finest second basemen. "I have nothing but good memories of the Vet," said Seattle's Brett Boone, whose dad Bob caught for the Phillies during the club's golden era. "I still remember some of the people who worked there—ushers, peanut vendors. I knew them and always said hello to them when I came to the Vet as a player."

Many players had interesting reactions the first time they saw the Vet.

"I was like a deer in headlights," said catcher Darren Daulton. "In 1983, I was up for a cup of coffee, and I walked into the clubhouse and there's Mike Schmidt, Steve Carlton, Pete Rose, Garry Maddox, Tony Perez, Joe Morgan. Then I went down on the field and took it all in. I'd never been in a stadium like that, and it was overwhelming. And they were packing in big crowds, so it was all very intimidating."

Jim Thome had a similar experience. "When I first walked in, I instantly thought of Schmitty and Rose and Bowa and all the guys who had played there and won there," the first baseman said. "Then I went out on the field, and it looked really big. I remember looking at the fences and thinking, is it a good hitter's park? Is it a good pitcher's park?"

Outfielder Glenn Wilson came to the Phillies from the Detroit Tigers. The Vet was a sharp contrast to Tiger Stadium. "I will never, ever forget coming across the bridge from the airport and seeing Veterans Stadium and how massive it was," he said. "It was so thrilling to think that I was going to get the opportunity to play in front of so many people in a park that big. It just made me feel like a big-time athlete."

"When I came here from Cleveland and I saw the Vet for the first time, my eyes just jumped up," said outfielder Del Unser. "I thought as a hitter, I would really enjoy it, which I did. And they actually put people in the stadium instead of the 4–5,000 we drew in Cleveland. It was exciting."

"The first impression I had," said third baseman Dave Hollins, "was the size. It was overwhelming when you first saw it because it was so big and so high. You always have fond memories of your first big league park, so it was very special to me."

Second baseman Juan Samuel also experienced feelings of awe when he walked into the stadium for the first time. "I looked up and saw all the people," he said, "and I thought, wow, so this is what a major league park looks like. The feeling was overwhelming."

One of the biggest jobs at the Vet involved maintaining the stadium. That included countless tasks. It was the city's responsibility to take care of the stadium and the Phillies' and Eagles' obligations to maintain the playing field.

"The biggest issue for us was keeping the place clean," said Joel Ralph, the city's director of operations at the Vet from 1973 to 1987. "A lot of dirt is generated in a stadium. Keeping it clean and staying within your budget is a big job."

Cleaning the stands after games was a major job at the Vet.

Although it was taken for granted, another big job was hanging the foul poles—or nylon lines as they actually were—at the start of each season. After the nylon lines were removed from storage, they were fastened by cables as an engineer peered from home plate with a sighting glass and made sure the material dropped directly on the foul line. It was a touchy operation, which required precision work to get the "poles" exactly in the right place.

Ralph, who had been the city's deputy commissioner of recreation before he replaced Lloyd Vye at the Vet, often worked around the clock at the ballpark. Once, he stayed at the Vet for 21 straight days because he didn't want to cross the picket line of his striking workers. Overall, he said, the city was very supportive of his stadium operation.

"Anything we needed, we got," he said. "We never had problems with the politicians. Every mayor supported us. Each mayor had different interests. [Frank] Rizzo was hardly ever there. [Ed] Rendell was always there."

A bigger problem was the occasional fracas between the Phillies and Eagles. "In the beginning it [their relationship] wasn't very good," Ralph said. "Vye had big problems with them, especially over the way their leases, which favored baseball, were structured. But eventually the situation improved greatly. They got to understand each other's problems and cooperated with each other."

As stadium manager, Joel Ralph guided the operation of the Vet for 15 years.

Bill Giles, Phillies president from 1981 to 1997, and before that the club's executive vice president, recalled a sometimes rocky existence between the two teams. "From year to year, things cropped up that made it difficult. We got along pretty well, but we did have some fights over some things and Vye or Ralph had to step in and referee. There were a lot of conversion issues. The biggest fight we always had was about the paint on the field. Getting the football lines cleaned up so that it was a clean-looking baseball field was always an issue.

"Actually," Giles added, "we had more fights with the city than we did with the Eagles. The city maintained the structure. The Phillies' responsibility was the ground crew and the day-game people. We had no plumbers, no carpenters. If there was a leak or the electric went bad, the city had to fix it. And they were often not very quick to react and sometimes not very efficient."

The Phillies were in charge of general upkeep during their season. That meant keeping the concourses, ramps, and seats clean and in satisfactory condition. The ground crew, of course, maintained the playing area but also handled general maintenance, even in the winter when jobs included replacing light bulbs, painting, even delivering and storing supplies and other items to be used in season.

Likewise, the Eagles took over the operation during their seasons. "We always tried to make sure everything was working," said former general manager Pete Retzlaff. "When you have a stadium that big holding that many people, a lot of things can go wrong." Once, the ceiling of Retzlaff's office, which sat under a commissary, developed a leak. It turned out that the leaking substance was Coke syrup.

Despite its patriotic connotation, the name Veterans Stadium was sometimes criticized for its lack of imagination. In an *Inquirer* column headlined "Vet honored people, not products, profit," writer Frank Fitzpatrick eloquently defended the name while calling the stadium "one of the last sports facilities to have saved its soul from the devil of commercialism."

"The Vet (was) free of any corporate connection," Fitzpatrick wrote. "It wasn't saddled with a dot-com prefix. It didn't represent a carpetbagger bank or a fat-fueled fast-food chain. You didn't feel as though you were stepping into a focus group each time you walked inside. Instead, it carried a simple name that suggested millions of simple men and women whose lives had a purpose beyond the pursuits of SUVs, 401Ks, and McMansions." And the fans, he said, "went there to watch ball games, not to endure a marketing experience. It was a venue, not a mall. Sports and the surroundings were what mattered at Veterans Stadium."

Certainly, the Vet had some tragedies. A fan fell out of the upper deck in the 1970s and was killed. A worker also died when a cart he was driving plunged through a guardrail on the 600 level. And in 1998, nine cadets at an Army-Navy game fell out of the stands when a railing collapsed (see Chapter 16).

It also had it share of other problems and idiosyncrasies. One involved the Vet's animal population.

Squirrels sometimes scurried around the field. Mice were often spotted, even in the dugouts. Pigeons lived in the eaves. And some two dozen cats resided at the stadium. They helped to keep the rodent population under control. On occasion, one would run onto the field in the middle of a game. Once, according to Tampa Bay Bucs football coach Joe Gruden, while he was an assistant coach with the Eagles and working in the wee hours of the morning, a cat and two rats fell through the ceiling onto his desk. Another Eagles assistant coach once claimed that a cat urinated on his sheaf of papers.

Before the Vet was imploded, the cats were rounded up, and homes were found for the tamer ones, some were sent to shelters, and others were transferred to Citizens Bank Park to resume their duties on the rodent patrol.

Rats have always been a major part of Veterans Stadium lore. Depending on who's doing the talking, either there are no rats at the Vet or there are scores of them, some the size of small dogs.

"I can honestly say that in my 33 years at the Vet, I never saw a rat inside the building," said Mike DiMuzio, who began at the Vet as a groundskeeper and eventually became the director of facility management. "The only time rats showed up at all was when the construction started (on Citizens Park) and they were displaced."

Ralph concurred. "I never saw a rat," he said. "Mice, yes. You get mice in this kind of facility. And I'll tell you something about the cats, too. They never bothered anyone. All the stories about cats attacking people was just folklore."

Among those in disagreement was Daulton. "Sometimes we'd come back from a road trip and be unloading our stuff in the clubhouse at 3:30 in the morning, and we'd hear the rats running around behind the walls," he said.

Down through the years, Eagles players have also supported the view claiming the presence of rats at the Vet. Ex–offensive guard Brian Baldinger said the players called them wharf rats. "They were so big, they should have been tested for steroids," he said. "I never saw rats that size before. And you never knew where they'd be. They could be in your shoe, in the coaches' room, or having races across the floor." Eagles defensive end N. D. Kalu told columnist Bob Ford in the *Inquirer* that rats frequently ran across his feet as he moved about from one room to another.

Former linebacker Bill Bergey claimed he once saw a large rat run across the floor of the locker room and into a hole. "We looked at each other in bewilderment," he said. "Is this the NFL? But guess what, he was our rat, and we didn't think anything more about it."

There were, of course, other complaints about the Vet. Many of them came from the Eagles. "The stadium was living proof that baseball and football were not compatible sports," said Retzlaff. "You can't play baseball in a football stadium, and you can't play football in a baseball stadium."

Mike DiMuzio worked with a painter touching up one of the early signs at the Vet.

Frank Dolson, a columnist for more than four decades at the *Inquirer*, added this view: "It was a lousy place for baseball fans," he said. "Most seats were too far from the field, especially those in the upper deck."

Present Eagles owner Jeffrey Laurie, who couldn't wait to get out of the Vet, once called it a "dump." Former Eagles receiver Harold Carmichael called it a "toilet."

"When Laurie called the Vet a dump, that really pissed me off," fumed Ralph. "The Vet was never a dump. Most of the bad publicity that it got had to do with the Eagles. They really knocked the facility. And reporters always said it was the worst stadium. It wasn't the worst stadium.

"The Phillies had complaints sometimes, too," Ralph added. "But they approached it in a different manner than the Eagles. The Phillies were professional and low key. They never knocked the facility the way others did."

Not all Eagles criticized the Vet. One who didn't was safety Randy Logan. "The Vet was a place that was comfortable for me," he said. "I came from Michigan, and when you talk about facilities and seating capacity, we had over 100,000 every game. So the Vet was a lot smaller. To me, that made it nice and comfortable. Sure, some things could've been better. But the Vet was at least as good as other stadiums I played in."

Another former Eagle who chose not to rip the Vet was defensive back Al Nelson. "I thought making the transition from Franklin Field to Veterans Stadium was pretty easy," he said. "Going to the Vet was like going to heaven. Sure, you had to be careful with the turf because there were soft spots and you could trip. But overall, it was a good place to play. It was very exciting, especially because the fans were so passionate. It was always a madhouse."

Except for the artificial turf and a few minor problems, most baseball players themselves seldom criticized the Vet. One time, Mike Schmidt groused about the "cat stink" in the runway leading from the clubhouse to the dugout. Kevin Stocker said there were beer and garbage odors in that same runway. And Jimmy Rollins said that his first impression of the Vet when he saw it in 1997 was that it "was real ugly. But I guess I appreciated it, though," he added, "because I wanted to get to the big leagues and that was where I wanted to play."

Added pitcher Mitch Williams: "The smell underneath was not attractive, and it smelled a little ripe down in the bullpen sometimes. By then, of course, the facility was getting behind the times. But I came to work every day and never had a problem with it."

In a sampling of managers, there was hardly overwhelming support of the Vet.

"I don't have real special memories about the ballpark because of what it was," said former Phillies and present Boston Red Sox pilot Terry Francona. "It didn't have a lot of personality. It had the cookie-cutter feeling. Plus, it was built a long time ago. Ballparks have changed. People don't like that kind of park anymore."

"One of my strongest memories of the place," added Francona, "was having to put a trash can in my office because the roof was leaking."

Said St. Louis Cardinals manager Tony LaRussa: "It wasn't anything special. It was better than a minor league park. Sometimes, the turf was difficult."

Bobby Cox, the skipper of the Atlanta Braves added: "It was not exactly Wrigley Field or Fenway Park. It wasn't one of those old, traditional stadiums. So when it went down, I really didn't have any regrets. We had some great battles there. And at one time it was a good stadium. But there comes a time when you have to get a new one."

While it lived, the Vet was also accused of having cracked concrete, broken plumbing (in 1982, a water pipe burst and drenched the Phillies offices), ceiling tiles that fell, flooded floors, peeling paint, broken restrooms, broken seats, and all kinds of other flaws. Its distance from the stands to the field was criticized. The stadium's detractors in its latter years were relentless in their condemnations of the Vet.

Was the Vet unfairly maligned? Did it really deserve all the insults and slurs thrown its way?

The Vet took on a special look for the 1993 World Series.

Should it have pleaded guilty when network broadcaster John Madden called the Vet his least favorite stadium, saying it deserved to be blown up? Or when *Sports Illustrated* labeled it the "second worst stadium" in baseball (behind Montreal's Olympic Stadium)? Or when visiting players, fans, or neighborhood residents called it a concrete doughnut and complained—sometimes loudly—about various parts of the facility?

Ralph bristled when he thought about the unfavorable treatment given the Vet. "It was unfairly maligned," he said. "Absolutely. To say it was crumbling, falling down, was simply not true. It got a bad rap. It was basically a good, solid building. It was well kept. It was way above similar stadiums in upgrades and amenities. It was a nice complex. It was safe. It was designed to serve two teams, which it did. It brought a very diverse activity into the city."

The Eagles' Bergey put a different twist on the controversy. "It was a dump, " he said. "It was a stinkhole. It was a piece of garbage. But it was our stinkhole. It was our garbage. And it was home, and we loved it."

It was home to legions of players who wore the colors of Philadelphia teams. And because it was, it played an important role in their games, one reason being that it made the home field advantage especially strong.

But one did not have to be a player to appreciate the Vet. It also had its supporters among nonuniformed people.

"It was a good feeling coming to work at the Vet," said general manager Ed Wade, who got his start in baseball in 1977 as an intern in the Phillies public relations office. "I say that against the backdrop of a lot of people maligning the facility. But we'd go to other parks, and they weren't as well kept as the Vet. I ran at lunchtime, and if I ran in the upper deck, there were guys power-washing the concrete every day.

"The sight lines could have been better," he added. "It would have been better not to play on artificial turf. The offices leaked a little too much. But all things considered, the place was fun and full of good memories. There was a lot of very positive history there, and because of that, it was a special place."

Chris Wheeler also began working at the Vet at an early age, starting in the public relations office in 1971 before moving into broadcasting in 1977. He left the old stadium with many fond memories. "I drove down there every day, and I couldn't wait to get there," he said. "I loved the place. I have a lot of great memories. I saw so many wonderful games. Plus, I got a chance to pursue a lifelong dream—doing what I do for a living."

Retired sportswriter Bill Carroll of the Lancaster *New Era* also shunned criticism of the Vet. "I never thought it was a dump or an abomination as a lot of people said," he noted. "I always thought it was one of the better stadiums. It was where I did my work and where I saw some great games."

Even though he fell and suffered a serious injury inflicted by a broken elevator, and wound up successfully suing the city for a healthy sum, another person touched by his years at the Vet was strength and conditioning coach Gus Hoefling, who came to Philadelphia to work with the Eagles in 1973, then two years later moved to the Phillies and spent the next 17 years with the club. "It was a wonderful place to work," he said. "I'd drive up to the Vet, and think it was an honor to work there. It was like working in a rose garden. You knew everybody. They'd always say hello. I loved the place."

For most Phillies players, Veterans Stadium was an ideal place to perform. Here's a sampling of their comments.

Outfielder Lenny Dykstra: "It was the best. Electrifying. Playing there and being able to win, there was nothing better. And the fans were probably the best in baseball because they know the game. It was a place I'll never forget. You just can't duplicate the memories."

Catcher Tim McCarver: "It was similar to other ballparks, but it had its own flavor. What I especially liked about the Vet was that it was in South Philly, which gave it an atmosphere unlike any other park. Cincinnati was downtown. Pittsburgh was downtown. But the Vet was a big-time stadium in a neighborhood. There was such a distinctive thing about it because of the people and the area. I always found that being in South Philly was very, very nice."

Outfielder Jeff Stone: "I loved Veterans Stadium. It was one of the best ballparks for me. I always played good there. The fans were great. It was a good ballpark for hitters. It had a special history. It was one of the parks I enjoyed playing in the most."

Catcher Mike Lieberthal: "I enjoyed playing there because I liked it from the standpoint of both hitting and catching. I was always in the dirt, and the Vet's dirt was pretty good. I liked hitting there. The wind hardly ever blew. And with the turf, you got more hits."

Pitcher Steve Bedrosian: "There were a lot of things I liked about playing at the Vet. My teammates. Mike Ryan in the bullpen with his pet squirrel Issac who had no back legs and pulled himself around by his front legs. Watching Lefty [Steve Carlton] and Schmitty retire. I really enjoyed it there."

Infielder Tony Taylor: "It was a tremendous stadium to play in. It was great for the fans because they had a good view of everything that was going on. I enjoyed coming to the stadium every day."

Outfielder Jay Johnstone: "There are many great memories about how good the Vet was to play in. The '70s teams, the '80s teams, the '93 team. They were great times, and so many things from those eras happened at the Vet."

Pitcher Randy Wolf: "It was an interesting place. It seemed more like a football stadium, and you didn't get as much of a baseball feeling. But when the team was winning and the place was sold out, there was nothing like it."

Shortstop Kevin Stocker: "I really enjoyed playing at the Vet. The turf was both good and bad. It had some seams that were tough. Once they got the blue seats in, it was especially good because the multi-colored seats looked old and didn't give you very good visibility."

Pitcher Curt Schilling: "It looked like a flying saucer. But it was *thee* place to play baseball in the National League for 15 years."

Catcher Ozzie Virgil: "It made a good impression on me right from the first time I stepped out onto the field. All my memories at the Vet were good. The fans, the administration, the owners . . . everything was very pleasant."

Outfielder Bake McBride: "I loved playing at the Vet because of the players, the fans, and the city. This was where I had a lot of success. The Vet was one of the best parks that I hit in because the ball carried. You saw it better, too. I just really enjoyed playing in that ballpark, even when I was playing with the Cardinals."

Pitcher Tommy Greene: "I felt privileged to play there. I knew it was older, but to me it was a big league ballpark. It was the cream of the crop. It may not have been the most modern stadium, but it was the place where you worked and it had a lot of memories. Some pretty good teams played there. I was just glad to be a part of it."

Infielder/coach John Vukovich: "It was a good place to play. No question about it. A lot of great things happened to me at the Vet. First, I met my wife there. Second was the 1980 World Series, a memory I'll always cherish. Third was winning the pennant in 1993."

Catcher Lance Parrish: "I liked it. After coming from Tiger Stadium, I finally got to experience what a bigger clubhouse and big dugouts were like. That was really nice. The atmosphere was good, and the field was good, too. Of course, being a catcher, I was in the dirt all the time, but that was never a problem for me."

Outfielder Jim Eisenreich: "It was fun to play in. Physically, it was old, but it was a great place for me. I loved the atmosphere. The ballpark had flavor. It was one of those places that it didn't matter what it looked like. When it had people in the stands and you were playing, there wasn't anything better. I enjoyed every minute."

And so did millions of others who visited the stadium during its 33 years.

PHILLIES' FINEST

*The team's best 25 players
at the Vet*

While they played at Veterans Stadium, the Phillies never had a shortage of good players. Some were even better than good.

Five players who have gone to the Hall of Fame—Mike Schmidt, Steve Carlton, Jim Bunning, Joe Morgan, and Tony Perez—wore Phillies uniforms at the Vet, although only the first three spent more than one year there. Some 41 Phils players who played at the Vet were selected a total of 83 times to All-Star teams.

Three pitchers, including Carlton four times and John Denny and Steve Bedrosian each once, won six Cy Young awards. Schmidt captured three Most Valuable Player awards and a World Series Most Valuable Player

Above: Shortstop Larry Bowa.

(MVP). Manny Trillo, Gary Matthews, and Curt Schilling each won League Championship Series (LCS) MVPs.

While playing at the Vet, nine Phillies players won a total of 32 Gold Gloves, 10 of them by Schmidt and 8 by Garry Maddox. There were three National League Rookies of the Year—Lonnie Smith, Juan Samuel, and Scott Rolen. Al Holland and Bedrosian each won Fireman of the Year honors.

Countless times, Phillies led the league in various hitting, pitching, and fielding categories. And many players who graced the field at the Vet rank among the club's all-time leaders in these departments.

Overall, some 517 players wore the uniform of the Phillies during the team's 33 years at the Vet. When the Vet opened in 1971, the team's total payroll was $1,150,000, roughly the average salary of one player in today's market. In the final season at the ballpark in 2003, the Phils shelled out some $73 million in players' wages.

No book on Veterans Stadium would be complete without a closer look at the top Phillies players who performed there. Accordingly, this chapter is devoted to the top 25 Phillies who played for the team while it was stationed at the Vet. The selections were based on the players' achievements solely while playing with the Phillies, and not what they did with other teams. In each case, the individual's most memorable Phillies game at the Vet has also been selected.

Bobby Abreu
Right Fielder
Phillies—1998–2003

No other regular in the Phillies' 33 years at the Vet hit as consistently over .300 as Bobby Abreu. In his six seasons at Veterans Stadium, Abreu missed a .300 average just once. His best mark came in 1999 when he hit .335. He also reached double figures in home runs each year, his high being 31 in 2001. That year, he also had a career-high 110 RBI. Abreu is only the second Phillies player (the other is Roy Thomas, 1899–1904) ever to have walked 100 or more times five straight years, and the third to have hit 50 or more doubles in one season.

September 28, 2003—If Abreu played the numbers, 99 would have been a perfect choice. He went into the last game at the Vet with a .299 batting average, 99 RBI, and 99 runs scored. Uncanny. Although the Phillies lost to the Atlanta Braves, 8–3, Abreu got one hit and two RBI to finish with a .300 average, 101 RBI. His runs total stayed at 99.

Steve Bedrosian
Pitcher
Phillies—1986–89

Among Phillies relief pitchers, one of the best was Steve Bedrosian, a hard-throwing righthander. A strikeout artist who fanned just slightly less than

Right fielder Bobby Abreu.

one batter per inning, Bedrosian held the club record for career saves for 14 years with 103. His best season came in 1987 when he led the league with 40 saves, the first time a Phillies pitcher had ever done that. That year, Bedrosian became only the third National League relief pitcher to win the Cy Young Award. Bedrock also won 21 and posted a 3.04 ERA as a Phillie.

June 30, 1987—Scoring a pair of runs in the top of the ninth inning, the Pittsburgh Pirates had closed the gap to 6–4. Bedrosian was summoned to the mound with one out and a man on base. He got the next two batters to end the game and earn the save. It was his 13th consecutive save, a major league record for relief pitchers.

Bob Boone
Catcher
Phillies—1972–81

Among his many assets, one that described Bob Boone was "durable." He caught more games than any other Phillies catcher. He holds the major league record for most years, catching 100 or more games (15). For a while, he had the record for most games caught in a career. A Stanford graduate, Boone was smart, rock-solid behind the plate, had a strong arm, and was a decent hitter. He hit .259 in 1,125 games with the Phillies, including three straight years over .280. His father and two sons played in the majors.

October 14, 1980—When the Phillies overcame a 4–0 deficit to defeat the Kansas City Royals, 7–6, in Game One of the 1980 World Series, it was the Phils' first Series win since 1915. Boone played a key role, blasting three hits and driving in two runs. His third inning single drove in the first run, and his fourth inning double scored the sixth run.

Larry Bowa
Shortstop
Phillies—1970–81

Larry Bowa was arguably the finest shortstop in Phillies history. He had a career batting average with the team of .264, but his greatest work was done on defense. Only two other shortstops in the major leagues and none in the National League top Bowa's career fielding percentage of .980. Just one other player in history (Ozzie Smith) appeared in more games at shortstop than Bowa's 2,222. He led the NL in fielding six times and holds the club record for most assists (560) in one season.

September 26, 1979—It was the Phillies' last home game of the season. The fact that they beat the St. Louis Cardinals, 11–5, was really secondary. When Bowa ran off the field in the ninth inning, he completed the amazing feat of having not made an error all season at the Vet. Bowa finished the year with a then–NL record .991 fielding percentage.

Rico Brogna
First Baseman
Phillies—1997–2000

Any ranking of the top fielding first basemen in Phillies history includes Rico Brogna. In fact, a case could be made that he *was* the best. In 1998, Brogna fielded .996. He holds the club record for most assists (144) in one season by a first baseman. Few balls, either thrown or batted, ever got by the slick-fielding first sacker. And Brogna was no slouch as a hitter. In three full seasons with the Phils, he batted .265 and never hit less than 20 home runs. In 1998, he drove in 104, the most by a Phillies first baseman in 66 years.

August 25, 1999—No Phillies first baseman ever drove in more than 100 runs two years in a row until Brogna collected 102 RBI in 1999. The highlight of that season came when the Phillies blasted the San Diego Padres, 15–1. In one of the biggest outbursts in Phillies history, Brogna drove in seven runs with two doubles and two home runs.

Steve Carlton
Pitcher
Phillies—1972–86

Unquestionably, the best Phillies pitcher ever to step on the mound at the Vet was Steve Carlton. One of just 22 300-game winners in baseball history (329–244), Carlton posted a 241–161 record with the Phils, winning 20 or more games five times. Only four pitchers have recorded more than 4,000 career strikeouts, with Carlton (4,136) registering 3,031 of his with the Phillies. He pitched five one-hitters, won four Cy Young awards, and posted a 3.09 ERA with the Phillies en route to the Hall of Fame.

August 17, 1972—Some say it was one of the greatest years any pitcher ever had. Carlton won 27 games for a woeful Phillies team that was victorious only 59 times all season. At one point, Carlton won an incredible 15 straight games, longest in Phillies history. The memorable 15th came in a seven-hit, 9–4 win over the Cincinnati Reds.

Dave Cash
Second Baseman
Phillies—1974–76

No trade made by general manager Paul Owens was more astute than the one that brought Dave Cash to the Phillies. Cash was just what the doctor ordered. He gave the Phils steady play at second base. More importantly, he convinced a young team that badly needed a leader that it could be a winner. Cash's "Yes We Can" slogan spread through the clubhouse and helped to launch the Phils into their finest era. Cash missed only two games in his three years as the Phils' leadoff batter. He hit .296.

September 27, 1975—In the next-to-last game of the season, Cash had his biggest game of the year, going 4-for-5 with two RBI to lead the Phillies to an 8–1 win over the New York Mets. The game was especially significant for Cash because he solidified his league lead in hits. He finished with 213 safeties and set an NL record with 699 at-bats.

Darren Daulton
Catcher
Phillies—1983, 1985–97

Not only was Darren Daulton one of the top catchers the Phillies ever had, he was a team leader and hugely popular with the fans. Among catchers, Daulton hit more home runs and had the second-highest career fielding average (.988) in club history. Injuries sometimes got in the way, but he hit 137 home runs overall with the Phils. In 1992, he became only the fourth catcher in National League history to win an RBI title, when he drove in 109. He had 105 RBI in 1993, while hitting 51 homers over those two years.

Above: Catcher Darren Daulton.
Left: Center fielder Garry Maddox.

July 28, 1993—No one played a bigger role in the Phillies' 1993 pennant-winning season than Daulton. And no one had a bigger game than Daulton did in a 14–6 win over the St. Louis Cardinals. On the way to his second straight big season, Daulton slammed a triple and a grand slam home run while collecting six RBI to lead the route.

Lenny Dykstra
Center Fielder
Phillies—1989–98

Despite injuries that allowed him to play just two full seasons, Dykstra was one of the main cogs of the club's off-again, on-again 1990s teams. A fine leadoff hitter, base-runner, and center fielder, Dykstra was one of the more aggressive players in modern Phillies history. With the Phillies, he hit .289. He hit .325 in 1990, then had a spectacular season in 1993, hitting .305, while leading the league in at-bats (637), hits (194), runs (143), and walks (129). He also had a career-high 19 home runs.

October 20, 1993—The fourth game of the 1993 World Series was the highest-scoring game in history with the Toronto Blue Jays handing the Phillies a devastating 15–14 loss. The Phils had a 14–9 lead entering the eighth inning. Dykstra had a monster game, hammering two home runs and a double, and scoring and driving in four runs apiece.

Jim Eisenreich
Outfielder
Phillies—1993–96

Even though he was not a regular, Jim Eisenreich etched his name in Phillies lore with his solid play. His best asset was his bat, and he used it to hit over .300 four straight years. His high was .361 in 1996. While usually playing in well over one 100 games, he also went .318, .300, and .316. His three-run homer won Game Two of the 1993 World Series. Eisenreich was also a flawless fielder. He was widely admired for overcoming Tourette syndrome, an affliction that cost him nearly four years of his career.

June 14, 1993—A consummate pro, Eisenreich had many key hits for the Phillies, but his biggest came in a 10–3 victory over the Montreal Expos. Although not noted as a home run hitter, Eisenreich walloped a grand slam homer. It was not only his first Phillies slam, it sent the team to its sixth straight win and best start (45–17) in club history.

Von Hayes
Outfielder/First Baseman
Phillies—1983–91

Traded to the Phillies from the Cleveland Indians for five players, including Manny Trillo, Von Hayes never quite won the hearts of Phillies fans. He should have. Hayes was one of the club's premier players in the 1980s, a solid hitter with pop in his bat. He hit .272 with the Phillies with 124 home runs. Hayes had the third-highest number of homers (77) at the Vet. He reached double figures in home runs six times, including 26 in 1989. In 1986, he had a banner season, hitting .305 with 19 homers, 98 RBI, and 107 runs.

June 11, 1985—In one of the most lopsided games in big league history, Hayes had a starring role. Blasting 27 hits, the Phillies crushed the New York Mets, 26–7. Hayes did what no other big leaguer ever did, hitting two home runs in the first inning. He hit a leadoff homer, then followed with a grand slam as the Phils jumped out to a 9–0 lead.

John Kruk
First Baseman/Outfielder
Phillies—1989–94

It might have been true that John Kruk didn't look like a hitter. But looks could be deceiving. Kruk could flat out hit. And he did it about as well as anybody in the modern Phillies era. In six years with the Phillies, Kruk never hit below .291. He hit more than .300 four times, including .331 after joining the Phils during the 1989 season, .323 in 1992, and .316 in 1993, a year in which he twice had five hits in one game. With the Phillies overall, Kruk batted .309. He collected a .348 average in the 1993 World Series.

April 11, 1994—It wasn't so much what Kruk did on the field as what he did to get there. Kruk had been diagnosed with testicular cancer and had missed all of spring training while undergoing radiation treatment. Although not expected to be back yet, Kruk was in the lineup on opening day. He laced three hits, including a double in his first at-bat.

Mike Lieberthal
Catcher
Phillies—1994–2003

He went about his job quietly and without a lot of fanfare. But while he played at the Vet, Mike Lieberthal was one of the steadiest Phillies players of the last decade. He was an excellent receiver, rated one of the league's best. In 1999, he recorded the highest fielding percentage (.994) of any catcher in Phillies history, making just three errors all season. Entering the 2004 season, Lieberthal had a .266 lifetime batting average. In 2003, he hit a career-high .313, the third highest mark among major league catchers.

September 30, 1999—There have been a number of big games in Lieberthal's career, but none bigger than the Phillies 2–1 victory over the Chicago Cubs. In that game, Lieberthal hit his 31st home run of the season. The blast gave him more round-trippers than any other Phillies catcher, breaking a 43-year-old record held by Stan Lopata.

Greg Luzinski
Left Fielder
Phillies—1970–80

Of those who played at the Vet, there was only one power-hitter more deadly than Greg Luzinski. That, of course, was Mike Schmidt. But "the Bull," as he was called, did more than his share of heavy damage. He hit home runs in double figures eight times, three times going over 30. He hit 39 in 1977 to go along with a .309 batting average and 130 RBI. Two years earlier, he had gone .300 with 34 home runs and 120 RBI. Luzinski ranks second in most homers (130) at the Vet and fourth on the club's all-time list with 223. As a Phillie, he hit .281.

May 16, 1972—There was never any question about Luzinski's power. The only question was, how far would the ball travel once it collided with his bat? Of Bull's tape-measure homers, none was more memorable than his smash off the Liberty Bell, then hanging from the 400 level in dead center field. The ball traveled an estimated 500 feet.

Garry Maddox
Center Fielder
Phillies—1975–86

It was said that two-thirds of Earth is covered with water and the other third by Garry Maddox. Maybe that was a slight exaggeration, but few center fielders covered more territory than the "Secretary of Defense." He had a career fielding average of .983. Maddox was also a top base-stealer who could hit. His average with the Phillies was .284. He was second in the league in batting in 1976 with a .330 mark. His 10th inning RBI double gave the Phillies an 8–7 win in the deciding Game Five of the 1980 LCS.

October 3, 1982—As the Phillies defeated the New York Mets, 4–1, on the final day of the season, Maddox clinched a Gold Glove as the National League's finest-fielding outfielder. It was his eighth Gold Glove. That was particularly noteworthy because only Roberto Clemente and Willie Mays won more Gold Gloves in the National League.

Gary Matthews
Left Fielder
Phillies—1981–83

Although he didn't stay long, Gary Matthews had a major impact on Phillies fortunes. The Sarge was the man who took charge. He was a hard-driving, hustling, team leader. And he could play the game. Matthews hit .301 in 1981, then had a fine year in 1982 with 19 home runs, 83 RBI, and a .281 batting mark. But his biggest contribution was in 1983 when, despite just a .258 average, the left fielder played a big role in the Phils' pennant with his fiery, no-nonsense play. Matthews wound up hitting .279 in his Phillies career.

October 8, 1983—The 1983 League Championship Series belonged to Matthews. He hit home runs in three straight games and was the Series MVP. After a home run and four RBI in a 7–2 Phils win over the Los Angeles Dodgers in Game Three, Matthews drilled a three-run homer that gave the Phils another 7–2 win and the National League pennant.

Bake McBride
Right Fielder
Phillies—1977–81

In the judgment of many experts, the Phillies would not have been the team that they were if they hadn't acquired Bake McBride. McBride was one of the final pieces that put the Phils over the top, and his contributions were considerable. He batted in different spots in the order, but always produced. In his first year with the Phillies, he hit .339 in 85 games. He hit .309 in 1980, slugging a number of key hits, including a three-run homer in the first game of the World Series. Overall, his average with the Phils was .292.

September 26, 1980—As the end of the season approached, the Phillies were still unable to break away from the Montreal Expos. So every victory was critical. In a win the Phils had to have, they beat the Expos, 2–1. McBride's clutch home run provided the winning margin and kept the Phils ahead in a race that went to the season's last day.

Tug McGraw
Pitcher
Phillies—1975–84

Throughout their first decade at the Vet, there was no shortage of excellent relief pitchers on the Phillies. One, though, stood out above all the others. Tug McGraw was the one. And not only could he pitch. He had a great sense of humor, an always positive attitude, and a relentlessly enthusiastic spirit. Eventually, he became a folk hero in Philadelphia, a player revered by fans everywhere. McGraw ranks third in games pitched (463), fourth in saves (94), and second in relief wins (49) on the Phillies' all-time list.

October 21, 1980—It is fitting that the greatest moment in Phillies history featured one of the most beloved players in Phillies history. Excitement, police dogs, a roaring crowd filling the Vet to capacity, a moment without precedent in Philadelphia sports. McGraw struck out the Kansas City Royals' Willie Wilson to give the Phillies their only World Championship.

Scott Rolen
Third Baseman
Phillies—1996–2002

Toward the end of their tenure at the Vet, the Phillies were amply endowed with weak teams. One of the few beacons in the darkness, however, was Scott Rolen. He was what they call a five-tool player. He could hit, hit for power, field, run, and throw. And despite his less than amicable departure, he'll go down as one of the top third basemen in Phils history. Rolen had a .282 batting average with the Phillies with 150 home runs. In 1998, he hit .290 with 31 homers and 110 RBI. He hit .298 with 26 home runs in 2000.

July 2, 1999—Of his many fine games, both offensively and defensively, Rolen's signature game was possibly the one in which he became the first player at the Vet to hit inside-the-park and conventional home runs in the same game. Showing both speed and power, Rolen accomplished the rare feat during a 14–1 victory over the Chicago Cubs.

Pete Rose
First Baseman
Phillies—1979–83

When Bill Giles engineered a contract with Pete Rose, it gave the Phillies exactly what they needed: an aggressive player, a fierce competitor who would hustle his socks off and light a fire under his laid-back teammates. Rose did not disappoint. With the spirited style he brought from the Cincinnati Reds, he sparked the Phils to a pennant and World Series victory in 1980 and another flag in 1983. Rose had some banner years at the plate with the Phillies, hitting .331 in 1979 and .325 in 1981. Overall, he hit .291.

August 10, 1981—Exactly two months earlier, Rose had tied Stan Musial as the National League's all-time leader in hits. But then came a players' strike. No games for 60 days. In the first game after play resumed and with 60,651 fans, plus Musial, in the stands, Rose grounded an eighth inning single to left off Mark Littell for his record-breaking 3,631th hit.

Juan Samuel
Second Baseman
Phillies—1983–89

It would take some digging to find a more exciting player than Juan Samuel during the Phillies years at the Vet. Sammy created excitement the way a boom box creates noise. He flew on the bases. He hit with gusto. And although his defense wasn't the greatest, it was always exciting when a ball was hit his way. Samuel hit .263 with the Phils, his best year being 1987 when he batted .272 with 28 home runs, 100 RBI, and 113 runs. He stole 72 bases in 1984, the most for a Phillie in the 20th century. He also swiped 53 in 1985.

August 12, 1987—The Phillies beat the Chicago Cubs, 13–7. Although Samuel hit a grand slam and a single and drove in five runs, his triple was the significant hit. It was his 10th of the season and made him the first player in major league history to reach double figures in doubles, triples, home runs, and stolen bases in each of his first four years.

Curt Schilling
Pitcher
Phillies—1992–2000

For a guy who was a relief pitcher when the Phillies traded for him, Curt Schilling turned into a pretty good starter. So good, in fact, that in the 1990s he was the club's premier hurler. He won in double figures five times, reaching a high of 17 in 1997. He went 16–7 in 1993. Schilling, who had a 101–78 record with the Phils, struck out 319 batters in 1997 to set a modern National League record for righthanders. In 1998, he fanned 300 to become only the sixth big league pitcher to register back-to-back 300-strikeout seasons.

Second baseman Juan Samuel.

Pitcher Curt Schilling.

October 21, 1993—One of the most gritty pitching performances in Phillies history was Schilling's masterpiece in the fifth game of the 1993 World Series against Toronto. Having lost a demoralizing 15–14 game the day before, the Phillies had their backs to the wall. But a fiercely determined Schilling fired a 2–0, five-hitter to keep the Phils' hopes alive.

Mike Schmidt
Third Baseman
Phillies—1972–89

What can be said about Mike Schmidt that hasn't already been said? Hall of Famer. Best third baseman in baseball history. Won or tied for eight home run titles. Ranks 11th on the all-time home run list. Winner of 10 Gold Gloves.

Three-time MVP winner. Eight-time All-Star Game starter. Phillies all-time leader in most hitting categories. Schmidt was simply the best Phillies player ever to set foot on the Vet turf. While spending his entire career with the Phils, he hit 548 home runs, drove in 1,595, scored 1,506, and hit .267.

July 7, 1979—Many of Schmidt's memorable feats happened on the road. Of his top games at home, none was bigger than the time he hit three homers in his first three at-bats in an 8–6 win over the San Francisco Giants. In his final at-bat the game before, Schmidt had also homered. The outburst gave him four consecutive home runs.

Jim Thome
First Baseman
Phillies—2003

It doesn't matter that Jim Thome played only one season at the Vet. In that one season, he carved a niche for himself in Phillies history that is impossible to ignore. After signing as a free agent following a long career with the Cleveland Indians, Thome came to Philadelphia and promptly won over the tough Phillies fans with both his bat and his down-to-earth demeanor. While batting .266 with 131 RBI, his 47 home runs not only won the National League crown, but ranked as the second highest total in club history.

September 27, 2003—In the next-to-last game at Veterans Stadium, the Phillies won for the final time there, 7–6 over the Atlanta Braves in 10 innings. Thome, who finished fourth in the league's MVP voting, hit two home runs to set a Vet record with 28 home runs in one season. His eighth inning blast was the last homer to be hit at the Vet.

Manny Trillo
Second Baseman
Phillies—1979–82

With no reasonable doubt, it can be said that the Phillies never had a better second baseman with the glove than Manny Trillo. The slick-fielding, whip-armed Trillo holds the team record for highest one-season fielding percentage (.994), set in 1982. In four years with the Phils, he made just 33 errors. Trillo also could deliver with the bat. He batted .277 as a Phillie. He hit .292 in 1980, and as MVP in the LCS, he socked a key RBI double in Game Four and a go-ahead two-run triple in the pennant-clinching Game Five.

July 30, 1982—The Phillies' 3–1 win over the Chicago Cubs marked a special occasion for Trillo. In that game, he set an extraordinary record by playing in his 89th straight game without an error, then a National League record. During his streak, Trillo also set a major league record that still stands for most consecutive errorless chances (479).

THE GREATEST MOMENT

Nothing tops the last game of the 1980 World Series

It was 11:29 on the night of October 21, 1980. Sixth game of the World Series. Top of the ninth inning. Bases loaded. Two outs. Phillies leading the Kansas City Royals, 4–1 in the game and three games to two in the Series.

Policemen, some with dogs, some on horseback, rimmed the field at Veterans Stadium. Players inched up to the tops of the dugouts. The stands pulsated with excitement and anxiety. Fans, 65,839 of them, sat on the edge

Above: Right after the Phillies clinched the World Series, Mike Schmidt jumped on his happy teammates.

of their seats, many struggling to catch their breaths. The tension was almost unbearable.

Out on the mound, Tug McGraw got set to deliver a 1–2 pitch to Willie Wilson. Just one batter earlier, Pete Rose had reached under the outstretched glove of Bob Boone to grab a foul pop up that the catcher had bobbled in front of the Phillies dugout. And then, summoning one last pitch from his aching arm, McGraw, admittedly "out of gas," struck out Wilson to crown what stands as the greatest moment in Phillies history.

It was also the greatest moment in the 33-year history of Veterans Stadium.

There were, of course, many other great moments at the Vet. Quite a few of them came as a result of Phillies post-season appearances.

Overall, Veterans Stadium was the site of nine World Series games; three in 1980, three in 1983, and three in 1993. The Phils won four of those games, three in 1980. The Phillies also appeared in 13 National League Championship Series (NLCS) games at the Vet. After losing their first six games, they had a 5–8 home record in the NLCS.

In addition to their one World Series victory, the Phillies clinched two National League pennants at the Vet. The team never captured an NL East Division crown at home.

Of the post-season baseball games held at the Vet, some were particularly memorable. None, of course, topped the 1980 finale.

The 1980 World Series cast the spotlight on the Vet in a way that had not occurred before. Previously, the stadium had never served as the site of a sporting event of this magnitude. But the World Series attracts nationwide—even worldwide—attention, and with two highly appealing teams performing, the Vet became a focal point of the crown jewel of baseball.

The Phillies were coming off an NLCS with the Houston Astros that even now is widely regarded as one of the best—if not the best—in playoff history. It took five games—four that went into extra innings and four that were decided by either one or two runs—to reach a conclusion.

Finally crowned the National League champion, the Phillies moved into the World Series against the Kansas City Royals. The first game, played October 14, was memorable in its own right simply because it was the first Series battle staged in Philadelphia in 30 years.

Manager Dallas Green tapped Bob Walk as the Phils starting pitcher. It was the first time a rookie started a Series opener since Joe Black did it for the Brooklyn Dodgers in 1952. Walk gave up eight hits and six runs in seven innings.

Trailing, 4–0, the Phillies rallied for five runs in the third, with Bake McBride's three-run homer being the big blow. Two innings later, Garry Maddox's sacrifice fly drove in what proved the winning run as the Phillies squeaked out a 7–6 verdict with Walk getting the win and McGraw the save. It was the Phillies' first World Series victory in 65 years.

A major issue as the 1980 World Series concluded was the presence of police dogs on the field.

The Phillies won Game Two at the Vet, 6–4, but lost two out of three in Kansas City. The Series then returned to Philadelphia for the sixth game.

Some 65,838 fans, the largest crowd of the Series, jammed into every available space at the Vet. The cheers were deafening as the Phillies built a 4–0 lead behind Steve Carlton, two of the runs having been driven in by Mike Schmidt and one each by Boone and McBride.

As the eighth inning began, McGraw was asked to warm up. Tug reached for his glove, only to find that a German shepherd was lying on it. The police dog's handler rescued the glove, and a little later, McGraw was summoned to the mound after Carlton put the first two runners on base.

Paul Owens (left), Dallas Green, and Ruly Carpenter (right) accepted the winners' trophy from baseball commissioner Bowie Kuhn as announcer Bryant Gumble watched.

Tug walked Wilson to load the bases, then gave up a sacrifice fly to U. L. Washington. After the Royals reloaded the bases on George Brett's infield hit, McGraw threw three straight balls to Hal McRae before getting the future Phillies coach to ground out to end the inning.

With the score now 4–1, and the tension raging to a nearly unfathomable level, the Phillies went down in the eighth. As dogs, horses, and cops rimmed the playing field, the Royals came to bat in the ninth.

Up in the 400 level in the Phillies executive box, the club's then–vice president, Bill Giles, was sweating buckets. And it wasn't because the Phillies were on the verge of victory.

"I was the guy who had been negotiating about bringing in the horses and dogs with Wilson Goode, who at the time was the city managing director," Giles recalled. "I was very nervous about what might happen if people ran out on the field. I was very upset that Goode [a future Philadelphia mayor] decided to bring the dogs out. I said, 'Bring the horses out,' but he brought the dogs, too. I thought that presented a bad picture and image for the city."

And it did. The next day, newspapers and television stations throughout the country carried pictures showing the extensive four-legged menagerie and commentaries that were highly critical of their presence. But, in the final analysis, the law-enforcement group proved a strong deterrent in controlling what could otherwise have been an ugly situation with fans ripping up the field and perhaps worse. Making the matter more critical was the fact that the Eagles had a game at the Vet that Sunday.

McGraw struck out Amos Otis leading off the ninth. But then he loaded the bases on a walk to Willie Aikens and singles by John Wathan and Jose Cardenal. That brought Frank White to the plate. White lofted a high pop foul in front of the Phillies dugout. Boone camped under it, but at the last minute, the ball popped out of his glove. As it headed for the ground, Rose reached under Boone's mitt and made the catch. Two outs.

Now it was Wilson's turn. In another of life's many ironies, the Phillies had considered drafting Wilson in the early 1970s and had even brought him to the Vet for a tryout.

"We were selecting early, and who we would take was between Wilson, Dale Murphy, and Lonnie Smith," recalled Ruly Carpenter, the team president in 1980. "At that time, Dale was a catcher. We had also worked him out at the Vet, but we didn't think he could make it as a catcher. Wilson was only a righthanded batter then. We could see his great speed, but we thought his only way to play in the major leagues was if he became a switch-hitter. So we had questions about what both he and Murphy could do, and we went with Lonnie, who we'd worked out in California, and really liked."

As Carpenter thought back to those days, Wilson could do nothing more on a 1–2 count than swing and miss at a McGraw fastball. Tug leaped into the air in what turned into the most triumphant demonstration in Phillies history. The Phillies had finally won the World Series after 97 years of futility.

Fans stood in the stands cheering as loudly as their vocal chords would allow them, many with tears streaming down their faces. The tears flowed elsewhere, too.

Carpenter, who had replaced his father, Bob, as team president in 1973, watched with his dad from his box on the 400 level as the players celebrated on the field. "The first thing I did," he said, "was to start crying. I'm not ashamed to admit it. It was like all the years of frustration that had come before were finally over."

Afterward, in the tumultuous Phillies clubhouse, the media crowded around McGraw, who had given himself the nickname "the Tylenol Kid" because he was taking eight of those pills each day trying to quell the pain in his exhausted left arm. What pitch had he thrown to strike out Wilson? he was asked.

"The slowest fastball in the history of baseball," Tug said. How did he figure that? "It took 97 years to get there," McGraw replied.

Green, who had become manager the year before, would say years later that the outcome was never in doubt. "We knew in the clubhouse from the beginning that we were going to win the thing," he said. "It was just a case of when. Rose had said to me, 'Dallas, if we can get past the playoffs, the World Series will be a piece of cake.' And he was right. No offense to Kansas City, but we had the momentum, we had everything in place, the guys were playing great, and we had all our troubles behind us. And we had decided, we were going to go and beat Kansas City.

"And then we did it in front of our home fans, and it was just great for [general manager] Paul Owens and I, for the players, the organization, the fans. I was a home-grown guy and I had grown up in the organization and then Paul and I had put the team together, so it was very, very special to win the World Series," said Green, who long after the team had been called back onto the field and the wild victory celebration had finally ended, wound up with his wife and several of his children at 3 A.M. at the nearby Penrose Diner, where a number of policemen from the Vet had also congregated.

Without question, the night provided a memory that everybody who was there would never forget. "It was certainly my fondest memory," said Mike Schmidt. "It was the fondest memory for everybody on that team."

There were, of course, other fond memories emanating from the Vet. One was the pennant-clinching game on October 8, 1983. In that unforget-table battle, Gary Matthews slammed a first-inning, three-run homer to send the Phillies on their way to a 7–2 victory over the Los Angeles Dodgers in the fourth game of the NLCS.

Known as the Wheeze Kids because of the presence of a number of grizzled veterans such as Rose, Joe Morgan, and Tony Perez, all one-time members of the Cincinnati Reds' famed Big Red Machine, the Phillies had not been overwhelmed by the admiration of their fans during most of the regular season. But, led by the resurgent bat of Morgan, the Phils won 14 of their last 16 games to clinch the NL East title. Suddenly, the popularity of the team was unrestrained as the Philadelphia area tingled with excitement.

"That was kind of the last hurrah for Pete and Tony and me together," Morgan said. "And that made it very special. When you're at the end [of your career], you probably appreciate things a little bit more than you do in the middle or the beginning. So I loved it in Philly in 1983. It was a great year."

The team, which had lost 11 of 12 games during the regular season to the Dodgers, was, however, a decided underdog in the NLCS. But after splitting the Series in Los Angeles, the Phillies returned home and climbed ahead in the best-of-five Series, two games to one. Owens, who had come down from his front-office perch to manage the team at mid-season after Pat

MVP Gary Matthews sparked the Phillies to their first pennant won at the Vet.

Corrales was fired, sent Carlton to the mound in Game Four in search of his second win of the Series.

Matthews, who was to be named MVP of the Series, got the Phils started with a three-run homer in the first inning. By the sixth inning, the Phils had a 7–1 lead after Sixto Lezcano's two-run homer. The Dodgers' only run had come on a home run by Dusty Baker.

Carlton was lifted after the sixth inning with a 7–1 lead. Ron Reed and Al Holland finished out with the latter retiring five of the last six batters. The Phillies were on their way to their second World Series in four years and a date with the Baltimore Orioles.

"The 1983 season was the highlight of my career," Matthews said. "Having Carlton on the mound with John Denny and Tug there, too. Playing with my best friend, Garry Maddox, and with Pete Rose. It was a feeling that will forever be very special to me. We didn't win the World Series. But the fact that we were finally able to knock off the Dodgers was just awesome."

The Phillies had no winning outings at the Vet in the 1983 World Series. And there would not be another post-season home game of note until

1993. When such a game did occur, however, it took a place among the Vet's most memorable moments.

Again, it was the pennant-clinching game. This time the opponent was the Atlanta Braves. On October 13, the Phillies captured the flag with a 6–3 victory in the sixth game of the best-of-seven Series.

To get to that point, the Phillies had roared through the regular season, roosting in first place in the NL East for all but one game of the season. Stymied by injuries, the team had finished in last place in 1992, but a healthy club in 1993, bolstered by some key acquisitions, made it an altogether different situation.

"It was just electric that year," said Jim Eisenreich, one of the most valuable acquisitions. "The fans were like a 10th man; they enjoyed themselves so much and they were behind us all the way. It was an awful lot of fun playing that year."

Starting the Series at the Vet, the Phillies split the first two games, then came back from three games in Atlanta needing just one more win to claim the pennant. Tommy Greene took the mound to face future Hall of Famer Greg Maddux.

Darren Daulton's bases-loaded, ground-rule double gave the Phillies two runs in the third. Then, after an RBI single by the Braves' Jeff Blauser, the Phils added two more runs in the fifth on a two-run homer by Dave Hollins.

"We needed guys to step up, and that's what we did," said Hollins.

Mickey Morandini tripled in two more runs in the sixth to send Maddux to the showers. But even with a 6–1 lead, the Phils were by no means home free. Atlanta got to Greene in the seventh as Otis Nixon clubbed a two-run homer. Exhausted, Greene departed after that inning.

By then, the stadium was pulsating with fans screaming and stamping their feet as the action on the field became tenser by the minute. There was no less tension in the Phillies dugout.

"The atmosphere was unbelievable," recalled Morandini. "There we were, on the verge of going to the World Series, and there were 65,000 people in the stands going crazy. It was quite overwhelming. In fact, that whole season was the most fun I ever had playing baseball."

"I was just so damn excited, I was out of breath," manager Jim Fregosi said.

David West came on to retire the Braves in order in the eighth, and Mitch Williams did likewise in the ninth. When pinch-hitter Bill Pecota struck out to end the game, Williams leaped into the air while his teammates sprinted to the mound, where they formed a mass of howling, happy humanity. And out of the stands came a massive roar that must have been heard as far away as Chester.

"People said the Braves were better on paper," Daulton recalled. "I don't think you can put desire on paper."

Having just clinched the 1993 pennant, Darren Daulton and Mitch Williams began
the celebration as teammates rushed to join in.

While becoming only the third team in baseball history to go from last place to first in back-to-back seasons, the Phillies rode a wave of ecstasy into the World Series against the Toronto Blue Jays. In Canada, where the Series opened, the Phils managed to half the first two games. Back at the Vet, they lost the next two games.

The second loss was a memorable 15–14 slugfest on October 20 in Game Four. The teams combined for 31 hits, both that and the total runs scored being World Series records. Twelve of the hits were for extra bases.

Lenny Dykstra hit two home runs while driving in four and scoring four. Daulton also homered, Mariano Duncan and Milt Thompson added three hits apiece for the Phillies, and Devon White, Roberto Alomar, and Tony Fernandez each matched that total for Toronto.

Neither starter—Greene for the Phillies and Todd Stottlemyre for the Blue Jays—lasted three innings. Thompson's bases-loaded triple helped the Phillies to a 4–3 lead in the first. Toronto led 7–6 after three innings. A five-run fifth featuring two-run homers by Dykstra and Daulton put the Phils up, 12–7.

Eventually, the Blue Jays raked Phillies relievers Larry Andersen and Williams for six runs in the eighth to overcome a 14–9 Phillies lead and squeak by with a one-run victory.

Blowing such a big lead, not to mention the chance to tie the Series, ranked as one of the more excruciating losses the Phillies ever suffered. After such a devastating defeat, the Phillies could easily have folded. But on October 21, Curt Schilling, MVP in the NLCS, came to the rescue.

In a game that undisputedly ranks among the most memorable post-season tussles at the Vet, Schilling brought the Phillies back from the brink of elimination with a spectacular five-hit shutout, beating the Blue Jays, 2–0, and sending the Series back to Toronto. It was one of the strongest pitching performances in a long history of stellar Phillies mound efforts.

"I was upset because the previous night we'd given a game away," Schilling said. "So I wanted the ball. I wanted the responsibility. If you didn't want the ball in those situations, why show up?"

While Schilling stymied the Blue Jays inning after inning, the Phillies scratched for runs against Toronto pitcher Juan Guzman. They scored once in the first when Dykstra walked, stole second, went to third on a wild throw from catcher Pat Borders, and romped home on John Kruk's ground out. In the second, Daulton doubled and scored on Kevin Stocker's single for the Phils' final run. Stocker said later that it was "the most satisfying hit I ever had."

The euphoria that engulfed the Phillies was, of course, short-lived. Two days later in Toronto, the Series ended when Joe Carter touched Williams for a walkoff, three-run homer that brought the Blue Jays from a 6–5 deficit to an 8–6 win.

While Schilling's win in Game Five stands as the Vet's last memorable post-season skirmish, several others with unfavorable results rank on the stadium's never-to-be-forgotten list.

One was the Vet's first encounter with post-season play on October 9, 1976, when the Phillies met the Cincinnati Reds in what was then a best-of-five NLCS. After seeing a 15 $\frac{1}{2}$-game lead shrivel to three, the Phillies had finished nine games in front, winning 101 jousts during the regular season, the highest total in team history. The Reds had won 102 games and were the defending World Champions, having beaten the Boston Red Sox in 1975 in a rousing seven-game Series.

"We were playing the hottest team in baseball," recalled Phillies manager Danny Ozark. "I wanted to win so badly."

The Reds, popularized as "The Big Red Machine" for being the dominant team of the era, featured a lineup that included future Hall of Famers Morgan, Perez, and Johnny Bench, plus Rose, Ken Griffey, George Foster, and a band of other top professionals. Cincinnati's manager was George (Sparky) Anderson, also a future Hall of Famer and the Phillies second baseman during his only big league season in 1959.

The opening game marked the Phillies' first appearance in post-season play since they'd faced the New York Yankees in the 1950 World Series. Carlton drew the starting assignment for the Phils against the Reds' Don Gullett.

Greg Luzinski's sacrifice fly gave the Phillies a 1–0 lead in the first inning. But Foster's solo homer, two hits and three RBI by Gullett, and Rose's three hits led the Reds to a 6–3 victory. Gullett allowed just two hits before leaving after eight innings with a leg injury. Rawly Eastwick came on to surrender RBI singles to Schmidt and Jay Johnstone in the ninth.

The Vets' losing streak in memorable games continued in 1977 after the Phils had again clinched the NL East, again with 101 wins. This time the competition was the Los Angeles Dodgers under rookie manager Tom Lasorda. It was a Series that lives in infamy in Phillies history.

In Game Three on October 7—Black Friday as it became known—in the first game of the Series at the Vet, the Phils sent Larry Christenson to the mound against Burt Hooton. The Dodgers took an early 2–0 lead, but in the bottom of the second, one of the most bizarre incidents ever to find its way into a baseball game happened.

The Phillies loaded the bases, and as each batter reached, Hooton became more unnerved. Sensing this, the crowd—which numbered 63,719—got involved. Each time Hooton went into his windup, the crowd hooted. And the hooting got louder with each pitch. Hooton, who had already been experiencing control problems, walked Christenson. Then, as the crowd got even louder, he walked McBride. Hooton, now totally unraveled, then walked Larry Bowa. By this time, the Dodgers pitcher had walked home three runs. He was removed without further adieu.

"That whole episode was incredible," said Phillies president David Montgomery, who at the time was the team's director of sales. "Has there ever been a crowd that literally got a pitcher out of a game? I don't think so."

Eventually, the Phillies took a 5–3 lead into the ninth inning. Dependable reliever Gene Garber was on the mound for the Phils, and after the second out, he had retired eight straight batters on ground balls, and it looked like the Phillies would finally win their first post-season game at home since 1915.

But then disaster struck. Aging Vic Davalillo, a member of the Dodgers' unimpressive bench and a Mexican Leaguer as recently as August, beat out a drag bunt. Then with two strikes, Manny Mota launched a drive to deep left field. Luzinski, who in these kinds of situations was usually replaced by defensive whiz Jerry Martin, was still in the game in left. He drifted back for the catch, but the ball hit his glove and fell to the ground as Davalillo scooted home. Second baseman Ted Sizemore booted the relay throw, allowing Mota to go to third.

Davey Lopes followed with a shot off the glove of Schmidt. The ball bounced toward short, where Bowa alertly picked it up and fired a bullet to first. Lopes appeared to be out, but umpire Bruce Froemming ruled otherwise. The Phillies screamed in protest, but to no avail. The call stood, and Mota scored on the play to tie the score.

The debacle wasn't over yet. Garber threw away a pickoff attempt, and Lopes went to second. Then, Bill Russell bounced a single up the middle with Lopes scoring on the hit to give the Dodgers a 6–5 victory.

To say that the Phillies were a somber bunch as they trudged back to the clubhouse would be a gross understatement. They were completely destroyed. And for all intents and purposes, the Series was over.

Many years later, Ozark, a former Dodgers coach, would recall that evening and cringe. "I wanted to beat the Dodgers more than anybody," he said. "But I messed up. I should have taken Greg out. But I didn't know he [Davalillo] was going to bunt, and that nobody was going to cover first. And I didn't know that the ball was going to hit Schmitty and bounce over to Bowa. I didn't know that the umpire was going to miss the call. They ran some pictures in the papers that showed he [Lopes] was definitely out. It was just one of those darned things that didn't work out. Mota wasn't supposed to pull the ball. I never saw the ball. I don't think a lot of others did either. It was hit so hard."

If the perception of that game as one of the most disappointing ever played at the Vet—or, for that matter, in all of Phillies history—wasn't bad enough, the situation was no better the next night. Adversity was again an ugly visitor to the Phillies cause.

It rained. And it rained. And it continued to rain. It was hard rain, too, not just light sprinkles. Commissioner Bowie Kuhn and National League president Chub Feeney, who had the authority to call a postponement, sat stalwartly in the downpour, apparently oblivious to the terrible conditions on the field and—obviously under the influence of the dictums of television—unwilling to make the right decision. The game was played.

Performing through a steady downpour that drenched the field and obliterated almost any semblance of a baseball game, the teams slogged through the night with the Phillies unable to solve the offerings of Tommy John's rain-soaked sinker-ball. Dusty Baker poked a two-run homer off Carlton in the second inning, and the Dodgers went on to slide to a 4–1 victory and clinch the NLCS as John went the distance, allowing just seven hits.

Other Post-Season Games at Veterans Stadium

October 10, 1976 – With the largest crowd (62,651) ever to see a playoff game up to that point, the Phillies lost to the Reds in Game Two of the NLCS, 6–2. Jim Lonborg pitched a no-hitter for five innings, but an error by Dick Allen helped Cincinnati to a four-run sixth that paved the way for a 6–2 Reds victory. Luzinski's home run and three hits by Johnstone provided the Phillies' main offense against Cinci starter and winner Pat Zachry and reliever Pedro Borbon. The Series ended two days later in Cincinnati with a 7–6 Reds victory.

October 4, 1978 – Misfortune was proving to be the Phillies' unrelenting mistress. The playoffs opened against the Dodgers at the Vet with Christenson getting the call against the fans' old friend, Hooton. Burt gave up 10 hits and four runs in less than five innings, but during the same time, his teammates raked Christenson for seven runs. With Steve Garvey belting two home runs, and Lopes and Steve Yeager each homering once, LA romped to an easy 9–5 victory. Bob Welch gave up one run over the final four and one-third innings to get the win. Bowa had three hits for the Phils.

October 5, 1978 – Another loss followed in Game Two, extending the Phillies' playoff losing streak at Vet Stadium to six games. The Dodgers' John hurled a complete game four-hitter and got 18 ground outs with his masterful sinker to blank the Phillies, 4–0. Lopes homered off Dick Ruthven after the Phils starter had fired three perfect innings, then drove in two more runs. Phillies fans were booing loudly by the sixth inning. Ultimately, the Phillies lost the Series in four games as Maddox bobbled a fly ball that led to a run in the 10th inning that gave the Dodgers a 4–3 victory.

October 7, 1980 – The opening game was the only one of the five NLCS games against the Houston Astros that was completed in the regulation nine innings. A crowd of 65,277 flocked to the stadium to see if the Phillies could start to shed the bonds of three straight NLCS losses. They did while winning their first NLCS game at the Vet, 3-1. Luzinski smacked a two-run homer in the sixth to put the Phillies ahead. Carlton scattered seven hits over seven innings to get the win, and McGraw got the save with two innings of hitless relief. Losing pitcher Bob Forsch went the distance, allowing eight hits.

October 8, 1980 – Third base coach Lee Elia admitted he made a mistake when he held up McBride at third on Lonnie Smith's single to right with the score tied at 3–3 in the bottom of the ninth. The result of the blunder was a 7–4 Houston victory in Game Two. Ruthven allowed just three hits and two runs in seven innings, but his teammates could get just two runs off Nolan Ryan. Each team scored in the eighth. Then Elia's blunder sent the game into extra innings. Houston scored four runs off Ron Reed in the 10th with Jose Cruz knocking in the winning run. The Phils outhit the Astros, 14–8.

October 15, 1980 – George Brett made national headlines when he had to leave after six innings because of an attack of hemorrhoids. But Game Two of the World Series belonged to the Phillies. Carlton and the Royals' Larry Gura matched shutouts for four innings before the Phils broke ahead on a sacrifice fly by Maddox and an RBI single by Bowa. A three-run seventh fueled by Otis's two-run double gave a 4–2 pad to Kansas City. The Phillies then came back with a four-run eighth to win, 6–4, as Del Unser's pinch-hit RBI double began the rally. McBride singled home the tying run before Schmidt got the game-winner with an RBI double. Reed saved the win for Carlton.

October 9, 1981 – A 60-day players' strike during the season fostered a plan to decide division winners by declaring first and second half champions who would meet in a special playoff. The Phillies won the first half, the Montreal Expos captured the second half, and the two met in a best-of-five Series. With Montreal ahead two games to none, the Series moved to the Vet, where the Phillies snatched a 6–2 victory behind Christenson, who scattered four hits and one run over six innings. Matthews slugged three hits, while the Phils took advantage of four Expos errors.

October 10, 1981 – George Vukovich belted a pinch-hit home run in the 10th inning to give the Phillies a 6–5 victory in a wild and wooly fourth game of the Series. Schmidt and Matthews also homered for the Phils, while Gary Carter poked a four-bagger for the Expos. Phils' starter Dickie Noles pitched well before leaving with a 4–2 lead in the fifth. Afterward, the lead seesawed until Vukovich's blast off Jeff Reardon leading off the 10th. McGraw got the win.

October 11, 1981 – Although favored to win the Series, the defending World Series champions were no match for Steve Rogers as the Expos won the NL East with an easy 3–0 victory. Rogers, the winner in the Series opener, yielded just six hits in a complete game shutout. He also poked a two-run single in the sixth that broke a 0–0 deadlock. Carlton gave up seven hits over eight innings while absorbing his second loss of the Series.

October 7, 1983 – Phillies rookie Charley Hudson became the only pitcher of the four-game Series to hurl a complete game as he beat the Dodgers, 7–2, in Game Three of the NLCS. Hudson gave up just four hits while striking out nine. He surrendered a two-run homer to Mike Marshall in the fourth for the only Dodger damage. The Phillies scored two runs without a hit in the second, then added another run in the third on Joe Lefebvre's sacrifice fly. Matthews took care of the rest with a solo homer in the fourth, a two-run single in the fifth, and an RBI single in the seventh.

October 14, 1983 – It was billed as the I-95 Series. From the Phillies' standpoint, it could have been called "five and out." After splitting the first two games in Baltimore, the third game of the World Series was held at the Vet. The big news was that Rose was being benched in favor of Perez. Matthews and Morgan each homered to give the Phillies an early 2–0 lead. But the Orioles caught up with Carlton, and with two runs in the eighth rallied to take a 3–2 victory. Jim Palmer, working in relief of Mike Flanagan, became the first pitcher to win a Series game in three different decades.

October 15, 1983 – Cy Young Award winner John Denny, the victor in the Series opener, figured to pull the Phillies even in the Series. He didn't. The Orioles won the third one-run game of the Series, 5–4, as Rich Dauer cracked three hits and drove in three runs. The Phils had a 3–2 lead after a single by Denny and double by Rose each plated runs in the fifth. Baltimore answered with two runs in the sixth as four straight pinch-hitters paraded to the plate. Dauer doubled home the eventual winning run an inning later. Storm Davis got the win in the 20-hit affair.

October 16, 1983 – Going into Game Five, neither Mike Schmidt, Cal Ripken, nor Eddie Murray had been factors in the Series. Together, the three sluggers had six hits in four games. While the first two remained mired in dismal slumps (Schmidt wound up going 1-for-20 in the Series), Murray broke out of his with vengeance. He slammed two home runs and a single and collected three RBI to lead Baltimore to a 5–0 victory and the World Championship. Scott McGregor went the distance, allowing just five hits. The game was played before the largest crowd (67,064) in Philadelphia baseball history and the biggest World Series audience since 1964.

October 6, 1993 – In the first game of the NLCS, Kim Batiste went from goat to hero in the space of just one inning. With the Phillies leading, 3–2 in the ninth, Batiste threw a potential double play ball into right field, setting up the tying run for the Braves. One inning later, he drilled a one out single to score Kruk with the winning run in a 4–3 Phils victory. Earlier, the Phillies had trailed, 2–1, before Pete Incaviglia socked a 423-foot solo homer in the fourth. A wild pitch by Braves starter Steve Avery gave the Phils the lead run in the sixth. Schilling struck out the first five batters in the game and pitched eight gritty innings, giving up two runs and seven hits. Mitch Williams got the win.

October 7, 1993 – There was never any doubt about the strength of the Braves' offense. Especially after Game Two of the NLCS. Atlanta hitters pummeled six Phillies pitchers for 16 hits, four of them home runs in a lopsided 14–3 victory. Phils starter Tommy Greene gave up seven runs before leaving in the midst of a six-run Atlanta third. Jeff Blauser, Fred McGriff, Terry Pendelton, and Damon Berryhill all homered for the Braves. Joined by four-baggers off the bats of Dykstra and Hollins, the teams set an NLCS record for most homers in one game. Maddux had no trouble cruising to the win, yielding five hits and two runs in seven innings.

October 19, 1993 – A major rain storm, the first at the start of a World Series game since 1968, caused Game Three to be delayed for 72 minutes. Phillies pitchers probably wished it had kept raining. As the Series got its first exposure to the Vet, Toronto blasted 13 hits and twice staged three-run innings. The result was a 10–3 win for the Blue Jays and pitcher Pat Hentgen. Paul Molitor, curiously replacing American League batting champion John Olerud at first base, slapped a two-run triple in the first off Danny Jackson. Two innings later, he homered. Thompson hit a home run for the Phillies in the ninth.

SPECIAL OCCASIONS

Over the years, there were many memorable games

In every sport, there are moments that exceed the levels of mere normalcy. There is no particular measure that defines these moments. They are simply times when something happens that is clearly out of the ordinary. And they are savored because of that.

Above: Von Hayes became the first major leaguer to hit two home runs in the first inning in a 26–7 rout of the New York Mets.

Steve Carlton acknowledged the fans after completing his 15th straight victory while recording one of the greatest seasons of any pitcher.

Anything that survived more than three decades certainly would have a hearty share of these special moments. Such was the case with Veterans Stadium. Particularly where baseball was concerned, the Vet was richly endowed with moments that were above and beyond routine events.

Hitting feats, no-hitters, triple plays, oddities, special games, and unusual circumstances were among the many occurrences at the Vet that were defined as great moments. Some of the participants such as Mike Schmidt and Steve Carlton were future Hall of Famers. Others were one-time wonders enjoying their 15 minutes of glory.

During their 33 years at the Vet, the Phillies finished first in the East Division six times. They placed second five times, third seven times, fourth five times, fifth four times, and sixth six times (several finishes were ties). Their finest era, when general manager Paul Owens masterfully put together some of the best teams in Phillies history, occurred between 1974 and 1983, when the team finished no lower than second only three times, while winning five division titles, three pennants, and one World Series.

Those years, as well as most of the others, produced many special occasions. The ones described herein are those that occurred during the regular season. Special moments during post-season play were discussed in Chapter 5.

Two of the Vet's finest hours took place when it played host to All-Star Games.

The first occurred in 1976 in the year of Philadelphia's bicentennial celebration. Placed amid a summer-long series of festivities, the game was attended by 63,974 fans—at the time, the third largest crowd in All-Star Game history. Among the spectators was President Gerald Ford, who was escorted to his box by rival managers Sparky Anderson of the Cincinnati Reds and Darrell Johnson of the Boston Red Sox.

Due to a publicity campaign in Cincinnati, fans there stuffed the ballot box, selecting six Reds to the starting lineup. A club record five Phillies—Bob Boone, Larry Bowa, Dave Cash, Greg Luzinski, and Schmidt—were named to the squad. Luzinski was the lone starter, but the others all played.

Mark (The Bird) Fidrych, an eccentric Detroit Tigers rookie who talked to the ball and performed other strange antics, was the starting pitcher for the American League. Randy Jones of the San Diego Padres opened for the National League.

Fidrych gave up two runs in the first inning. With the Reds' George Foster and Cesar Cedeno of the Houston Astros each adding two-run homers, the NL cruised to an easy 7–1 victory, its 13th win in the last 14 outings. Foster was named Most Valuable Player. Boston's Fred Lynn homered for the AL, while Jones got the win, and Fidrych took the loss.

The Vet's second All-Star Game was held in 1996. By then, numerous side shows, held before the game, had become a regular part of All-Star Games. This one was no exception. An extravaganza called "FanFest" was held starting on the weekend before the game at the Pennsylvania Convention Center. A workout the day before the game was attended by some 62,000 fans. A gala center city party held by the Phillies took place that night. Other activities included a celebrity softball game featuring former players such as Lou Brock and Steve Garvey; Hollywood types including Ron Howard, Geena Davis, and Robert Wuhl; singer Meatloaf and skiier Picabo Street; the presence of 22 mascots; and the perfunctory home run derby, won by Barry Bonds.

Before the game, Cal Ripken of the Baltimore Orioles suffered a broken nose when a platform on which players were standing for a team picture tilted and caused another player to slam into him. With 62,670 watching, the game finally began with the Atlanta Braves' John Smoltz facing Charles Nagy of the Cleveland Indians.

The Nationals jumped out to a 1–0 lead in the first. Local guy Mike Piazza of the Los Angeles Dodgers then clubbed a solo home run in the second and an RBI double in the third to win the game's MVP award and pace his team to a 6–0 victory. Nine NL pitchers, including the Phillies' Ricky Bottalico, held the losers to seven hits with Smoltz earning the win and Nagy getting the loss.

One of the most memorable regular-season games at the Vet occurred when Pete Rose slammed his 3,361st hit to break Stan Musial's National

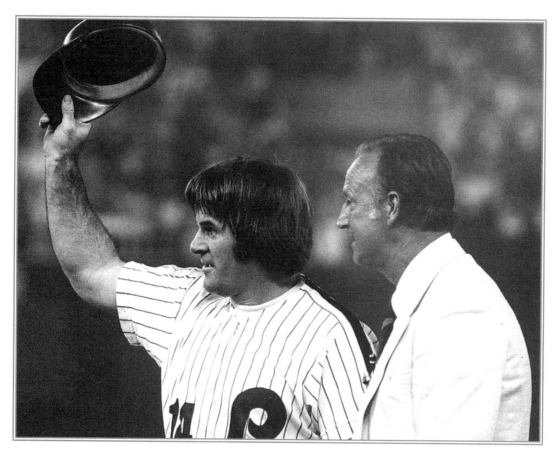

Moments after he became the National League's all-time leader in hits, Pete Rose was joined by Stan Musial, whose record just fell.

League record. Rose had tied the record on June 10, 1981 at the Vet with a first-inning single off Nolan Ryan. The Phillies first baseman failed to break the record that night, striking out the next three times, although the Phillies rallied to gain a 5–4 victory over the Astros.

A players strike began the following day. Exactly 60 days later, play resumed. Playing against the St. Louis Cardinals and with Musial in the stands, Rose went hitless in his first three trips to the plate. Then in the eighth inning with Mark Littell on the mound, Rose lashed a single between shortstop and third base for the record-breaking hit. Some 60,561 fans in attendance cheered wildly as Musial took the field to congratulate Rose. The Phillies lost, 7–3, but it mattered little on this star-studded night.

Another highly memorable regular-season game at the Vet took place on June 11, 1985, when the Phillies slammed 27 hits, including 14 for extra bases, to destroy the New York Mets, 26–7. It was a Phillies modern club record for runs scored. The Phils racked up 47 total bases while collecting 10 doubles and batting around four times. Between them, the Phils and Mets slugged 40 hits.

Ironically, the Phillies went into the game having scored just 25 runs in their previous nine games and had the third lowest team batting average (.230) in the league. But the draught was quickly over when the Phils scored nine runs in the first inning and seven more in the second.

Von Hayes, who was mired in a 9-for-63 slump and batting in the leadoff spot for the first time in his career, got the Phils started with a home run. Before the inning was over, Hayes had crushed a grand slam homer, making him the first major league player ever to hit two home runs in the first inning.

"Obviously, it was my best game," Hayes—who also singled, drove in six runs and scored four—said years later. "But what was really amazing was the way the whole team hit. Even a relief pitcher—Mark Rucker—got two hits. It was unbelievable."

Juan Samuel bashed five hits, Rick Schu slugged four, Bo Diaz lashed three doubles, and Glenn Wilson poked two doubles and a single and scored four runs. Diaz and Wilson both picked up three RBI, while Samuel, Diaz, and Garry Maddox each scored three times. Charley Hudson got the win, although he gave up 13 hits in five innings.

On May 15, 1989, the Phillies staged one of the most implausible finishes ever seen at the Vet when Bob Dernier hit an inside-the-park home run in the bottom of the 12th inning. The hit gave the Phillies a thrilling 3–2 victory over the San Francisco Giants.

Don Carman and the Giants' Scott Garrelts had matched shutouts over the first nine innings with the former yielding just four hits and the latter three. Both hurlers exited after the ninth, but the game remained scoreless until the top of the 12th, when Will Clark and Kevin Mitchell unloaded back-to-back homers off Steve Bedrosian, working his third inning in relief.

The Phillies, however, weren't dead. With two outs, Dickie Thon and Steve Lake singled. That set the stage for Dernier, who—inserted into right field in the ninth for defensive purposes—had thrown out Clark at the plate. Dernier lined a shot off Craig Lefferts to the left field corner that eluded Mitchell. As the Giants' left fielder tracked down the ball, Thon and Lake scored, and the speedy Dernier raced around the bases. Running out of gas as he reached the plate, Dernier dove home well ahead of the throw.

Nearly 15 years later, Dernier vividly recalled the play. "When I hit the ball," he said, "I knew Dickie could score and I thought Lake could, too, after I saw the ball bouncing around in the corner. As I came around second, I looked at [Larry] Bowa who was coaching at third, and since we had a chance to win, I knew he was going to keep me going. So I kicked it in a little. But there's a wall that you hit about 10 feet beyond third. You're not used to running that far. After I hit that wall, those last six or eight steps were the longest I've ever taken."

"What I remember most was the energy in the stadium," Dernier added. "You could feel it building as the play developed. The excitement was awesome. Of course, once I scored, I remember Chris James jumping

A three-run, inside-the-park, walkoff home run by Bob Dernier was one of the single most exciting plays in Vet history.

around like a jackrabbit. I got patted so hard on the head that I got a headache. Then Bedrock threw me over his shoulder and carried me up the tunnel to the clubhouse. A few of us stuck around in the locker room and celebrated until three or four o'clock in the morning."

More excitement occurred on August 15, 1990, when Terry Mulholland became the first Phillies pitcher to fire a no-hitter at home in the 20th century and the first Phillies lefthander to toss blanks. Mullholland, owner of a 13–21 career record at the time and a 6–6 mark for the season, beat the Giants, 6–0, with 32,156 fans in attendance. Darren Daulton hit a two-run homer in the fifth.

Mulholland, who struck out eight, came within one batter of pitching a perfect game. In the seventh inning, after fielding Rick Parker's grounder, third baseman Charlie Hayes was charged with an error on a throw to first that pulled John Kruk off the bag. Parker, a former Phillies minor leaguer, was the only runner to reach base but was quickly erased on a double play.

Hayes redeemed himself in the top of the ninth when with two outs, pinch-hitter Gary Carter smoked a wicked line drive down the third base line. Hayes made a spectacular backhanded catch to preserve the no-hitter.

The only other Phillies no-hitter at the Vet was thrown on April 27, 2003, by Kevin Millwood. The big righthander, acquired during the off-season in a trade with the Braves, downed the Giants, 1–0. The game's only run came on a first-inning home run by number two batter Ricky Ledee, who ironically caught a fly ball for the final out of the game.

Before a Sunday afternoon attendance of 40,016, the largest crowd ever to watch a Phillies no-hitter, Millwood struck out 10 and walked three to run his record to 4–1. It was just the third 1–0 no-hitter in major league history and the only no-hitter during the 2003 season.

Of all the memorable events at the Vet, nothing tops the one that began on the night of July 2, 1993, and finished on the morning of July 3. The occasion was a doubleheader between the Phillies and Padres.

Under normal conditions, the first game would have started at 4:35 P.M. But these weren't normal conditions. It rained and rained, then rained some more. As a result, the game didn't start until 5:45. Two more rain delays of one hour, 56 minutes and two hours, 48 minutes followed, bringing the a total of rain delays to five hours and 54 minutes. For some unfathomable reason, the game was played to its completion, finally ending at 1 A.M. on July 3 with San Diego winning, 5–2.

In the overall scheme of things, that game was virtually irrelevant. Curiously, a second game was started at 1:25 A.M. It went on and on, the Padres taking a 5–0 lead in the fourth inning, then the Phillies coming back with four runs, including a three-run homer by Ricky Jordan, and finally tying the score in the eighth.

The announced crowd for the first game was 54,617. But as the night wore into what broadcaster Richie Ashburn called "the shank of the night," most fans left the ballpark. Eventually, only about 6,000 people remained. But as word got around as the second game progressed, hundreds of new fans began appearing at the Vet in hopes of seeing a history-making event. They were not disappointed.

The score was tied at 5–5 in the bottom of the 10th inning when the Phillies, having used all available pinch-hitters, sent relief pitcher Mitch Williams to bat. A notoriously poor hitter, Williams had not batted all season. Naturally, he singled to drive in Pete Incaviglia from second with the winning run and give the Phillies a 6–5 victory. The clock read 4:40 A.M. It was the latest a major league game had ever finished.

There have been many other special baseball games at the Vet. It would be impossible to recap all of them. But here are some of the best ones:

September 18, 1971 – Rick Wise retired 32 consecutive batters to set a club record in a 12 inning, 3–2 win over the Chicago Cubs. Wise also slugged the game-winning single.

September 30, 1971 – A team rookie record for home runs was set by Willie Montanez, when he slammed his 30th in a 4–3 loss to the Pittsburgh Pirates.

April 19, 1972 – In a battle of future Hall of Famers, Steve Carlton, making his Vet debut, bested Bob Gibson and the St. Louis Cardinals, 1–0, in a game that took only one hour, 33 minutes and that was played before just 8,184 spectators. Carlton allowed three hits.

August 17, 1972 – Steve Carlton set a Phillies record with his 15th straight win beating the Cincinnati Reds, 9–4. Carlton allowed seven hits.

September 16, 1972 – Mike Schmidt hit his first major league home run. A three-run belt off Balor Moore, it gave the Phils a 3–1 win over the Montreal Expos.

May 4, 1973 – In their longest game since 1919, the Phillies downed the Atlanta Braves, 5–4, with Jose Pagan's sacrifice fly driving in the winning run in the 20th inning.

April 6, 1974 – A two-run homer in the bottom of the ninth by Schmidt off Tug McGraw gave the Phillies a 5–4 decision over the New York Mets on opening day.

May 12, 1974 – The Phillies went into first place for the first time since the Vet opened with an 8–7 win over the Pirates. Eddie Watt got the win in relief.

August 5, 1975 – A major league record was set when the first eight Phillies batters hit safely in a 10-run inning against the Cubs. Included in the barrage were home runs by Maddox and Schmidt, two doubles, and four singles. The Phils won, 13–5, getting 18 hits altogether.

September 27, 1975 – Tony Taylor, who had collected his 1,000th hit at Connie Mack Stadium, slammed his 2,000th career hit in an 8–1 win over the Mets. Carlton pitched a one-hitter.

October 3, 1976 – In the last game of the season, the Phillies beat the Reds, 6–2, to set a club record with 101 wins. The Phils also went over two million in attendance for the first time with 2,480,150.

June 22, 1977 – Larry Bowa's only grand slam of his career was one of eight home runs (five by the Phillies) hit in a 15–9 victory over the Reds that featured a five-run Phils seventh.

October 2, 1977 – A home run by Jay Johnstone powered a 5–3 triumph over the Expos as the Phillies closed the season with their second straight 101-win year and a Vet record 60 wins in 81 games.

April 8, 1978 – While driving in four runs with a single and home run, Larry Christenson won his eighth straight game and 16th win in 17 decisions in a 7–0 victory over the Cardinals.

June 3, 1978 – Reserve infielder Dave Johnson slugged a grand slam home run in the bottom of the ninth to give the Phillies a 5–1 win over the Dodgers. With it, Johnson became the first major leaguer ever to hit two pinch-hit grand slams in the same season.

May 19, 1979 – The Phillies wore burgundy uniforms in a 10–5 loss to Montreal. It was the first and last time the ugly duds would be seen.

July 10, 1979 – A major league record was set when Del Unser hit his third consecutive pinch-hit home run, a three-run blast in the ninth that gave the Phils a 6–5 win over the Padres.

April 26, 1980 – Carlton set a modern National League record with his sixth one-hitter in a 7–0 win over the Cardinals. A second-inning single by Ted Simmons was St. Louis's only hit.

July 25, 1980 – With his 260th home run, Schmidt broke Del Ennis's club record while Dick Ruthven threw a Vet record 12 innings in a complete game, 5–4 victory over the Braves.

September 29, 1980 – Fans booed unmercifully after the Cubs scored twice in the top of the 15th to break a 3–3 tie in one of the Vet's wildest games. But the Phillies scored three times in the bottom of the inning to take a 6–5 verdict with Manny Trillo's single plating the winning run.

April 29, 1981 – Striking out the side in the first inning, Carlton became the first lefthanded pitcher in baseball history to whiff 3,000 batters as the Phils beat Montreal, 6–2.

April 6, 1982 – For the only time in Veterans Stadium history, the opening game with the Mets was postponed because of snow. Cold weather again forced cancellation of the game the following day.

October 1, 1982 – In one of the greatest pitching duels in Phillies history, John Denny and Terry Leach of the Mets matched one-hit shutouts for nine innings. Denny gave up a second inning single to Dave Kingman, and Leach served up a fifth inning triple to Luis Aguayo. New York won in the 10th, 1–0.

April 13, 1983 – Following four walks, Bo Diaz blasted a grand slam homer with two outs in the bottom of the ninth to give the Phillies a 10–9 triumph over the Mets in one of the team's greatest comebacks in Vet history.

May 1, 1983 – Exactly 100 years after the Phillies played their first game, they clobbered the Mets, 11–3, as Tony Perez drove in five runs on three hits.

May 28, 1983 – In one of his most quixotic games, Schmidt, who was hitless in his previous 22 at-bats and who had struck out four times in the game, gave the Phillies a dramatic 5–3 decision over Montreal with a two-run homer in the bottom of the ninth.

September 2, 1983 – In yet another dramatic finish, Ozzie Virgil's pinch-hit, grand slam homer with two outs in the bottom of the ninth delivered a 5–3 win to the Phillies over San Francisco.

April 10, 1984 – An unforgettable opening day was decided when Schmidt touched Nolan Ryan for a three-run homer in the eighth inning to give the Phillies a 3–1 victory over Houston.

July 29, 1984 – The Phillies got back-to-back leadoff home runs for the first time in their history as Juan Samuel and Von Hayes drilled first-inning round-trippers. Len Matuszek's second game-winning pinch-hit homer in the last five days downed the Expos, 6–4.

June 23, 1986 – With a major league record 15 extra base hits and a club record 11 doubles, the Phillies annihilated the Cubs, 19–1. Samuel collected six RBI with two home runs and a double, while Rick Schu drove in four runs with two doubles and two singles.

September 28, 1987 – Don Carman came within one batter of pitching a perfect game when Mookie Wilson beat out an infield single in the fourth inning of a 3–0 victory over the Mets. Carman struck out five.

July 26, 1988 – After two rain delays totaling three hours and 25 minutes, New York beat the Phillies, 7–5, in a game that ended at 2:13 A.M.

June 8, 1989 – Steve Jeltz became the first Phillies player to hit a home run from both sides of the plate in the same game, but that was only part of the story. Pittsburgh scored 10 runs in the first inning, but the Phillies came back to capture a 15–11 victory.

July 29, 1989 – With a crowd of 47,277 watching, the Phillies retired Carlton's number 32 in a pregame ceremony in which the untalkative ex-hurler actually gave a speech.

May 26, 1990 – In a similar pregame ceremony attended by 56,789, the Phillies retired Schmidt's number 20.

April 28, 1991 – The Phillies pulled off the first triple play in Vet history when the Padres' Tony Gwynn lined a shot to second baseman Randy Ready. After catching the ball, Ready stepped on second, then, although he could easily have tagged the runner, threw to first baseman Ricky Jordan for the third out.

September 14, 1992 – An RBI single in the sixth inning of a 6–2 win over the Expos made Darren Daulton the first Phillies catcher ever to drive in 100 runs in one season.

July 7, 1993 – Lenny Dykstra's two-run double gave the Phillies a 7–6 decision in the 20th inning of a marathon with the Dodgers. The game tied for the longest in Vet history.

July 27, 1993 – John Kruk collected five hits for the second time in the season as he led an 18-hit attack that gave the Phillies a 10–7 victory over the Cardinals.

August 13, 1993 – A ninth inning grand slam by Kim Batiste downed the Mets, 9–5. The hit was the seventh of a club record eight grand slams during the season.

September 24, 1993 – The Phillies went over the three million mark in attendance for the first time in club history while beating Atlanta, 3–0. Mitch Williams set a team record with his 41st save.

August 25, 1995 – Gregg Jefferies became the first Phillies player to hit for the cycle since Johnny Callison did it in 1963 as the Phils slammed the Dodgers, 17–4. Winning pitcher Jeff Juden became the first Phillies hurler to hit a grand slam since 1984.

June 13, 1997 – In their first interleague game, the Phillies defeated the Toronto Blue Jays, 4–3, with Wayne Gomes getting the win in relief in his major league debut.

August 18, 1997 – For only the second time in Phillies history, two players hit grand slams in the same game. Mike Lieberthal and Billy McMillon did the honors in a 12–3 win over the Giants. The Phils' only other two-slam game was in 1921.

September 1, 1997 – In the start of an amazing three-game sweep of the New York Yankees in the first meeting of the two teams since the 1950 World Series, Curt Schilling struck out 16 in a scintillating 5–1 victory. Schilling would finish the season with a club record 319 strikeouts.

September 11, 1997 – A somber pregame tribute was paid to Phillies favorite Richie Ashburn, who died two days earlier in New York. Ashburn had been a Phillies broadcaster for 35 years and before that a player with the team for 12 seasons.

September 8, 1998 – Phillies batters set a club record with seven home runs in one game in a 16–4 shellacking of the Mets. Rico Brogna, Bobby Estalella, and Kevin Sefcik each homered twice, while Marlon Anderson hit one out in his first big league at-bat.

May 19, 1999 – The second and last Vet Stadium triple play by the Phillies resulted after a liner by the Mets' Mike Piazza. Shortstop Alex Arias snared the smash, touched second base, and threw to Brogna at first to complete the tri-killing.

August 8, 2000 – An eighth inning, upper deck grand slam gave Pat Burrell his second homer of the game and made him the first Phillies player to hit two slams in his rookie season in a 10–4 victory over the Padres.

September 17, 2001 – On one of the most emotional nights ever held at the Vet, baseball returned to action for the first time after the terrorist attacks of

September 11. A gripping pre-game tribute to the victims was followed with a 5–2 defeat of the Braves as Scott Rolen homered twice off Greg Maddux.

June 2, 2002 – A grand slam and a three-run homer by Robert Person gave him a club record for most RBI in one game by a pitcher in an 18–3 thumping of the Florida Marlins. The Phils scored 10 runs in the first inning.

April 9, 2003 – Jim Thome and Burrell each homered twice and collected five RBI as the Phillies battered Maddux and the Braves in an astonishing route, 16–2.

May 9, 2003 – Thome hit only the second home run ever to reach the Vet's 600 level in right field as the Phillies edged the Houston Astros, 5–3. The only other player to outdistance Thome was the Pirates' Willie Stargell in 1971.

June 6, 2003 – In their first trip back to Philadelphia since they left town in 1954, the Athletics—now playing in Oakland—defeated the Phillies, 7–4. Two days later, after rain cancelled the second game, the Phils swept a doubleheader, 7–1 and 8–3, with Kevin Millwood and Randy Wolf getting the wins.

June 12, 2003 – Another inter-league game was especially memorable as the Phillies nipped the Boston Red Sox, 6–5, on Todd Pratt's two-run homer in the 13th inning. Thome had hit game-tying home runs in both the eighth and 12th innings.

While the Phillies staged numerous special moments at the Vet, opposing teams and players were not without their memorable performances. For instance, on May 9, 1973, Johnny Bench collected seven RBI and became the first visiting player to slug three home runs in one game at the Vet in a 9-7 Reds victory. On May 31, 1975, the Astros set a Vet record with 12 runs in the eighth inning en route to a 15–3 rout of the Phillies. On August 6, 1980, the Phils suffered their most one-sided loss at the Vet, a 14–0 lacing by St. Louis and complete game pitcher Bob Sykes.

George Hendrick drove in seven runs to lead the Cardinals to a 15–3 triumph on June 29, 1982. On the night of August 4, 1982, Joel Youngblood, having just been traded, singled for the Expos in a 15–11 Phillies win. A few hours earlier at Wrigley Field in Chicago, Youngblood had singled for the Mets. He was the only major leaguer ever to get hits for two teams on the same day.

Fernando Valenzuela struck out 15 and drove in the game's only run to lead the Dodgers to a 1–0 win on May 23, 1984. Dwight Gooden fanned 16 for the Mets on September 17, 1984, but lost, 2–1, when he balked home the winning run in the eighth. And on April 13, 1987, Jamie Moyer's bid for a no-hitter was ended by Samuel's ninth-inning single in a 5–2 Cubs win.

Among other near no-hitters by the visitors, Tom Browning had a perfect game broken up by Dickie Thon's ninth-inning double, but the Reds won, 2–1, on July 4, 1989. Another near no-hitter was spoiled on August 3, 1990, when Doug Drabek surrendered a two-out single in the bottom of the ninth to Sil Capusano in an 11–0 victory for the Pirates. Good pitching performances by the opposition continued, and on October 6, 1991, the Mets' David Cone tied a National League record with 19 strikeouts while hurling a 7-0 shutout.

En route to his 70–home run season, Mark McGwire had one of just two three–home run games that year when he led the Cards to a 10–8 victory on May 19, 1998. In another slugging outburst, eight different players hit home runs for Cincinnati in a 22–3 drubbing of the Phillies on September 4, 1999. Overall, the Reds walloped nine homers, and Brogna added one for the Phillies to set Vet and National League records for the most home runs in a nine-inning game.

All of the special moments at the Vet, of course, haven't been headline grabbers. In fact, quite a few of them were downright bizarre.

For instance, there was the time in 1976 when Phillies outfielder Rick Biosetti in his first major league appearance was installed as a pinch-runner. Biosetti was promptly picked off first. In 1994, Phils pitcher Andy Carter was ejected while making his major league debut after he hit two of the first three batters he faced.

Slow-footed catcher Bob Boone hit an inside-the-park home run in 1976, and when a Phillies official was asked years later how such a thing could have happened, his reply was, "three outfielders died." Also on the hitting front, in 1987, Carman got his first major league hit after going 0-for-48. That same year, pitcher Kevin Gross was ejected from a game and subsequently suspended when a piece of sandpaper was discovered glued to the heel of his glove. Gross denied ever scuffing balls.

Once in 1985, after fans had given him an especially hard time the night before, Schmidt wore a wig onto the field before a game. Seeing through the disguise, fans appreciated the attempted humor and gave Schmidt a standing ovation.

Mike Maddux beat his brother Greg of the Chicago Cubs, 6–3, in 1988 in the only time the two started against each other. In an amazing piece of work in 1991, Andy Ashby struck out the side on nine pitches. In 1996, the Phillies tied a National League record when a pitcher named Glenn Dishman became the 54th player used by the club during the season. Three years later, the Phils made history again when they employed a same-name battery of Bennett and Bennett, Joel on the mound and Gary behind the plate.

RARELY A DULL MOMENT

Games were often accompanied by grand promotions

Stuntman Karl Wallenda walked across the top of Veterans Stadium, one side to the other, on a wire. Not once, but twice.

There was Kiteman, Cannonman, and Rocketman, plus the Wondrous Winns, Benny the Bomb, and the Playboy Bunnies. There were trapeze acts, a motorcycle ridden on a high wire, and parachute jumpers. And there were ostrich races, duck races, cows milked, and numerous other animal acts.

All at one time or another were involved with promotions staged at Veterans Stadium.

During its 33 years, the Vet was the scene of virtually every kind of promotion imaginable. Some were very good; a few were very bad. But regardless of the quality of the event, anyone attending a Phillies game over

Above: No Phillies' promotions were more spectacular than The Great Wallenda's two trips across the top of the Vet.

the years was likely to encounter some kind of promotion. There was a good chance it would not be ordinary.

The biggest promotions were usually staged on opening day. The last home game of the season also was always good for some kind of special activity. During the season, Sunday afternoon games were big in the Phillies' specially created world of fun and games.

Celebrities often took part in the events. But the entertainment wasn't always summoned from the outside. Sometimes, fans or players or the media or even umpires took part. And numerous times during any given season, a Phillies promotion involved some kind of a giveaway.

Collectively, this great variety of activities made Veterans Stadium and the Phillies a national leader in the field of sports promotions. The Vet was a place whose name was synonymous with the word "showmanship."

And the reason for that was hardly accidental. The Phils' extensive promotional activities were the centerpiece of a deliberate plan to get people into the ballpark. Such a technique might conflict sharply with the ideals of some baseball purists, whose view is that a baseball game in and of itself is enough to attract fans and shouldn't be cluttered with intrusive sideshows. But to the Phillies, the rationale was simple: Give the fans a reason to enjoy themselves, regardless of what happens in the game, and they'll come back again.

Bill Giles, the driving force behind the idea and the man who engaged most of the Phillies promotions over the years, had successfully tested the theory while serving as an executive with the Houston Astros. After he joined the Phillies, he initiated what he called his "staircase marketing concept."

"I wanted to do something unusual to attract a fan who was either not a died-in-the-wool fan or who may never have been to a baseball game," he said. "Theoretically, they would sample the product once, have a good time, and end up coming three or four times a year. Then they'd graduate to a 16-game plan, then become a season-ticket holder with a small plan, then—if you've produced a good enough product—they'd become full-season ticket holders. It was a kind of staircase effect.

"That was one phase of the concept. The other phase was that I wanted to make it enjoyable so that Mom, Dad and the kids could say on the way home, 'Gee, it's too bad the Phillies didn't win the game, but we had a good time.' We wanted them not to be completely dependent on the team's won-lost record."

To accomplish that objective, the Phillies staged some of the gaudiest promotions ever held in a ballpark. None, however, was bigger than The Great Wallenda's two journeys across the top of the Vet.

The first one was held on August 13, 1972. It was a Sunday afternoon game, and a crowd slightly in excess of 32,000 was in attendance. The idea was for Wallenda, the head of a world-famous family of high-wire artists, to walk on a two-inch wide steel cable close to 900 feet from foul pole to foul

The creative genius of Bill Giles was the driving force behind most of the Phillies' spectacular promotions at the Vet.

pole across the top of the Vet at a height of nearly 200 feet without a net. The feat, which required Wallenda in the early and late stages of his trip to walk above fans in parts of the upper deck, had never before been performed at a major league stadium.

Some time prior to the walk, Bill Hall, an entertainment agent who had sold the idea to Giles, took Wallenda to the Vet to look at the task he was being asked to perform. "He looked up," Hall remembered, "and said in his thick German accent, 'this will be spectacular.'" Wallenda had never walked that far on a high-wire.

The day of the walk, a crew of 20 men assembled at the Vet at 7 A.M. to raise and anchor the wire with the aide of a crane. With Wallenda and Hall helping, they finished the job five hours later. Wallenda, who had been performing his stunt since 1926, then took a nap in the stadium's first aid room. When he awoke, he drank a glass of milk (reports that he downed

Three-time national basketball championship coach Cathy Rush of Immaculata College participated in a sports celebrity contest.

something much stronger were erroneous), then climbed to a catwalk on the roof of the Vet.

"We had to go to Lloyds of London for insurance," then Phils president Ruly Carpenter recalled. "I talked to him before he went up. He made it seem like it was just another day at the office."

Wallenda, then 67 years old and earning $3,000 for the job, began his walk holding a 40-pound balancing pole. As he started, he spoke briefly with his daughter, who just two weeks earlier had lost her husband in a high-wire accident.

About 30 feet away from the start, Wallenda abruptly sat down on the wire. He motioned to the people back on the roof, but they were unable to figure out what he wanted. Finally, then stadium operations manager Pat Cassidy stationed on the floor of the Vet, determined that Wallenda was complaining that the guide ropes held by 38 people on the ground were too loose. The situation was remedied, and Wallenda proceeded on his journey.

At the halfway point, while hovering high above second base, Wallenda stopped and did a headstand. Those who were still watching went crazy. Those who weren't watching—and there were many—hid in terror.

"I was scared to death," remembered Phillies manager Frank Lucchesi. "I couldn't watch. I went into the clubhouse. Quite a few others were already there."

Some fans ran into the corridors. Even some hardened veterans of the press box either turned away or sought cover inside.

"I just sat there and watched in amazement," said Carpenter, one of the brave viewers who stayed to observe. "It was incredible that a guy would have that kind of balance and courage."

It took Wallenda 17 minutes to get across. One of the loudest standing ovations in Vet history greeted him as he climbed onto the roof.

"At first, I thought, he's done this so many times, he's not scared," said Giles, then a Phillies vice president. "But when he came down from the roof and then had about six martinis, I knew he was scared."

Much later, emerging from an impromptu party staged by his family, Wallenda showed up back on the roof to help workman remove the wire. According to Hall, who over the years booked many of the special promotions with the Phillies, he would not have passed a sobriety test.

Regardless, the feat ranked as one of the most memorable occurrences in the history of the Vet. And the following morning, it commanded a major place in newspapers throughout the nation. The following week, *Life* magazine did a two-page spread on the event.

It would, however, not be Wallenda's last visit. He returned to the Vet in 1976 to perform the same stunt. This time, he did it on May 31 as part of the Phillies' bicentennial celebration. Some 52,211 fans were in the stands at the start of his act.

Wallenda, who two years later fell to his death while performing on a high wire in Puerto Rico, added something extra for the occasion. He wore a Bicentennial cap and had U.S. flags on each end of his balancing pole. As he did before, Wallenda performed a headstand at the halfway point. The now 71-year-old high-wire artist finished the trip in 21 minutes and was again greeted with a standing ovation.

While Wallenda's two performances ranked atop the list of Veterans Stadium promotions, there were many other breathtaking acts. Many were executed on opening day.

Kiteman appeared on opening day seven times, finally making it to the pitching mound in 1990.

One was done in 1992 by Benny the Bomb, real name Benny Coskey. At second base, Benny placed himself inside a two-foot-by-six-foot box, and with enough powder to blow up a one and-one-half ton safe, set off an explosion that reduced the box to rubble. Benny emerged from the debris, dazed and shaken, but not enough to prevent him from delivering the first ball.

Some of the most remembered opening-day promotions were the various attempts by Kiteman to deliver the first ball to home plate. Kiteman appeared seven times, during which he was portrayed by three different people.

The idea was for Kiteman to take off down a 120-foot ramp in the upper deck in center field and glide to the vicinity of the pitcher's mound with the ball. The first Kiteman, a water skier from Cypress Gardens named Dick Johnson who was paid $1,500 for his effort, crashed into the center field seats in his first attempt in 1972. One year later, his flight ended in the stands in left-center field.

Kiteman III—T. J. Beatty was his real name—made it to center field in 1980. Then in 1990, Pete Bonifay became the first Kiteman to make it all the way to the pitcher's mound. Bonifay also arrived at the scheduled destination in 1995, 1999, and 2003.

Another spectacular opening day promotion was performed in 1975 by Monique Guzman, who rode a motorcycle across a high wire from first base to third base with the first ball. A special ground rule had to be put into effect in case a ball hit the wire because it could not be removed before game time.

In 1978 and 1985, Dave Merrifield dangled from a trapeze suspended from a helicopter. A woman dressed as William Penn slid down a wire that extended from the left field roof to the visitors' dugout in 1982. The Wondrous Winns rode across the stadium in 1986 with the husband riding a motorcycle on a high wire with his wife on a wire suspended underneath, nearly 200 feet above the ground.

Rocketman was the headliner three times, once crashing in practice and being unable to perform on opening day. And Cannonman, who traveled at a speed of 90 miles per hour after getting fired into the air from center field, also appeared several times. In 2003, three members of the Smith family were fired in succession from cannons.

There were numerous parachute deliveries. The Golden Knights, an Army parachute team, dropped down in 1979. Two years later, TV weatherman Jim O'Brien led a team that parachuted into the park. The U.S. Navy Leap Frogs based in San Diego flew into the stadium five times.

A different kind of approach was taken in 1976 when a pair of cowboys known as the Peterson brothers, taking turns dressed as Paul Revere, rode horses from Boston to the Vet. When they arrived after 16 days on the road, they presented the first ball to Rocketman, who blasted down to the pitcher's mound, where he gave the ball to new Hall of Famer Robin Roberts.

Throughout the years, major attractions become significant parts of Phillies opening-day ceremonies. They were events that Giles had deemed necessary after his arrival from Houston.

"I grew up in Cincinnati [where his father was president of the Reds]," Giles said, "and the city made a very big deal of opening day. Schools were closed, they had a big parade downtown; there were bands and banners, and politicians spoke. The game was sold out. Opening day was almost as big a deal in Cincinnati as Christmas.

"When I came to Philadelphia in late 1969, I looked at the attendance for opening day [at Connie Mack Stadium] and it wasn't very good. I said, 'What do you do here on opening day?' They said, 'well, we have the Salvation Army Band, and salute the American flag. Some city council guy throws out the first ball.'

"I said, 'We have to change that. When we get to the Vet, we're going to do something quite different.' I wanted to create an atmosphere in which it seemed that something special was happening. I wanted to tell Philadelphia that baseball was a big deal, that opening day was a big deal. It meant that spring was here, and that meant baseball was here, and we're going to have a lot of fun at the ballpark for the next six months."

A prominent singer or group of singers usually vocalized the national anthem on opening day. Among those who did were television host Mike Douglas, The Four Aces, the Grease Band, The Lettermen, Robert Merrill, James Earl Jones, The University of Pennsylvania Glee Club, and the Philadelphia Boys Choir. Various Mummers string bands and high school bands also did the honors.

Throwing out the first ball, a practice that also occurred through much of the season, was often handled on opening day by people with a Phillies connection such as Ruly Carpenter, Jim Bunning, Tug McGraw, Greg Luzinski, Bill White, Paul Owens, Richie Ashburn, and Dick Allen (with Eddie Joost and Bobby Shantz). Other first-ball throwers included Mayors Frank Rizzo, Bill Green, and Wilson Goode, Governor Robert Casey, Cardinal John Kroll, and baseball commissioners Bart Giamatti and Peter Ueberroth.

Many prominent events, of course, were staged during the season. One of the most dramatic occurred September 17, 2001. That night, there was major league baseball for the first time since the horrific events of September 11.

A Marine color guard presented the flag, a band from Lansdale Catholic High School played, and the Valley Forge Chorus sang the national anthem. Mayor John Street was in attendance. Players, coaches, and managers from both teams, as well as the umpires, lined each baseline as the somber ceremony took place.

"It was very, very emotional," recalled Chris Long, the Phillies director of entertainment. An employee of the club since it began at the Vet in 1971, she ranked it as one of the most memorable events ever staged at the stadium.

"I don't think there was a person who wasn't emotional," said Long. "And the television cameras showed it. One of the most poignant pictures showed [Phillies manager] Larry Bowa standing there with tears rolling down his face."

Another memorable event was the closing ceremony September 28, 2003, at the final game at Veterans Stadium (see Chapter 17). It, too, was an emotional experience for many people with lengthy connections to the doomed ballpark.

Naturally, many activities held at the Vet were on the frivolous side. One of the more popular ones was the event called "cash scramble," in which fans raced around the field scooping up as much money as they could find. Birthday parties for the Phillie Phanatic were annual occurrences. There were old-timers' games pitting former major league players against each

A "cash scramble" when fans tried to scoop up as much money as they could was a popular Vet promotion.

other. The Playboy Bunnies once participated in a softball game. And then there was a man dressed as the "High-Jumping Bunny Rabbit," who leaped off a hot air balloon only to crash land.

There were frequent acts involving real animals such as trained elephants, camels, baboons, goats, pigs, and sea lions. Several times, players participated in cow-milking contests. Dog and horse acts visited the field on occasion, too. Always, when animals were on the field, they were followed by a clean-up crew.

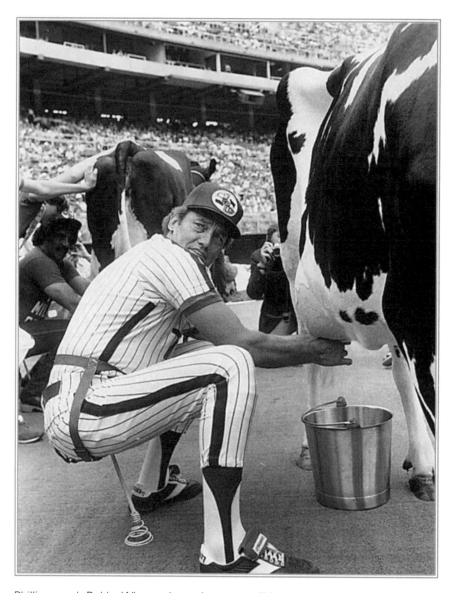

Phillies coach Bobby Wine took part in a cow-milking contest.

Some of the animal acts bombed. Such was the case with the infamous duck race. Twenty ducks were supposed to run across the infield from first to third but instead ran in every other direction, some heading for the Phillies dugout. Worse yet was the ostrich race. That event ended in disaster when, instead of racing from right field to the infield, the big birds bit, spit, and refused to run. Thereafter, one of the riders, a guy named Ashburn, harbored a lifelong distaste for ostriches.

When he was Mayor, Ed Rendell conducted the Philadelphia Orchestra. Baseball comic Max Patkin performed his routine. Harry Kalas, in addition to participating in the ostrich race, rode on a tricycle. And never to be forgotten were the annual Fourth of July fireworks, which

Mayor Ed Rendell directed the Philadelphia Orchestra with the help of the Phillie Phanatic.

always attracted a huge crowd both inside and outside the stadium; the late-season Fan Appreciation Day; or Camera Night, when fans could photograph Phillies players parading past rows of shutterbugs lining the field.

There were the occasional weekday afternoon games called "businessperson specials," games when communities, companies, or other groups were recognized, and games when specific groups were honored.

Phillies players wore burgundy uniforms during a game in 1979. The attire was supposed to be worn every Saturday. But the garb was so ugly that it was never seen again. In 1993, the Phillies and visiting Pittsburgh Pirates wore 1933 replica uniforms. The highlight of the day was a brawl between the teams.

The numbers of Ashburn, Roberts, Steve Carlton, and Mike Schmidt were retired in special ceremonies. The last two were major productions, attended by numerous former players and other guests and with both players receiving loads of gifts. The first two occurred without any advance publicity. "It really took me by surprise," Ashburn said at the time. "I didn't know anything about it until they told me while I was standing on the field. But . . . I never had a nicer thing happen to me."

Vet promotions weren't limited to the playing field. Nearly every Sunday throughout much of the life of the Vet, fans who attended games received clothing or souvenir items from different companies affiliated with the Phillies. In the 200-level concourse beneath the stands, there were always games. Fans could bat against a pitching machine, see how fast they could

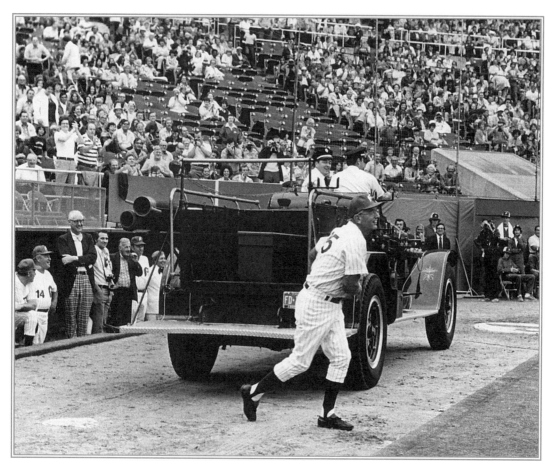

Relief ace Jim Konstanty, the 1950 National League MVP, headed from a fire truck to the mound as part of the 25-year reunion of the Whiz Kids.

throw, do a mock broadcast, make a baseball card, or test their skills on video games. They were levied minimal charges for these activities, with most of the money going toward research for ALS (amyotrophic lateral sclerosis, or Lou Gehrig's disease).

The concourse also had various displays. One of particular note were the plaques of players and managers from the Phillies and Athletics who were elected to the Philadelphia Baseball Wall of Fame. Started in 1978, the group included 50 all-time greats. Another display paid tribute to the Negro Leagues with pictures, memorabilia, and hats and jerseys. Yet another display listed up-to-date records of current Phillies along with pictures of Schmidt, Carlton, and others.

Over the years, there were many other promotional activities at the Vet. Originally, they came under the direction of Frank Sullivan, a Phillies employee since the mid-1950s. Sullivan ran the club's promotions department from 1971 until he retired in 1994. Long was Sullivan's assistant before taking over. Her office now comes under the broad umbrella of the Phillies' marketing department.

The Phillies often saluted visiting stars, such as Willie Mays on his 41st birthday.

"We did a lot of fun things over the years," Long said. "The fan reaction was always very positive. They understood that we were trying to make the game more interesting."

Long said that the one thing that changed noticeably over the years was the participation of the players. "They used to be willing to go on the field and do things," she said. "Most players won't do that today."

With all the memorable events that occurred at the Vet, it's likely that the players weren't missed.

BALLPARK PERSONALITIES

There were a number of familiar figures at Phillies games

He strutted around the field. He danced on the dugout roof. He badgered umpires and opposing players. He careened through the stands. He showered fans with hugs and kisses.

According to his bio, he stood six-feet tall, weighed 300 pounds, and came from the Galapagos Islands. He had a big nose, a long red tongue, huge feet, and a belly that extended far beyond practical limits. He was green, gifted, and gleeful.

He went by the name of Phillie Phanatic, and throughout much of the life of Veterans Stadium, this odd creature was a popular figure at every home

Above: Wearing colonial costumes, Phil and Phyllis (with Mary Sue Styles) were the Phillies' original mascots.

game. He was furry, funny, and friendly. And in the process of becoming synonymous with Phillies baseball, he established a worldwide image as the premier mascot in all of sports.

Played first by Dave Raymond and then by Tom Burgoyne, the Phanatic was one of a number of regular, long-term fixtures at the Vet. In some cases, they were as familiar to fans as were some of the players.

Some were known for their work. Others were known as "characters." Some were only heard. Some were only seen. But over the years at the Vet, all made significant contributions to Phillies games, either individually or in groups.

They were people such as Dan Baker and Paul Richardson. Mary Sue Styles, Froggy (also known as Mark Carfagno) and Jack Donnelly. And the Hot Pants Patrol, the Whiz Kids Band, and Phil and Phyllis.

The Phanatic, of course, was the most visual persona for the longest length of time. He made his debut April 25, 1978, and was still making merry when the Vet closed in 2003.

When the stadium originally opened in 1971, the Phillies had introduced a pair of mascots named Phil and Phyllis. Dressed in colonial costumes and wearing oversized head pieces with comic book faces, they wandered—somewhat stiffly—around the stadium greeting fans.

Although the couple became part of the Phillies' regular routine, the act was not overly inspiring. Some people thought the team could do better. One of them was Dennis Lehman, now the executive vice president of the Cleveland Indians, but then a young assistant in the Phils' public relations department.

"Denny kept telling me that we needed a mascot," Bill Giles, then the Phillies vice president, recalled. "I resisted when he kept telling me how much fun the San Diego Chicken was, but he kept pursuing it with me, and eventually I created the idea of the Phanatic."

Giles asked the club's promotions director, Frank Sullivan, to contact Harrison/Erickson Inc. of Brooklyn, New York—the creators of Big Bird, the enormously popular creature on the television show *Sesame Street*, as well as Miss Piggy and characters on the Muppets—and design a costume for a Phillies mascot.

"I wanted an undefinable, lovable character who kids would like," Giles said. "I asked them to make it fat with a big nose. But I didn't want anybody to say that it was a hippopotamus or any specific animal."

When the first design came in, Giles didn't like it. The creature wasn't fat enough, and its nose wasn't long enough. He sent it back to the drawing board with instructions to fatten the Phanatic, make its nose longer, and add something that would shoot out from its mouth. Eventually, a suitable creation arrived.

The Phillie Phanatic clowned his way into becoming professional sports' most acclaimed mascot.

"Still, I honestly didn't think it would work," said Giles. "But I said, 'We'll try it. How much is it going to cost?' They said, 'It'll cost $2,900 and we control the copyright, or it's $5,100 and you can have the copyright.' I said to myself, 'This isn't going to go over. Major league baseball doesn't have mascots. This is college and high school stuff.'

"So I said, 'All right, I'll save the money and give you $2,900.' What happened? It worked. And three years later, I paid $250,000 for the copyright."

The Whiz Kids Band offered both music and nostalgia to Phillies fans.

It was, however, money well spent. With Raymond in the suit, the Phanatic became a popular mainstay at Phillies home games. And not just kids, but adults, too, developed a fondness for the creature.

At first, Raymond, then a 21-year-old college student serving part-time as a clerk in the Phillies promotions department, had to develop a routine. The son of former University of Delaware football coach Tubby Raymond, he had no background in performing. But when he was asked by Giles to give the role a try, he readily consented. "Just go out and have fun with it," Giles said.

"I think the Phanatic's personality evolved very quickly," Raymond said in an interview several years ago. "Within about one year's time, I had down in my mind what I wanted the Phanantic to do. Then there was some refinement. But the fans were the guides for what I could or couldn't do."

Raymond developed some unforgettable routines. The Phanatic shook his belly at opponents. He shook his rear at fans. He roared across the outfield in his four-wheeled cart. He mutilated dummies dressed as opposing players. He smashed plastic batting helmets. He danced with groundskeepers and umpires. All the while, fans laughed, applauded, and loved every minute of it.

The Phanatic's favorite umpire was Philadelphian Eric Gregg. Much to the entertainment of fans, the two began to perform together in 1979. It started when Raymond called Gregg to ask him if he would dance with him. At first, Gregg demurred, saying an umpire couldn't dance with a mascot. But Raymond persisted, and Eric finally consented if two conditions were met: he could get clearance from his crew chief Doug Harvey, and he could select the music. Gregg picked a Michael Jackson song called "Rock with You," a big hit at the time.

"Harvey said I could do it if there were no arguments going on and there weren't any disputes at that point between the umpires and the Phillies," Gregg said. "So in the bottom of the fifth, the song came on. The Phanatic drove up in his cart, got out, hit me in the back, and we started rockin'. The crowd went nuts. And that was the start of the routine we did for many years."

Sometimes, the Phanatic's antics didn't go over well with opponents. Such was the case when he began spoofing Los Angeles Dodgers manager Tom Lasorda. Becoming increasingly unhappy with the stunt each time it was performed, Lasorda eventually came to regard the Phanatic with considerable scorn and irritation.

The Phanatic, who annually made upwards of 200 appearances away from the Vet, spoofed quite a few others, too. During the NLCS in 1993, he did an imitation of actress Jane Fonda—an exercise devotee and then the wife of Atlanta Braves owner Ted Turner—doing a workout. Fonda, sitting in a field box nearby, signaled her approval of the skit.

Raymond spent 16 years as the Phanatic before retiring prior to the 1994 season. He was replaced by 28-year-old Burgoyne, Raymond's backup and occasional setup man, who over the previous five years had made more

One of the Phanatic's most popular routines over the years was dancing with Philadelphia-bred umpire Eric Gregg.

Who played in more games at the Vet than anyone? The answer is organist Paul Richardson.

than 1,000 appearances outside the Vet as the Phanatic. Burgoyne first got the job after answering a newspaper classified ad and beating 15 other applicants in a tryout.

Burgoyne ably carried on the duties of the Phanatic while adding a few twists of his own. The basic objectives, however, remained the same: have fun; entertain the fans.

"I think the fans have always taken the Phanatic to be one of their own," Burgoyne said. "He wears his emotions on his sleeve. Sometimes, he has a little attitude. But he always likes to have fun, and the fans like to have fun with him.

"The Phillies," Burgoyne added, "always gave me complete freedom. They never told me where to go or what to do at certain times. The beauty of that is the spontaneity it creates. You don't sit around all day dreaming up skits. You just go out and keep it simple. Maybe you ruffle some feathers or maybe you dance with an umpire who doesn't want to dance. Then that becomes part of the act. Part of the charm of the Phanatic is that you never know what's going to happen from one day to the next."

On hot days, the Phanatic knows what will happen: he'll roast in his heavy, furry costume. After a 20-minute stint, even with ice packs strapped to him, he's soaked, his clothes are drenched. And the Phanatic has, as Burgoyne calls it, "a bad case of body odor."

As the Phanatic, one of Burgoyne's more noteworthy skits came in 1997 during the Phillies first inter-league game. The team was playing the Toronto Blue Jays at the Vet. The Phanantic engaged Toronto outfielder Joe Carter in a wrestling match. Carter, of course, hit the walkoff home run that beat the Phillies in the final game of the 1993 World Series.

Who threw that home run pitch (Mitch Williams) has become one of the Phillies more infamous trivia questions. Here's a more pleasant question: Who played the most games at Veterans Stadium?

The answer is organist Paul Richardson. The esteemed maestro of the keyboard estimated that he missed no more than five games while playing in every one of the Phillies' 33 years at the Vet.

Richardson began taking piano lessons at the age of five, progressed to the organ in high school, once had his own trio, sold organs and pianos, and taught the organ for many years. In 1969, while playing at a Phillies Christmas party, he said to Giles: "Here's what you need [at the new stadium] . . . a new organ that has rhythm."

Shortly thereafter, Giles gave Richardson the job. He began with the Phillies in 1970 at Connie Mack Stadium. When the Phillies moved to the Vet the following year, he went with them and was a fixture there until the stadium closed.

At first, Richardson played jazzed up versions of songs such as *Tarantella*, *Can Can*, and *Hava Nagila*, and, of course, the three most sung songs in the nation, *The Star Spangled Banner*, *Happy Birthday*, and *Take Me Out to the Ball Game.* Once when a streaker ran onto the field, he played *Is That All There Is?* When players from opposing team made errors, Richardson often played *These Boots Are Made for Walking.* Another time while groundskeepers chased a loose dog, the organist offered a rendition of *How Much Is That Doggie in the Window?*

"I played a lot more before Phanavision," Richardson said. "In the early days when the Phillies weren't too good, I played a lot of sarcastic or comical songs. Back then, I did my own script. After Phanavision came along, they put together a script for each game and gave it to me."

Richardson, who for five years also played on weekends at Yankee Stadium when the Phillies were on the road, performed before night games for an hour on the concourse level of the Vet. Then, in his booth on the first base side of the press box, operating a synthesizer as well as the organ, Richardson demonstrated his keyboard proficiency in a variety of situations throughout the game.

"I played during player introductions, after certain plays on the field, between innings, with the Phanatic, and even during rain delays," Richardson said. "Major League Baseball has a rule that you don't play when a ball is in play or when a pitcher has his foot on the rubber. And you can't play anything that reflected on the umpire. I always had to concentrate on what was happening on the field."

Similar concentration was also required of public address (PA) announcer Dan Baker, another long-time fixture at the Vet. It was Baker's job to make sure the fans were aware of the identity of every batter, every new pitcher, and every substitution during a game. "Now batting . . . number 25 . . . first baseman Jim Thome," was one of Baker's familiar refrains.

Baker, one of only two PA announcers in the major leagues who also worked the scoreboard, began with the Phillies in 1972. He added the Eagles' PA job in 1985 and did similar duties for numerous other teams and events in the Philadelphia area as well as handle play-by-play for various games and serve as executive director of the Big 5.

Although not flamboyant, but with an unmistakable voice and distinctive style, Baker was known to add a little drama to his pronunciations. "Mic-key Mor-an-dini" or "Greg Luz-in-ski" were names that Baker often announced with emphasis on different syllables while raising and lowering his voice.

At times, players over the years looked up to the side of the press box where Baker sat and signaled their approval of his introductions. Once in a while, he was also accused of making derisive introductions of visiting players. One in particular was J. D. Drew, the outfielder who refused a Phillies contract after the team made him its number one draft pick.

"I've been accused of stirring up fans, especially when it involved Drew and umpire Ed Montague," Baker said. "But I would never try to incite

Public address announcer Dan Baker worked both the Phillies and Eagles games at the Vet for many years.

Phillies ball girl Mary Sue Styles left an indelible image in the minds of fans, especially if they were male.

the crowd. In the case of Drew, the fans were booing him long before he got to the plate the first time [in Philadelphia]."

"My job," Baker added, "is to provide informational service. I always try to announce pretty much the same way unless a particular name lends itself to a little different twist. Sometimes, I've called down to the dugout to find out the way a visiting player pronounces his name. I want to be accurate."

Baker, who figured he missed only about 16 games during his 32 years at the Vet, also admonished fans over the Vet's elaborate PA system when they either ran or threw something onto the field. "I dislike boorish behavior," he said.

While Baker and Richardson were heard much more often than they were seen, another familiar Vet Stadium persona who was seen but not heard was an attractive blonde whose good looks, shapely figure, and strong throwing arm made her almost as well known as some of the Phillies players. Her name then was Mary Sue Styles, and she was a ball girl who patrolled the left field line at the Vet.

The Phillies were one of the first teams to break the on-field gender barrier when in the early 1970s they hired lovely young women to serve as ball girls. It was an attempt to add window dressing to a game that shouldn't have needed it. But in an era before such things would be considered politically incorrect, it was hugely popular with fans, especially those of the male gender.

Starting in 1974 and for seven seasons, Styles—Mary Sue to almost all fans—tracked down foul balls at every home game. She sat on a stool along the left field line in front of the stands. When a foul ball rolled down the field, she'd leap from her perch, make the pickup, and fire a well-directed toss back to one of the ball boys near the opposing dugout.

Styles, who as a soon-to-be high school graduate from Collingswood, New Jersey, had been spotted by Giles while she sought a job with the Phillies. The then vice president immediately offered her the post as a ball girl.

"I loved sports, so I accepted," said Styles, whose married name is Owens (no relation to Paul). "It was a case of being at the right place at the right time. I was hired right before the start of the season, and the Phillies provided me with a red glove—I only had two gloves the whole time I was there—and told me that the idea was to expedite the game."

Guys at the Vet were collectively in love. Players and fans proposed. The ones in the stands swooned, one even dashing to the edge of the stands once in a misguided attempt to kiss her. "It was all part of the fun," Owens said. "Nothing was taken seriously. But it was very flattering."

Mary Sue was sought for modeling jobs. She was even approached once by *Playboy*. She did TV commercials. And eventually, she said, the job became "very lucrative." But, before leaving the post at the age of 23, she always conducted herself with class and dignity, seldom talking to the players, even the Phillies.

A fabled moment for Styles came at the Vet during a game in 1979 between the Phillies and the Pittsburgh Pirates. It was a misty night with poor visibility, and when Keith Moreland smashed a drive with two men on base down the left field line and into the stands, Gregg, umpiring third base, hesitated, then signaled home run.

The Pirates went berserk. Eventually, crew chief Frank Pulli, umpiring at second base, said to Gregg, "Hey, big guy, that ball was foul. We have to turn [the call] over." With that, home plate umpire Harvey reversed the call. Naturally, that brought Phils manager Dallas Green storming out of the dugout. In the midst of one of his all-time tirades, Green, of course, was invited to leave the premises.

After the game, won by the Pirates, Gregg defended his decision. He said he saw Styles jumping up and down, waving her arms, so he figured it was a home run. "If it was good enough for Mary Sue, it was good enough for me," the beleaguered umpire explained. (Some years later, Styles admitted that she wasn't wearing her contacts and hadn't seen the ball.)

While Styles was the pre-eminent Phillies ball girl, many others patrolled the sidelines with style and distinction. One of them was Cathy Schneberger, who guarded the right field line much of the time that Styles was in left. Another was Gail Clements, who before her marriage to the Phillies' John Russell, once fielded a fair ball when she cut in front of left fielder Gary Matthews.

Phillies ball girls, a species that was eventually benched in the late 1980s, no doubt as at least a partial concession to changing social mores, were not the only feminine attractions at the Vet. Another was the Hot Pants Patrol, a group that also captured a share of the spotlight in the early Vet years.

Originally hired in 1971 as usherettes and hostesses, the decidedly unliberated-named Hot Pants Patrol (HPP) evolved into a group of eye-catching, shapely young women dressed first in mini-skirts, then in short-short pants and form-fitting jackets who circulated through the stands, mostly helping fans find their seats. As many as 125—college students, housewives, working women—were employed for a single game.

The original group was hired at the rate of $10.75 per game (plus tips) after the Phillies advertised and sent letters to colleges seeking interested women. There were more than 1,000 applicants for the group that was first called "Fillies." In the beginning, the 145 who were hired, of which 36 were assigned to the hot pants brigade, wore white uniforms. That outfit soon was replaced by the more suggestive attire.

"The shorts and jacket were considered fashionable at the time," said the original HPP captain Rosie (Sudders) Rahn, who had been a secretary for the Phillies at Connie Mack Stadium before Giles put her in charge of the group. "Most of the women felt it was a nice, prestigious job. We considered ourselves like a sorority. It was a happy job, and we all really liked each other."

Along with their jobs in the stands, which were rotated between upper and lower decks, the women participated in various pre-game activities such as softball games and other contests. They received lots of fan mail. And one member even appeared on the television show *What's My Line?* Others wound up working full-time for the Phillies, some of whom are now employed by the team in high-level positions.

Still another Hot Pants member married a Phillies ballplayer. Former infielder John Vukovich said meeting and marrying Bonnie Loughran was the best thing he did at Veterans Stadium.

Like the ball girls, the Hot Pants Patrol eventually yielded to the times. Blatant sexism was replaced by emancipation, and the HPP was ousted in favor of ushers wearing substantially more clothes.

A few other ballpark characters remained. One was Jack Donnelly, custodian of the left field line in the early years of the Vet before the advent of the ball girls. After their arrival, Donnelly, who began working for the Phillies in 1938 as an usher, was relegated to the role of warming up the left fielders between innings. Then, as before, the seemingly ageless Donnelly wowed fans with his strong throwing arm.

While patrolling the left field foul territory, Jack Donnelly impressed fans with his strong throwing arm.

Another fan favorite was the estimable Mark (Froggy) Carfagno, a delightful character who in real life was a full-time Phillies groundskeeper who doubled in a series of other roles. Froggy, as he was known to all, was a favorite dancing partner of the Phanatic. He was a confidant of players. He even took a turn once as public address announcer in one of Baker's rare absences.

Carfagno joined the grounds crew in July 1971. Through all the years he worked, his diligence and the joy of doing his job were always obvious. So was his devotion to the Philadelphia players and team.

"I idolized the players when I worked as a kid at Connie Mack Stadium selling newspapers and programs and giving out things like All-Star ballots," he said. "And I never stopped. Some of them, like Dick Allen, Tony Taylor, and Jay Johnstone, became good friends."

Good friends. Special people. Those were things that the Vet had in abundance.

HITTER FRIENDLY

A good park for the long ball

Between 1971 when it opened and 2003 when it closed, 4,349 home runs were hit at Veterans Stadium. Ninety-three of them reached the upper deck.

In the Vet's inaugural season, Willie Stargell hit the first home run into the 600 level. In the Vet's final year, Jim Thome slammed the fourth and last homer into the 600 level. In between, Greg Luzinski swatted 10 balls into the Vet's upper deck, including one titanic blast that smacked into the Liberty Bell, then located on the façade of the 400 level in center field. Mike Schmidt, whose 265 home runs were the highest individual total at the Vet, clubbed six shots into the upper deck.

Mark McGwire, Barry Bonds, Roberto Clemente, and Johnny Bench also reached the Vet's upper deck with mighty shots. So did Luis Salazar, Chili Davis, Butch Huskey, and Kelly Stinnett.

What this suggests is that Veterans Stadium was a place that was highly conducive to long-distance clouting. And it didn't always matter that

Above: Mike Schmidt hit the most home runs at the Vet while also leading in many other offensive categories.

the hitter lacked the pedigree of some of baseball's more prominent long-ball clouters.

Although there is no scientific evidence to document the conclusion, the Vet was an easier place to poke a ball into the stands than most of its modern-day counterparts with roughly equivalent dimensions. For instance, while the Vet averaged 127.4 home runs each year, in 27 seasons at Montreal's Olympic Stadium, an average of 120.6 home runs were hit each year. Pittsburgh's Three Rivers Stadium averaged 117.5 homers per year, while the norm at Dodgers Stadium in Los Angeles was 114.6 and at Busch Stadium in St. Louis 104.6. Among similar ballparks, only Atlanta's Fulton County Stadium with 145.7 and Cincinnati's Riverfront Stadium with 140.6 had higher averages than the Vet.

Of the teams that keep track of upper-deck home runs, in 31 seasons at Fulton County Stadium only 13 balls reached the upper deck. Ironically, 13 home runs made it to the upper deck in 31 years at Three Rivers Stadium. In 35 seasons, 35 hits carried to the upper levels at San Diego's Jack Murphy (later called Qualcomm) Stadium. And nine balls landed upstairs over a similar 35 years at Houston's Astrodome.

"The Vet was a wonderful park to hit in," said Schmidt, the Phillies' Hall of Fame third baseman who not only had the most home runs, but also the most at-bats (4,020), hits (1,094), doubles (220), and RBI (825) of all players who batted at the Vet. Larry Bowa had the most triples (49), and Lonnie Smith had the highest batting average (.368).

"I could reach all fields," Schmidt added. "It had a big center field. You had to hit the ball really well to get it out in center field. But I could hit a fly ball, a wall-scraper, and get it out in right. And the ball carried really well to left. You could see the ball real well at home plate."

And the Vet was not just a place where balls left the park with crowd-pleasing frequency. It was also a place where ordinary singles, doubles, and triples landed with abundance. Of course, it helped that the artificial turf (see Chapter 12) played a major role in helping hard-hit balls skid quickly past the outstretched arms of fielders.

Ironically, Phillies batters were credited with just 20 inside-the-park homers during 33 years at the Vet. Three of them were hit by Schmidt, and two each by Bowa and Bobby Abreu.

"It was a good-hitting park for any kind of hitter," first baseman John Kruk said. "I could always hit here. It started when I was playing with San Diego. When I got traded here, I thought, this is really going to be fun. The backdrop is great. With the turf, any hard-hit ground ball had a great chance of going through. Of course, as you get comfortable in a place, you get more confidence."

Kruk wasn't the only player who rejoiced when he was traded to the Phillies. First baseman Rico Brogna watched longingly from a distance before finding out one day that he would be playing his home games at the Vet.

John Kruk, who got his World Series ring from National League president Bill White, general manager Lee Thomas, and manager Jim Fregosi on opening day in 1984, was thrilled when he was traded to the Phillies.

"When I first played in the National League with the Mets and we came to the Vet," he said, "I remember thinking that this was a great hitter's ballpark. Even though the surface was rough, I always thought this was a good place for a hitter. So, when I got traded to the Phillies, I was really excited because one of the first things position players think about is what kind of hitter's park is it? I already knew it was very favorable to hitters."

Right fielder Dale Murphy had similar views. "One of the reasons I came here," he said after getting swapped to the Phillies, "was because I always liked to hit here. It's a very good park for a hitter."

Although he didn't get dealt to the Phillies, Atlanta Braves' center fielder Andruw Jones was another of many visiting players who looked forward to swinging a bat at the Vet. Jones hit one of the Vet's longest homers when he powdered a drive into section 545 in the center field upper deck in 1997.

"It was a really good park to hit in, and I always seemed to hit well there," Jones said. "The walls are high and the stands are up, so you get a very good background, and you don't get distracted by anything."

In 1998, when he set an all-time record with 70 home runs in one season, McGwire of the St. Louis Cardinals hit three home runs in a single game just twice. One of those times was at the Vet, when he hit drives out of the park in the third, fifth, and eighth innings, the third one reaching the upper deck in section 541.

The Vet was a hitter-friendly ballpark not only because the ball carried well. Because of the background, hitters could see pitched balls clearly. And, of course, the artificial turf was always a factor.

"As a hitters' park, it was not just good, it was great," said first baseman Thome, who set a club record in his first season with the Phillies in 2003 with 28 home runs hit at home. "When the weather turned warmer and the heat rose off the turf, the ball carried especially well. And with the artificial turf, the ball got through the infield pretty quickly."

"It was always a very fair ballpark," added outfielder/first baseman Von Hayes. "It wasn't one of those parks where one day you hit a ball good and it goes out of the park, and the next day it lands in the infield. The dimensions were very fair, too."

According to outfielder Doug Glanville, the lights helped to make the Vet a good hitters' park. "During day games, there was a little glare," he said. "But at night, with the lights, you could see the ball real well. It was a good hitters' park, but it had a nice balance because it was also a good pitchers' park."

"It was a real good place for pitchers," said catcher Ozzie Virgil. "The only place you could really get into trouble was when the ball was hit down the line."

The distance from home plate down the line to the left field fence was 330 feet. It was the same distance down the right field line. The power alleys stood 371 feet from home plate, and the fence in straightaway center was 408 feet. The outfield fences stood 12 feet high.

The symmetry of the park gave hitters another advantage.

"As a ballpark, I didn't like the symmetry or the sameness that the Vet had," said outfielder and pinch-hitter deluxe Del Unser, who also spent time as the Phillies' hitting coach. "But it was good for hitters. For instance, it made Schmitty a better hitter later in his career when he became a .300 hitter because he could drive the ball out in right field as well as left field. It was fair for him that way because it didn't penalize him if he hit the ball to the gap in right-center."

Infielder Tony Taylor also liked the gaps. "The Vet was especially good for a gap hitter like me because of the AstroTurf," he said. "Anybody who could hit the ball in the gap had a chance to hit 25 to 30 doubles or 15 triples."

Outfielder Lenny Dykstra also put his name on the list of hitters who counted the Vet as a friend. "I loved to hit there," he said. "The visibility was great. And I really liked hitting on the turf."

Ironically, not every pitcher saw Veterans Stadium as a hitter's park. Some thought it wasn't a bad place in which to pitch.

Above: Barry Bonds hit more home runs at the Vet than any other visiting player.
Right: Willie Stargell owned the longest homer ever hit at the Vet.

"I wouldn't call it a pitcher's park. But I wouldn't call it a hitter's park, either," said reliever Mitch Williams. "I don't think the ball carried extremely well. If you gave up a home run, you gave up a home run. It wasn't like there was a lot of cheap stuff. It was a legitimate ballpark. I didn't think it was bad to pitch in."

"It certainly wasn't like the homer-friendly parks today where the alleys are 360–370 feet and guys one-hand the ball out," pitcher Rick Wise said. "The distances were pretty fair."

The Vet was good for pitchers in Randy Wolf's estimation, too. "I always enjoyed pitching there," he said. "The lights are bright. The mound is nice and high. And the catcher always felt closer, although that was an optical illusion."

No optical illusions were some of the balls smashed to different parts of the grandstands, starting with the one Stargell hit off Jim Bunning on June 25, 1971. The ball landed in a runway next to section 601, making it the longest home run hit to right field at the Vet.

When the ball was hit, Phillies right fielder Roger Freed merely gazed up and without turning watched the ball fly far over his head. Players from both teams moved to the steps of their respective dugouts to observe the missile.

Stargell's Pittsburgh teammate Richie Hebner said he went up to inspect the spot where the ball landed. "It was a $25 cab ride," he said. Even Stargell admitted later that he had no idea the ball was going to carry that far.

The Phillies placed a plaque on the seat nearest the spot where the ball passed. Twice it was stolen. Eventually, the Phils painted a yellow star on top of the runway.

The last home run hit into the 600 level came off the bat of Thome on August 17, 2003, off Brett Tomko during a 6–4 win over the Cardinals. The ball smacked into a seat in section 600, just a foot or so short of Stargell's blast. It was Thome's second upper deck blast in his first season with the Phillies.

Only two other balls reached the 600 level at the Vet, both of them socked to left field. The Mets' Butch Huskey touched Matt Beech for a home run that reached section 638 in a game on September 15, 1997. Ruben Rivera of the San Diego Padres crushed a pitch thrown by Chad Ogea to the same section on May 3, 1999.

One of the most memorable long-distance clouts hit at the Vet was the one Luzinski clanked off the Liberty Bell on May 16, 1972. At the time, the bell was located on the facing on top of the 400 level in dead-center field. Hit off Burt Hooton of the Chicago Cubs, the flight of the ball was measured at 438 feet. It hit 50 feet above the playing field.

Luzinski had some other heroic homers. On July 13, 1977, he hit two upper-deck homers in the same game off ex-teammate Tommy Underwood of the Cardinals. One ball carried into section 575, the other to the aisle between 570 and 571. "In two pitches, Luzinski hit about 1,000 feet of baseballs off me," Underwood said.

Another gargantuan drive by Luzinski came on July 11, 1973, when he deposited a pitch by Jim Freeman of the Braves into section 580 in left-center field. A white bull's-eye marked the spot on the fifth row where the ball came down, which some believe was the longest ever hit at the Vet.

Luzinski had the second-highest number of homers at the Vet with 130. Rounding out the Phillies top 10 were Hayes (77), Scott Rolen (73), Abreu (69), Darren Daulton (67), Mike Lieberthal and Juan Samuel (both 52), Garry Maddox (47), and Pat Burrell (44). Bonds led all visiting players (27), one ahead of Gary Carter. Andre Dawson (21) was third, followed by Matt Williams (19), and Bench and Dave Parker (both 17).

As could be expected, Luzinski savored his at-bats at the Vet. "Veterans Stadium was one of the better ballparks to hit in," he claimed. "One of the big reasons was because the wind was blocked off and kept to a minimum."

Sometimes, though, the wind swirled at field level. And the flags atop the roof would blow one way while the wind blew another way on the field. Sometimes, it looked like the wind was blowing in and it actually was blowing out.

Slugger Greg Luzinski was greeted by another slugger, Dick Allen, after one of his frequent mighty blasts.

"Whichever way the flags were blowing, you knew the wind on the field was blowing the other way," said outfielder Milt Thompson. "That's just the way it was, and you learned to play it that way. Most stadiums that are open get a true carry. But in a fully enclosed one like the Vet, it can be kind of hard at times to read what the ball's going to do."

But the Vet wasn't like some other ballparks—especially Wrigley Field—where a ball could ride a jet stream into the stands. It was, instead, a fair ballpark with honest dimensions, good visibility for a hitter, and where a ball hit in the air did not die in mid-flight. It was a park where the crack of the bat was often followed by a single, a double, a triple, or even an upper-deck home run.

FLYING HIGH, FLYING LOW

The Eagles had their ups and downs at the Vet

Of all the fields where the Eagles played during their first 70 years, the one with which they were most closely connected was Veterans Stadium.

That affiliation was not necessarily because they reached any particular levels of grandeur there. It was simply because the Vet was the Eagles' home field for 32 years—or nearly one-half of the team's existence.

Above: Fan favorite Randall Cunningham completed 31 passes in a 1988 game at the Vet.

Originally, the Eagles had played home games at several other stadiums, most notably Baker Bowl in the beginning, Shibe Park/Connie Mack Stadium for 18 years, and for the 13 seasons leading up to their shift to the Vet at Franklin Field. Then in 1971, the Eagles joined the Phillies at the new multi-purpose stadium in South Philadelphia, and from then until their departure after the 2002 season, the Eagles and the Vet were inexorably linked.

The connection was not always smooth. Like a rocky marriage, it had its ups and downs.

Especially in their final years at the Vet, the Eagles went to great lengths to ridicule the place, choosing to ignore the fact that they had spent some rather productive years there. But to more than three decades of fans, and to many players and coaches, it had a special appeal.

Dick Vermeil, the coach who led the Eagles to their first Super Bowl, saw the liabilities that the Vet presented to his football teams. But he also saw the Vet for what it was: a place that on a crisp, fall Sunday afternoon could be so alive, so crackling with excitement, so full of the most noisy, passionate fans, that his team could be yanked to a higher level.

"To me," Vermeil said, "the Vet always gave us a very big home field advantage. Now, you have to realize that the stadium itself didn't make the atmosphere. It was the people who did. They had a love affair with the Philadelphia Eagles, and every Sunday they came to compete. They were a difference-maker. They were an inspirational tool."

In 32 years, they helped to inspire the Eagles to a 144–111–2 regular season record at the Vet, plus a 7–4 mark in the playoffs. Overall, the Eagles had 14 winning seasons, 16 losers, and twice finished at .500.

The Eagles, of course, played only one-tenth as many games at the Vet as the Phillies. Naturally, this made the baseball club the predominant occupant. But the Eagles had many memorable moments, spectacular plays, and outstanding players during their years at the Vet when the team's head coaches ran a quixotic gamut from Jerry Williams, Ed Khayat, Mike McCormack, Vermeil, Marion Campbell, Buddy Ryan, Rich Kotite, and Ray Rhodes to the present Andy Reid.

For the Eagles, coming to the Vet was, according to most members of the team, a welcome change from Franklin Field. "Compared to where we were before, Veterans Stadium was like a country club," said Eagles' center Mike Evans. "We thought it was neat to go there and play in a new stadium. It was pretty plush. Even the locker rooms were plush. We had only four showerheads at Franklin Field, so this was dramatically different."

Franklin Field had been enormously popular from a fans standpoint because it was a true football stadium and had outstanding sight lines from most seats except for some in the lower deck. But the 60,000-seat venue, which had been the scene of the Eagles' last championship in 1960 when they defeated the Green Bay Packers in a legendary battle for the NFL title, had major shortcomings. It had few amenities, almost no parking, terrible traffic jams, the seats were benches, and the players' and press facilities were right out of the Dark Ages.

Jimmy Gallagher, the Eagles' public relations director for nearly three decades and a man who worked for the team from 1949 until his retirement in 1995, looked at the move from a front-office perspective. "When we moved into the Vet, there were no carpets," he said. "It was cold, the offices were bare, and we had no windows. But it was terrific. It was kind of like when you buy a new home. You're proud of it. You want to show it off. Everybody was very happy. Stacked against what we had come from, it was heaven."

The Eagles' first game at the Vet was an exhibition game against the Buffalo Bills, at the time featuring O. J. Simpson. Thousands of tickets were available before the game, but a huge walkup crowd appeared, causing a major traffic jam outside the stadium. The game was a sellout.

"When the Vet opened, it was magnificent," said Ray Didinger, who covered the Eagles for the *Evening Bulletin* and *Daily News* before moving to NFL Films. "For the Eagles, it wasn't just a new playing field, it was also a new home. Compared to Franklin Field, which was very cumbersome and uncomfortable, the new place was terrific. It was very professional."

The first regular season game of the Eagles at the Vet took place on September 26 in the second game of the year. With 65,358, the largest home crowd in Eagles history up to that point in attendance, the Birds lost to the Dallas Cowboys, 42–7. After suffering their third straight one-sided loss the following week, 31–3, to the San Francisco 49ers at the Vet, head coach Williams was replaced by Khayat. The Eagles went on to finish the season with a 6–7–1 record while drawing more than 65,000 fans at every home game.

In the ensuing years, the Eagles had their ups and downs at the Vet. They failed to win a game there (although they tied one) during the entire 1972 season. They were thumped at the Vet, 44–27, by the Atlanta Falcons in 1973 and 42–3 by the Los Angeles Rams in 1975. And between 1971 and 1977, they had no winning seasons while losing considerably more games at the Vet than they won.

The picture brightened in Vermeil's third year, in 1978, when the Eagles posted their first winning record since 1966 and entered the play-offs for the first time since 1960. It remained bright during the rest of the Eagles' residency at the Vet, winning seasons outnumbering losers, despite six shoddy years in the 1980s and four more losers in the 1990s.

There were many memorable games at the Vet. One in particular came during the regular season in 1979, a 17–14 Eagles' victory over the Pittsburgh Steelers, one of the dominant teams of the decade and winners of three straight Super Bowl victories. A record crowd of 72,111 saw the Cowboys nip the Eagles, 17–14, in 1981. The Eagles roared back from a 23–0 fourth quarter deficit to edge the Washington Redskins, 28–23, in a game in 1985. And, of course, there were the always heavily followed Monday night games, including one in 1992 when the Eagles stopped the Arizona Cardinals seven times at the one-yard line before going on to a 7–3 victory.

In 1971, defensive back Al Nelson caught a missed field goal in the end zone and raced it back an NFL record 101 yards for a touchdown in a 42–7 loss to Dallas. Nelson remembered it well.

"I caught it just behind the goal line and took off," he said. "I had to make a couple of moves, and then Nate Ramsey threw a block on the Dallas kicker. I think some of the Dallas players were confused. But for me, it was a very big thrill, obviously my biggest moment as an Eagles player."

Three years later, in a Monday night game, linebacker Bill Bergey walloped Doug Dennison so hard that the Cowboy running back fumbled near the Eagles' goal line. Defensive back Joe Lavender scooped up the loose ball and raced 96 yards for a touchdown in a 13–10 win over Dallas.

"I remember escorting him down the field," said safety Randy Logan. "I threw a block on [Roger] Staubach, and then Joe just took off. Nobody could catch him. Then Tom Dempsey kicked a field goal to give us the win."

Among other special individual feats at the Vet, there was Dempsey's 54-yard field goal that helped to beat the St. Louis Cardinals, 19–7, in 1971. Wilbert Montgomery rushed for 197 yards in a 24–19 loss to the Cleveland Browns in 1979. He raced 90 yards for a touchdown in a 35–14 decision over the Houston Oilers in 1982. In 1985, in a 23–17 overtime victory over the Falcons, Ron Jaworski combined with Mike Quick on an NFL record-tying 99-yard touchdown pass for the winning score. Randall Cunningham completed 31 passes in a 24–13 victory over the Giants in 1988. Keith Jackson in a 1989 10–9 victory over the Vikings and Keith Byars in a 1990 24–23 loss to the Indianapolis Colts each caught 12 passes in the game. Fred Barnett gained 187 yards as a receiver in a 21–6 win over Houston in 1994. That same year, Herschel Walker became the first player in NFL history to have a 90-plus-yard run, reception, and kickoff return in the same game. And in 2001, Donovan McNabb connected on 32 aerials in a 20–17 overtime loss to the St. Louis Rams.

While the offensive heroics usually made the headlines, there were many others beside those mentioned above who performed nobly at the Vet. Not the least of these were offensive players such as tight ends Charley Young and Chad Lewis, tackles Stan Walters, Jerry Sizemore, and Jon Runyan, wide receivers Irving Fryar, Harold Jackson, and Harold Carmichael, and running backs Ricky Watters and Duce Staley.

Among defensive stalwarts were linemen Charley Johnson, Dennis Harrison, Clyde Simmons, Reggie White, Jerome Brown, William Fuller,

Although he had no toes on his kicking foot, Tom Dempsey set a Vet Stadium record with a 54-yard field goal.

William Thomas, and Hugh Douglas, linebackers Jerry Robinson, Seth Joyner, and Jeremiah Trotter, and defensive backs Bill Bradley, Herman Edwards, Wes Hopkins, Eric Allen, Brian Dawkins, Bobby Taylor, and Troy Vincent.

Special team players included kickers Paul McFadden and David Akers, punter Sean Landeta, and kick returners Vai Sikahema and Brian Mitchell. All played important roles, as did many others, in Eagles successes at the Vet.

There were, of course, many other examples of the Eagles' close connection to the Vet.

Eagles cheerleaders always attracted plenty of attention as they performed their routines.

Leonard Tose, who bought the Eagles for a reported $16.1 million in 1969 and owned the team until selling it in 1985 to Florida auto dealers Norman Braman and Ed Leibowitz for an estimated $65 million, once threatened to move the team to Phoenix. On game days, Tose flew a helicopter from his Main Line home to the Vet, landing on a grassy plot outside the Eagles' entrance.

Then there were the fabled Eagles' cheerleaders. First called Eaglettes, then the Liberty Belles, and finally just plain Eagles Cheerleaders, they were a highly select group of attractive young women who earned their places on the squad through tryouts. They were supposed to be cheerleaders, a group of them stationed at each of the four corners of the field, but to several generations of overheated males, they were much more than that.

Originally, they dressed in long pants, but over the years, their attire became increasingly skimpier. From long pants, they went to skirts, then short skirts, and finally to shorts with tops that were once described as "bikini size." So popular were the 36 cheerleaders that they even had their own calendar each year. It did not lack buyers.

"Fly Eagles Fly" was the so-called theme song of the team. It was played on radio shows, sung by the drunks in the stands, and could be heard

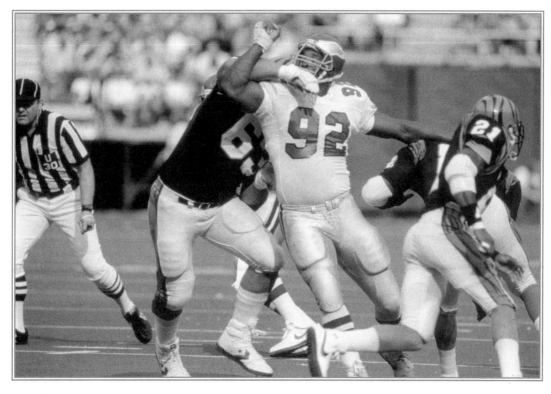

Defensive tackle Reggie White (92) was twice named the most valuable defensive player in the NFL.

just about anywhere else around the city where the Eagles' fortunes were being weighed.

In 1987, while fielding a squad of replacement players who were in uniform because the regular NFL players were on a three-week strike, the Eagles drew a crowd of 4,074—the smallest crowd in NFL history—to a game at the Vet against the Chicago Bears. The Eagles had played only nine games—five at home—in 1982 because of a 57-day players' strike that reduced the season from 16 weeks to nine.

After the Eagles, en route to a 4–10 record, suffered the 42–3 clobbering by the Rams in a game in 1975, McCormack, in his last year as head coach, was asked by someone in the media if the team had any dogs. Subsequently, the team was referred to as "dogs," and fans floated balloons with the name Alpo written on their sides.

Naturally, the games with Dallas attracted the most attention. The Eagles and Cowboys had built a bitter rivalry over the years that was second to none in professional sports. Each team passionately despised the other, and the feeling was possibly even stronger among the people in the stands.

Offensive lineman Brian Baldinger had an interesting perspective. He played for the Cowboys and then, after a stop at Indianapolis, joined the Eagles in 1992.

"When I was with Dallas, we loved coming to Philadelphia," he said, "because if we played well and kicked the stuffing out of the Eagles, we knew that the fans would turn on them. They would start to boo, and that would serve as a barometer for whether they were playing good or bad. That would be to our advantage."

Most of the time, though, the Vet played to the Eagles' advantage. That was not anything to be regarded lightly.

LAST STOP BEFORE THE SUPER BOWL

Eagles beat Dallas in a memorable Vet game

The most memorable game the Eagles played at Veterans Stadium took place on January 11, 1981. It was the game that sent the Eagles to the Super Bowl.

It had been a glorious year in Philadelphia. In the spring of 1980, the 76ers had reached the NBA finals. That fall, the Phillies had won the World Series. And before the year was over, the Eagles had capped their best season since 1960 by finishing first in the NFC East.

Four times during the year, the Eagles had drawn more than 70,000 spectators to games at the Vet, the first time they had done it that many

Above: A 42-yard touchdown run by Wilbert Montgomery (31) gave the Eagles an early lead in the NFL championship game against the Dallas Cowboys.

times in a single season. The team won seven of its eight home games, and finished the year with a 12–4 overall record, good for a first place tie in the NFL Eastern Division with the Dallas Cowboys. The Eagles had split two games during the season with the Cowboys, winning 17–10 at the Vet and losing 35–27 at Dallas.

As the calendar eased into 1981, the Eagles advanced to the divisional playoffs where they stormed to a 31–16 victory over the Minnesota Vikings. In that game, 68,434 crammed the Vet to watch the Eagles overcome a 14–0 deficit to win handily. Wilbert Montgomery ran for two touchdowns as the Birds pulled away with a 24-point second half.

The win vaulted the Eagles into the NFL championship game against the Cowboys, 34–13 winners over the Los Angeles Rams. Played on a bitter-cold, 16 degree, windy afternoon with the wind chill factor at 17 degrees below zero and before a crowd of 70,696, the game would attain legendary status on the list of unforgettable Eagles outings.

"It was one of the highlights of my career," said Dick Vermeil, who that season was in his fifth of seven years as the head coach of the Eagles and who later coached the St. Louis Rams to a Super Bowl victory. "It was truly one of my best memories in 14 years as an NFL coach.

"We had worked so hard to get there," he added. "We had been building toward that moment for five years. It all came to a head that day. That was our D-Day. Our level of focus and concentration was unbelievable. To a man, we believed that the Dallas Cowboys were going to be defeated."

As part of the battle of wits, the Eagles had made a stunning shift to their away white jerseys from their home green, forcing the Cowboys to wear their blue shirts, attire with which they won only 50 percent of the time while wearing.

From the coaches on down through the players, the Eagles were primed for the skirmish. And by the time the team reached the tunnel leading onto the field prior to the pre-game introductions, the level of excitement had virtually no bounds.

"I've never been so ready for a football game in 13 years of playing in the NFL," said linebacker Bill Bergey. "Vermeil had us sky high. We bought into his psych job. We knew we were going to win. It was only a matter of how much we would beat them by."

Safety Randy Logan also recalled the rush that engulfed the team. Logan had been an Eagle since 1973, but he, too, had a feeling unlike anything he experienced on the gridiron either before or since.

"It was almost like a mirage," he said. "We were so fired up. Coming out of the tunnel, I looked back at Harold Carmichael. He had a glare in his eyes like I never saw before. He had fire in his eyes, and he gave out a big yell, and we just exploded out of the tunnel."

And then the Eagles, who had practiced all week under the sunny skies of Tampa, Florida, exploded on the field for what would turn out to be their greatest game since 1960.

Dick Vermeil, who led the Eagles to their first Super Bowl, celebrated a victory with Harold Carmichael.

On the Birds' second offensive play of the game, 2:11 after the opening kickoff, quarterback Ron Jaworski handed off to Montgomery. With Dallas expecting the Eagles to come out passing, putting six defensive backs on the field, the great Eagles running back, who had missed four games and parts of three others during the season and had suffered a recurrence of a knee injury just a few days earlier, angled to his right, and—untouched by a single Cowboy—didn't stop until he reached the end zone 42 yards away.

"When I saw Montgomery burst off tackle and head for the end zone, I absolutely knew the Eagles were headed for the Super Bowl," said Merrill Reese, who was broadcasting what he would years later describe as the "single most memorable game of my life."

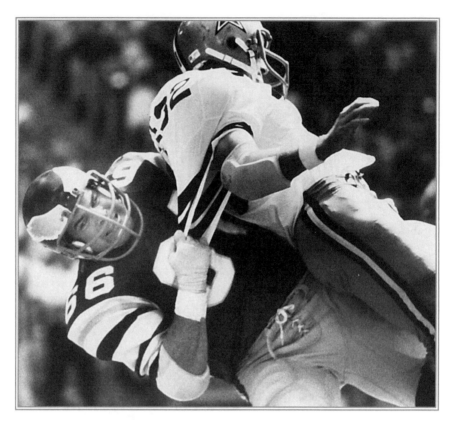

A Dallas runner had no chance against Bill Bergey (66), a defensive standout for the Eagles for seven seasons.

Jimmy Gallagher, then the Eagles' public relations director, wasn't any less excited. "I had a rush like I never had before," he recalled. "It was simply awesome. That run was probably the Eagles' greatest play at the Vet."

Dallas tied the score in the second quarter as Tony Dorsett went three yards for a touchdown to cap a 68-yard drive. But with Dorsett making two key fumbles and gaining only 44 yards while quarterback Randy White completed just 12 of 31 passes for 127 yards, the Cowboys didn't mount another serious threat for the rest of the game.

Undeterred by the weather, barefooted kicker Tony Franklin slammed through a 26-yard field goal in the third quarter after defensive end Carl Hairston had recovered a White fumble at the Dallas 11. A little while later, linebacker Jerry Robinson recovered a fumble by Dorsett and returned it 22 yards to the Cowboys' 28. Six plays later, Leroy Harris banged over from the 9. After Franklin's extra point, the Eagles had a 17–7 lead. He then added a 20-yard field goal in the fourth quarter to conclude the scoring at 20–7.

By the time the gun ended the clash, inspiring probably the most spirited celebration in Eagles history, Montgomery had picked up 194 yards rushing. Pulitzer Prize–winning New York *Times* columnist Red Smith called Montgomery "a greyhound with muscles."

Overall, the Eagles collected 263 yards on the ground to the Cowboys' 90. Jaworski completed just 9 of 29 passes for 91 yards.

"The Cowboys were the luckiest team in the league that day because they only got beat, 20–7," recalled Bergey. "The score was not indicative of the way the game went. It probably could've been 45–7, the game was that lopsided."

While Dallas coach Tom Landry, who wore a fur hat with the flaps down to ward off the cold, told writers that "our own mistakes got us in trouble," broadcaster Brent Musburger began telling his audience that Philadelphia was the "City of Champions." And no one was about to forget the role the fans had played.

"I've never heard the fans so loud, so into every single play," Bergey said. "They were on the edges of their seats the whole game. And we felt that excitement. Whenever you hear a football player say he is so engulfed in what he's doing that he never hears the fans, it's the biggest bunch of baloney in the world. You hear the fans. You feed off them. We surely did that day."

Sports writer and columnist Ray Didinger, who has covered the Eagles for more than three decades, also remembered what it was like to be at the Vet the day its seams nearly popped. "There was an atmosphere in the stadium the likes of which I've never seen before or since," he said. "The crowd was roaring even before the Eagles took the field. Emotion was so high. It's something I'll never forget."

Bergey remembered heading after the game up Broad Street to center city to have dinner with about 10 friends. "There was a girl in the car in front of us," he said. "Every time we stopped at a light, she took something else off."

The Eagles went on to face the Oakland Raiders in the Super Bowl at New Orleans. But they suffered a stunning loss, 27–10. And there would never again be another game at the Vet like the one when the Eagles won the NFL title.

Of course, there were other noteworthy playoff games at the Vet. Who could forget the Eagles' first playoff game at the Vet in the NFC wild card in 1979 against the Chicago Bears? Jaworski threw three touchdown passes, two to Carmichael, and Montgomery outgained the fabled Walter Payton, 87 yards to 67. Jaworski's third TD pass came in the fourth quarter on a 63-yard hookup with Billy Campfield that broke a 17–17 tie and sent the Eagles on their way to a 27–17 victory.

Other Eagles playoff games at the Vet included the following:

December 27, 1981 – With the help of two kickoff fumbles by Wally Henry, the New York Giants rushed off to a 20–0 lead in the first quarter of an NFC wild card playoff, then held off a late Eagles' surge to capture a 27–21 victory before a crowd of 71,611. In the second half, Jaworski passed to

Carmichael for one TD, and Montgomery ran for two more touchdowns for the Birds, while Scott Brunner hurled three TD passes for the Giants.

December 31, 1989 – In another NFC wild card playoff, Jim Everett uncorked a pair of first quarter TD passes, and the Los Angeles Rams held on to win a 21–7 decision with just 57,869 in the stands. Anthony Toney scored the Eagles' only touchdown on a one-yard run late in the fourth quarter. Randall Cunningham completed 24 of 40 passes for 238 yards.

January 5, 1991 – The Eagles got two first-half field goals from Roger Ruzek, but that was it as the Washington Redskins won, 20–6, in an NFC wild card game. Mark Rypien passed for two touchdowns for the winners. A major controversy was touched off in the third period, when coach Buddy Ryan pulled Cunningham and inserted Jim McMahon, who played for just one series of downs. Cunningham and some of his teammates loudly criticized the move. Ryan was fired soon afterward.

December 30, 1995 – In a wild, wild, NFC wild card game, the Eagles set a playoff scoring record while combining with the Detroit Lions for a two-team scoring mark in an unbelievable 58–37 triumph for the Birds. The Eagles broke open a 7–7 tie with 31 second-quarter points but were outscored 30–20 in the second half. Rodney Peete passed for three touchdowns, Ricky Watters scored twice, and Barry Wilburn and William Thomas returned interceptions for touchdowns for the Eagles.

December 31, 2000 – There was no bite in the Bucs as the Eagles downed an uninspired Tampa Bay team, 21–3, in frigid weather in an NFC wild card game. In his first playoff game, Donovan McNabb passed for two touchdowns and ran for another while completing 24 of 33 passes for 161 yards. McNabb passed to Na Brown and Jeff Thomason for second-quarter touchdowns as the Eagles built a 14–3 halftime lead. Then, with Hugh Douglas leading a fierce defense, the Eagles completely shut down the Bucs in the second half to win easily. Chris Warren ran for 85 yards for the winners.

January 12, 2002 – Again, the Buccaneers were no match for the Eagles in a lopsided NFC wild card 31–9 victory. McNabb threw second-quarter scoring passes to Chad Lewis and Duce Staley. Tampa, meanwhile, got only three first-half field goals and nothing in the second half. Correll Buckhalter romped 25 yards for a TD in the third period, and Damon Moore returned an interception 59 yards for another six-pointer as the Eagles dominated a comatose Tampa team. McNabb hit on 16 of 25 passes for 194 yards and rushed for another 57 yards, 39 in the first quarter.

January 11, 2003 – Playing for the first time in nearly two months after breaking his leg, McNabb completed 20 of 30 passes for 247 yards to lead

Eagles fans were often unruly, but they usually packed the house at the Vet and rooted fervently for their team.

the Eagles to a 20–6 victory over the Atlanta Falcons in an NFC divisional playoff. Bobby Taylor ran back an interception for a 39-yard TD, David Akers kicked two field goals, and McNabb hooked up with James Thrash on a 35-yard TD pass as the Eagles rode a 13–6 halftime lead to victory.

January 19, 2003 – The Eagles' last game at the Vet was one of their most disappointing. The favored Eagles were shocked by Tampa Bay, 27–10, in the NFC championship game. Brian Mitchell returned the opening kickoff 70 yards, and two plays later Staley scored from the 20 to give the Eagles a lead just 52 seconds into the game. But the Bucs roared back, taking a 17–10 cushion into halftime, then holding the Eagles scoreless in the second half to win easily. McNabb completed 26 of 49 passes for 243 yards, but it wasn't enough to overcome the eventual Super Bowl champs. Tampa's Brad Johnson completed 20 of 33 passes for 259 yards, while Ronde Barber scored with a 92-yard interception return.

FLAWS IN THE FIELD

Artificial turf was a controversial subject

In the rush to criticize Veterans Stadium during its 33 years, no part of the ballpark was subjected to more verbal abuse than its playing surface. Regardless of whether the sport was baseball or football, the artificial turf produced unfavorable comments from many players who ventured onto the field.

Generally, the objections were legitimate. The turf was hard, it was sharp, and it was a constant source of injuries. And those were just a few of its flaws.

"It was just horrible," said former Eagles linebacker Bill Bergey. "It was bad for your knees because it was so hard, and it was so sharp and abrasive that we'd get big strawberries on our elbows and knees. I never played on a field that was worse. I can not minimize how bad that surface was."

Because football players had much more physical contact with the turf as a result of endlessly getting their bodies slammed into it, they were much more prone to injuries and much more likely to complain than

Above: Workmen installed a new turf, one of six times that was done at the Vet.

baseball players. The men with bats and gloves did their share of grumbling, though.

"When I first came up, they still had the old turf, and when you dove for a ball, your arm was left on the field," said Phillies shortstop Jimmy Rollins. "It was just like they painted the cement green, and put in some white lines and dirt patches."

"It was a lot of trouble," complained outfielder Lenny Dykstra. Added pitcher Steve Bedrosian: "It was certainly not my favorite thing at the Vet." "I never liked it," said outfielder Greg Luzinski. "All the diving and running took a big toll on my legs," claimed second baseman Mickey Morandini. "I got a lot of bumps and bruises."

"The turf helped, but it hurt," first baseman John Kruk said. "It helped me get a lot more hits, but it always gave me a lot of problems with my knees. The game was meant to be played on natural grass, not on plastic."

Second baseman Juan Samuel recalled that during his first four years in Philadelphia, the turf didn't bother his knees. "But the last three years, my knees started to hurt," he recalled. "I remember at the time I was living in a two-story house in Cherry Hill. I'd come home from a game and I'd really feel it when I'd go up the stairs."

"I always felt," said broadcaster Chris Wheeler, "that if we hadn't had the artificial surface, the Vet would never have gotten quite the negative reputation it got. If it had been grass and dirt, I don't think it would have been as maligned as it was."

One of the great lines in Phillies history was a response to a question about the turf.

Asked how he compared grass with artificial turf, reliever Tug McGraw said, "I don't know, I never smoked turf."

Grass and dirt, however, were never a consideration when the Vet was in the planning stages. It was a foregone conclusion that the new ballpark would depart from the familiar natural surface of Connie Mack Stadium. In the long run, artificial turf was cheaper, easier to maintain, and required substantially less labor. And, of course, it was considered fashionable.

"When it was new, everybody wanted to play on AstroTurf," said infielder John Vukovich. "Now, nobody does."

Veterans Stadium was one of the early ballparks to use artificial turf. It was also one of the last to use it. By the time the Vet came down, all the stadiums built in recent years had real grass playing surfaces.

"By necessity, the field had to have artificial turf because it was going to be used for both baseball and football and would have to be changed back and forth," said architect Alexander Ewing, who took part in the original design of the stadium. "Both teams had very strong opinions on the surface."

When the stadium opened in 1971, 146,000 square feet of AstroTurf was installed in 15 foot rolls. The job was done by Monsanto at a cost of nearly $600,000. Only 15-foot-wide dirt circles at the pitchers' mound and home plate and 12-foot trapezoidal shapes for each of the three bases were left uncovered.

The turf produced uneasy feelings almost from the moment the Phillies stepped onto the field for their first game. "It changed the game for us," said third baseman Don Money. "You had to bunt a different way. On defense, if you were an infielder, you had to take four or five steps back. In the outfield, you had to be faster because you had to make sure you cut off balls hit into the gap. Even running the bases was different. I liked playing on dirt a lot more than AstroTurf."

More critical were the Eagles when they first used the field for an exhibition game in August against the Buffalo Bills. General manager Pete Retzlaff complained bitterly about the condition of the field, especially the soft spots on the part of the turf that covered the baseball infield. After his foot sank into one of the spots, Retzlaff was furious. "It isn't safe to play on," he told Ray Didinger of the *Evening Bulletin.* "Can you imagine a receiver planting his cleats and trying to make a cut? He could tear every ligament. It makes me sick just to look at it."

The city did its best to solve the problems. But much quicker than expected, the artificial surface wore down. Constant use, plus excessive heat in the summer, helped hasten the turf's demise. So did cold weather.

The turf was actually only a thin, three-quarter-inch thick pad that was glued to an undersurface of four-to-six-inch-deep asphalt. In the winter, the pad absorbed moisture, which would then freeze and cause contraction. As the winters passed, the pad, like a sponge, became smaller and smaller, never returning to its original size.

A new carpet was installed in 1977 at a cost of $800,000. That proved little better than the first AstroTurf. Knee injuries and pulled muscles hardly decreased. Manager Danny Ozark recalled that outfielders Greg Luzinski, Garry Maddox, and Bake McBride constantly showed the effects of the hard turf. "It took a toll on their backs and legs, and they were always walking around hurt," he said. "Grass certainly would've helped their durability and longevity. It would also have helped the pitchers. The ball got through the infield so fast that it was difficult even to knock it down."

Lumps developed on the surface. The turf had dead spots; yet, some balls would bounce high over infielders' heads. And balls hit on the ground roared past fielders, prompting someone to say that it was like playing baseball on a pool table.

That turf lasted until 1980. Another new surface was put down in 1988. This one had some advantages over the others. Its 315 foot rolls were sewn together, it had drainage ditches around the outfield that prevented puddles from forming, and the asphalt on which it was laid absorbed water much quicker than the material under previous turfs. That cut the length of time in half that it took to prepare the field after a rain delay.

More turf changes occurred in 1995, and in 2001, a surface called NexTurf was introduced. By far the most acceptable of the artificial surfaces,

NexTurf was a synthetic grass that was higher and softer than its predecessors.

As the Phillies farm system director, manager, and later an advisor, Dallas Green saw the evolution of the Vet's playing field. He had mixed emotions about the turf.

"Originally, I don't think anybody worried about the AstroTurf because it was state-of-the-art," he said. "It was what all the new stadiums were using. We didn't have second thoughts about it. We just played and tried to fill our teams with fast people in the outfield to stop the doubles and triples.

"As it got older, it got harder and contributed to some injuries. Of course, it was a multi-purpose stadium. You had everything there—elephants, football, you had all kinds of stuff going on in that stadium that took a toll on the turf. Eventually, it wasn't much fun for the guys to play on. It didn't become easier again until we got the NexTurf."

All the artificial surfaces required a vastly different kind of treatment than the old grass fields. With the fake turf, dirt, tobacco stains, and chewing gum had to be cleaned off the field. There was no mowing, sprinkling, pulling weeds, or keeping the field level. There was no reason to use fertilizer. Or, as the Phillies did at Baker Bowl, no need for sheep to keep the grass trim.

"Because the field was level, you couldn't bevel or shape the baselines based on who you were playing or whether you wanted a bunt to go foul or fair," said Mike DiMuzio, who began working at the Vet in 1971 and was the director of operations from 1982 until the park closed. "Instead, we had to concentrate on the things the players were most concerned with—the pitching mound, home plate, and the basepaths. We also had to concentrate on the bullpens because you didn't want a pitcher coming off a mound that's not in good shape in the bullpen to a very good mound on the field. You also wanted both mounds equal in height."

The Phillies bought 80 to 100,000 tons of clay and dirt each season. The material, used for the uncarpeted parts of the field and in the bullpens, was delivered periodically in 50 pound bags, which were stored in the subterranean level of the Vet.

Through most of their years at the Vet, the Phillies employed seven groundskeepers. Joe Meccariello and Ralph Frangipani were each head groundskeeper for much of the Vet's life. Two members of the seven-man crew worked all year, three were seasonal, and the others were on what was called a junior crew. The two full-timers went each year to spring training to work on the Phillies' fields in Clearwater.

An important job of the ground crew, Frangipani said, "was to keep the baselines drawn. The lines would usually last for a homestand, but then they'd start to fade, and we'd have to reline the field when the team came back from a road trip. We used water-soluble paint."

Mark (Froggy) Carfagno, a member of the grounds crew since 1971, was in charge of the dirt areas around all three bases. For night games, he

Above: Ralph Frangipani was head
groundskeeper overseeing a crew of seven.
Right: Mark Carfagno, with help from Dick Allen
Jr., had the job of keeping the areas around the
bases in top shape.

always got to the park at 1 P.M. and wouldn't leave for another 10 to 12 hours,
usually spending one hour after a game starting to prepare the field for the
next game. If the weather was threatening, he often arrived at the park around
9 A.M.

"People were always asking, 'Why do you come so early?'" Carfagno
said. "I always told them we need to make the field just right. After batting
practice, you had to make the field look perfect for that first pitch.

"The batter's box always had a good reputation," he added. "In some
parks, a batter had to dig real hard, maybe an inch into the dirt, to get
comfortable. Here, he didn't have to do that. It was nice, tight dirt that
players could dig their spikes into. I remember Luzinski used to say that all
he had to do was dig a couple of times with his spikes, plant his feet, and
he'd be set."

Of all the jobs that the grounds crew did at the Vet, none was more
critical than the upkeep of the pitching mound, a job performed for the last

15 years of the Vet by Fran Dunn. Nothing gets a hurler any testier than a flawed mound. But through many of the years at the Vet, the mound was regarded as one of the best in the big leagues. One reason was because it was always considered higher than other mounds. It also had a steeper slope, which especially benefited power pitchers but, in general, also Phillies pitchers who over the years compiled a much lower team earned run average at the Vet.

"It was always my favorite mound, even before I got here," pitcher Kevin Millwood told Jim Salisbury of the *Inquirer.*

"It was a very good mound," said Greg Maddux while pitching for the Atlanta Braves. "It was high. Higher than all the other mounds."

Many claimed the mound was higher than the allowable 10 inches. Periodically, umpires and at other times National League officials measured the height but never found it to be in violation of the rules. "It just looked higher," DiMuzio said, "because of the steepness of the slope."

The original mound had handle-like devices under the surface. When the field needed to be changed for football, a machine with hooks would perch over the mound, pick it up, and cart it away. Later, the mound, as was the home plate area, was placed on a hydraulic lift which raised or lowered it, depending on the sport being played.

"To maintain the mound," said Joel Ralph, the stadium's manager from 1973 to 1987, "you'd have to wet it, rake it, tamp it, water it again, let it dry, wet it again, and rake it again. It was a long process. Once, the mound had to be set on fire to dry it out. The groundskeepers poured gasoline on it."

Another special chore of the grounds crew and others was the conversion of the field from one sport to another. That was a regular occurrence in the fall, and also for a brief time in the summer when the Philadelphia Stars played football at the Vet.

"It was the biggest job, and the one that concerned me the most," Ralph said. "Originally, the job was designed to be done in 48 hours with a crew of 75 people. Then we got it down to 50 (a 35-man crew from the city, the rest from the Phillies' ground crew). They were all highly skilled, highly motivated people. By the end of the Vet, the conversion could be done in 12 to 13 hours."

Included in the effort were the jobs of adding (or removing) 10,000 seats that telescoped in under the 300 level, the visiting dugout, outfield fences and curtains, foul poles (or nets), scoreboards, the screen behind home plate, and various other items.

Once, there was a Phillies game, a Rolling Stones concert, and an Eagles game, all within six days. Another time, the Eagles had a Thursday night exhibition game, and the Phillies were due to take the field for batting practice at 4 P.M. the next day. "It (the conversion) went like clockwork," said DiMuzio of the highly trained group. "Everybody knew what he was doing."

The unforgettable Zamboni sucked water from the field after rainstorms.

Another advantage of the artificial surface was in evidence when it rained. Rather than have water soak the field and render it not playable, as was often the case with grass, the field was quickly cleared of water. The unforgettable Zamboni, with its engine droning endlessly while it worked, was originally used to suck up water and deposit it in drains on the field. With later surfaces, water was collected on tarpaulins and dumped into the turf, where it was absorbed in a matter of a few seconds and poured into a drainage system below the surface that could handle up to 10 inches per hour. A crew of 15 usually manned the tarps before and after a rainstorm. Games at the Vet were seldom cancelled because of rain, and only 82 games were postponed during the stadium's 33 years.

"We knew the system, and could cover the field in a matter of minutes," Frangipani said. "Getting the tarp off the field quickly when it was loaded with water was a little tricky, especially if the wind was blowing. You can't take too long because everybody is anxious to get the game resumed."

Once, as the crew began covering the field, a security guard who was helping the procedure slipped on the wet turf and slid under the tarp. "They didn't know I was under there until I tried to get out," said Ed Sickles. After several minutes of flailing away, Sickles was rescued and crawled out unharmed.

One situation that neither the grounds crew nor anybody else had control over was the way the playing surface reacted to a hot summer day. When the temperature rose to the 90s and the humidity was approaching an unbearable level, the artificial surface retained heat. Outfielder Milt Thompson claimed it would get so hot that heat waves would rise off the turf as high as a player's chest. As pitcher Rick Wise put it, "The field got hotter than Hades."

"I remember one time it got to 165 degrees on the field," said catcher Darren Daulton. "It was really unbearable, physically and psychologically. Before a game, you knew you were going to go out into it and that it was going to be very hot. It was always in your mind. I saw guys pass out. I almost passed out one time. I'd lose 10 to 15 pounds a game.

"You'd come into the dugout between innings," Daulton continued, "and the rubber in your shoes was melting, your feet were on fire. You'd put your feet on ice. It may be an old wives tale, but we'd put cabbage in our hats or helmets. It was supposed to keep you cool. By the end of the first inning, it was cooked cabbage.

"After a while, you wouldn't feel anything. You were soaking wet. The trainers had ammonia water, and you'd stick your head in it. They'd towel you down every inning, and you'd suck down as much water as you could."

Players learned how to deal with the terribly hot conditions. "The other team had to play on it, too," said third baseman Dave Hollins. "So there was really no use whining. There wasn't anything you could do about it."

"You had to learn to pace yourself during batting and infield practice," said shortstop Kevin Stocker, "or you'd just wear yourself out. But once you got used to it, it wasn't as bad as St. Louis or Kansas City."

For pitcher Tommy Greene, the excessive heat had another liability. "I was a fly ball pitcher," he said, "and when it got hot the ball carried a bit more. I had to try very hard to keep the ball down, or it would go out of the yard. But standing on the mound or catching or playing first were the best spots to be when it was real hot because it was cooler on the dirt than on the turf."

The heat, which once soared into the 160s on the field during a night game, wasn't the only condition that altered the way people played. Actually, the very presence of artificial turf changed the way players performed their jobs.

Shortstop Larry Bowa once told Mark Whicker of the *Evening Bulletin* that he had to play back on the heel of the infield. "It cuts down on double plays because you can't play up," Bowa said. Second baseman Manny Trillo claimed he always had to find a lump in the surface and play in front of it. "I can't take any chances," he said.

Visiting players never took too kindly to the artificial surface either. "Players from other teams would come in for three or four games, and their hips would start bothering them," said outfielder Doug Glanville, who played both for and against the Phillies. "Their knees would get sore. It wasn't much fun to play on."

"The turf made a lot of difference, and I didn't care for it" said Greg Maddux. "It was pretty hard around home plate, so you gave up a lot of high choppers. And the ball got through the infield and into the gaps real fast. As a pitcher, you always had to be thinking of that."

"AstroTurf changed the game," said Wise. "It was definitely not a pitcher's best friend.

"Balls went through the infield in the blink of an eye. Outfielders had to have more speed and play deeper so they could cut off balls in the gap."

That served as an advantage for some outfielders like Maddox. "I was very fortunate to have speed," he said. "The AstroTurf was designed for speed, and that allowed me to excel. I could get to balls fast. And I knew the bounces in the turf, the wall, how the wind blew . . . I knew everything there was to know about the outfield. Playing at the Vet for many years gave a big advantage to my game."

Whether or not the turf was good for all outfielders was a matter of opinion. "It made it harder to play defense," Luzinski said. Added Thompson: "The ball really bounced on the turf. It was very tough to make a play on a ball hit in front of you because it would bounce so high. When the turf got hot, it was almost like the ball was on a trampoline. The turf was good to hit on, but not necessarily good to play on."

Players sometimes slipped on loose dirt while rounding the bases. Sometimes balls would hit seams in the infield and take crazy bounces. Sometimes fly balls would drop and then careen far over an outfielder's head. But nothing in baseball quite compared with the problems the artificial turf caused in football.

Once, an Eagles punter stepped into a split in a seam just as he was about to kick the ball. He missed it completely. Another time, a player dislocated both elbows after he banged into the turf. Running back Wendell Davis of the Chicago Bears blew out both his knees at the Vet, a calamity for which the turf took the blame. And Dallas Cowboys running back Emmett Smith always brought 12 different pairs of shoes to the Vet, wearing whichever pair the surface dictated on the day of the game (such as hot, wet, dry, or frozen).

When Dick Vermeil was the Eagles' coach, the team practiced on the grass field at JFK Stadium and sometimes at the Navy Yard to avoid possible injuries that could be caused by the Vet's surface. "I hated the turf," he said many years later. "It was so hard, and it had seams, and when it got cold, it became even harder. It was just a very poor playing surface."

In 2001, an Eagles exhibition game with the Baltimore Ravens was cancelled shortly before game time after visiting coach Bill Belichick complained that some areas of the turf weren't level. He refused to play, and fans who had packed the stadium were refunded the price of their tickets, at considerable loss to the Eagles.

Visiting teams were always particularly wary of the Vet surface. For Eagles games, some teams would not run certain plays that required using the worst areas of the field. New York Giants quarterback Phil Simms was quoted on an NFL Films show as saying that when he moved from the huddle to the line of scrimmage at the Vet, the first thing he did—even before he scanned the opposing defensive alignment—was to look over his shoulder and search for soft spots in the turf. He wanted to know where they were so he could avoid them while fading back to pass.

For football, the worst section of the field was the area used by baseball as the infield. There were cracks between the pieces of turf laid over the bases. There were spots as soft as pillows. And although the pitcher's mound was removed for football, its cover stuck above the rest of the playing surface.

"Whenever we got down to that end of the field, we had to remember to keep our feet high," Bergey said. "You didn't scoot along like you normally would because if you got your foot caught in one of those cracks and it was planted there and somebody hit you, your foot might stay there. But something had to give. It wasn't going to be your foot. It was probably going to be your knee. We were all very conscious of that."

The turf was so hard, Bergey said, "that you would feel it the following morning. On Monday mornings after a Sunday game, I ran five or six miles just to work up a real good sweat to try to get the soreness out of my body. Once, I remember playing in a Monday night game against the Washington Redskins, and the game went into overtime. Can you imagine playing four hours on that crap?"

Strawberries, those ugly red splotches that occur when skin rubs across a hard surface, were so common in football that Eagles trainer Otho Davis developed a special solution made of cream and powder that when wrapped in gauze would heal the wound in about one week. For those with exposed strawberries, often, when they were watching game films, players sitting behind them would flick the injured area with their fingers, causing a yelp and a sudden burst of extreme pain.

Offensive guard Brian Baldinger said that his elbows bled after every game. "The turf was just terrible," he said. Baldinger claimed that the team walked the field every day that they played or practiced on it to spot both the soft and hard spots in the turf. "There were dead spots in different places," he said. "The rest of the field was rock hard. If you were an offensive lineman, you constantly had to look down to see where your feet were."

A few Eagles did not despise the artificial surface. One who didn't was safety Randy Logan, who never missed a game in 159 outings. "That's all I played on at Michigan," he said, "so I was used to it and didn't really have any complaints."

Despite its many imperfections, the Vet's playing field got better with each new surface. And the various turfs were not without some benefits, especially to baseball. Although many who witnessed the 1993 World Series still have a vivid recollection of a throw from Daulton that took a high

A throw during the 1993 World Series took a high bounce off the turf and whacked shortstop Kevin Stocker (left) in the throat.

bounce and hit Stocker in the throat as he tried to nail Roberto Alomar on an attempted steal of second base, most of the time, fielders got a true hop.

"For fielding, it was good because you knew what kind of hop you were going to get," said first baseman Rico Brogna. "You knew it was going to be true. You just had to be ready because it was going to get on you quickly. If you had good reflexes, you'd be all right. But it was definitely fast because it was matted down."

Added infielder Tony Taylor: "I thought the infield was tremendous, even better than the grass one at Connie Mack Stadium. I really enjoyed playing on it at the Vet. If you were quick with your hands and quick with your feet, you could make the play anytime because the bounce was going to be true."

Because he played more on the NexTurf, Rollins was partial to the Vet's final surface. "When the ball came up, it slid a little," he said. "But once you figured out the speed as the ball got to you, you knew it wasn't going to do anything funny. It kind of sat down like it does on grass."

"It was an easy-fielding ballpark because of the AstroTurf," said third baseman Mike Schmidt, who often came early and hit golf balls into the center field seats. "Plus, I could run faster because of the turf than I could on a natural grass field."

Like Schmidt, many players claimed that their speed was enhanced by playing on the artificial turf. More than one hitter got an extra base because of his increased speed. "It sure made me feel faster," said outfielder Glenn Wilson. "I loved playing on it."

"The turf was definitely good for me," said outfielder Jeff Stone. "It increased my speed. Running on turf, I could get a good jump and that just made me faster. Sometimes, I even ran too fast and tripped over my own feet."

Despite repeated complaints about the turf by third baseman Scott Rolen, an issue that fed into his desire to be traded, most players over the years learned to adjust to the surface. Many didn't like it, but they accepted it.

"You learned how to deal with it," said Brogna. "No matter where you played, you became used to your home surface. Your body learned it and got used to it. It tweaked my knees and back from time to time, but it was consistent. All you can ask for as a professional athlete is consistency from anything and anybody."

BEHIND THE SCENES

The lowest level was one of the most important areas

Well below street level, in the deep recesses of Veterans Stadium, another world existed. It was a world all to its own, a place that fans never saw, where only a highly select group was allowed entry.

In effect, though, it was the hub around which revolved the very reason anyone came to a game at the Vet. And especially before as well as after games, it buzzed with activity.

The subterranean level of the Vet had no name. It had no real identity either. And it certainly wasn't attractive. In fact, it was one of the most drab, dull parts of the stadium, windowless and without pretense, and the place where some of its loudest critics claimed to have collected some of their best ammunition.

But it was full of important places. And nooks and crannies. And areas that in effect served as "offices" for the people most vital to the game.

The area fed off a long, circular concourse. It was reached primarily by two elevators, one running from the Phillies offices upstairs, the other by the press elevator that came to be used by a lot more people than just the press.

Above: The Eagles' locker room, like the other ones, was mostly devoid of amenities.

Located at one end of the concourse were the indoor batting cages. At the opposite end were areas where food for the concessions stands as well as supplies for the playing field were stored. In between were more Phillies and Eagles offices, the office and dressing room of the Phillie Phanatic, a photo lab, a video room, the office of equipment manager Frank Coppenbarger, the umpires' dressing room, a media room where post-game and other interviews were held, and four locker rooms.

"There were a lot of neat little areas where people could hide," said Mike DiMuzio, the Vet's director of facility management, who in his 33 years at the stadium learned all the nooks and crannies. "The place had a lot of idiosyncrasies."

One of them was located off a tunnel that led to the field where there was a dressing room for groundskeepers and another room where they kept their equipment. The latter became known as the "mud room" because dirt and clay were stored there.

Perhaps that room contained the most interesting part of the entire area. It was where "the wall" stood.

The wall had its origin sometime in the 1970s when the room served mostly as an office and lounge for the groundskeepers. It also served as a lounge for players who would stop in after and even sometimes during or before a game for a quick drink, sometimes to eat, or just to talk a little baseball with the crew.

"A lot of baseball was talked in there," remembered slugger Dick Allen. "Some of the players gathered in there. Usually, that's where they could find me. Before the game, after the game. Sometimes, players have personal problems, too, and we'd hack them out in there. Sometimes, it wasn't all hacking things out. We'd have a little beverage."

Allen was the most frequent visitor. But lots of other players stopped in. Greg Luzinski often brought crabs to eat. Tony Taylor developed a reputation for making daiquiris. Even Steve Carlton as well as visiting players and occasionally a celebrity from some other field came to the room.

"It was," said groundskeeper Mark (Froggy) Carfagno, "a place where guys could get away from the pressure, relax a little bit, and enjoy themselves. It was a great place for all of us."

The room had a refrigerator and lounge chairs. And the wall.

During the 1970s, Gary Tinneny, a groundskeeper, got the bright idea to have players who came into the lounge sign their names to a painted, cinder block wall on one side of the room. The names quickly added up.

Carlton, Allen, Luzinski, Taylor, Tug McGraw, Pete Rose, Robin Roberts, Manny Trillo, Larry Christenson, and numerous other Phillies signed the wall. Then, as more players from other teams stopped in, a wall on the other side of the room became the designated spot for the signatures of visiting players.

Lou Brock, Tom Seaver, Willie Stargell, Joe Morgan, Willie McCovey, Don Drysdale, Dave Winfield, Tony Perez, Gary Carter, Bill

Madlock, Gaylord Perry, Steve Garvey, Walter Alston, and many others penned their names on the wall. Eventually, the wall contained the names of some 15 Hall of Famers. Nonplayers Howard Cosell, Joey Bishop, Max Patkin, an assortment of umpires, and a variety of others also signed.

"It got to be kind of neat," said DiMuzio, who was a groundskeeper in the 1970s when the signings began. "Gary started getting the guys who came in to sign, and it became a thing where the guys wanted to be asked to come in and sign. There were probably 150 signatures on the two walls."

As time went on, the room became less of a lounge and more of a storage area. Shovels and rakes were hung on the walls, covering the signatures. Shelves, cans of paint, boxes of materials, and other pieces of equipment stood in front of the walls. And by the late 1980s, attempts to get players to autograph the walls had pretty much ceased.

But the walls that fans never saw remained intact. Eventually, the walls that had been a vital part of the Vet's history were removed and, although expected to be relocated to Citizens Bank Park, were temporarily put in storage where they remain today.

While the walls developed their own kind of legendary status among Vet insiders, there were many other prominent areas located in the bowels of the stadium. Among them were the locker rooms.

One locker room made the kind of headlines not usually associated with such places. It was the dressing room of the Eagles cheerleaders, those scantily clad beauties who decorated the sidelines at every home game. In 2001, two anonymous cheerleaders filed a suit in U.S. district court alleging that players from visiting teams, who used an adjacent locker room, viewed them in various stages of undress, including before, during, and after they showered, through holes in the wall and cracks in doors. The misuse of the male libidos, the cheerleaders said, had been going on for more than 15 years.

The suit, claiming an invasion of privacy, originally asked for $75,000 in damages from 23 NFL teams. Eventually, additional cheerleaders, both past and present, joined the legal action, bringing the number of claimants to more than 100. According to a report by the *Associated Press*, the suit was expanded to 29 NFL teams (excluding the Eagles), and the amount of damages was increased many times over. The suit was eventually settled out of court.

For the players, the Eagles and the visiting team's football and baseball locker rooms were large, bare-bones rooms devoid of either luxuries or amenities. Large lockers unadorned by frills dominated the rooms. For football teams, even in the Eagles' clubhouse, there was no area large enough to hold a full team meeting. Players spilled through the doors and into the adjacent areas.

But the Eagles' clubhouse was not without some benefits. Linebacker Bill Bergey described some of them.

"The locker room wasn't really too bad," he said. "We shared the bathroom and the shower with the Phillies. We also shared saunas. There was a door between the teams' locker rooms. That was pretty neat. The Phillies would come in and visit us, and we would go over and visit them. It enabled us to become friends with a lot of them. Once, Tug took me down to the indoor batting cage.

"The weight room wasn't good," Bergey added. "It was probably worse than any college weight room in the country. It was a small dungeon. It did not have a pleasant atmosphere."

According to center Mike Evans, the Eagles often held their own version of the "home run derby," attempting to swat balls out of the park. Defensive back Bill Bradley was the club leader in that category. "Some of the Phillies would stand around and watch us," Evans said. "When we watched them take batting practice, we were always amazed at how hard they hit the ball."

More pleasant was the Phillies' clubhouse, the main part being, like the others, a large rectangular room surrounded by lockers jammed with players' clothes and equipment. Ironically, four players during the life of the Vet—Joe Lefebvre, Sixto Lezcano, Lenny Dykstra, and Roger Mason—had been traded in moves that merely required them to stroll down the hall from one baseball clubhouse to the other.

Side rooms in the home team clubhouse included the manager's office with a desk and a bathroom, sparsely decorated in the mode of who-ever was the present skipper. Other rooms, including the coaches' dressing room, a shower room and bathroom, an equipment room complete with facil-ities for washing uniforms, Jeff Cooper's trainer's room, a workout room, a room where players could watch their performances videotaped by Dan Stephenson, and a small players' lounge, stood around the perimeter of the main clubhouse where first Kenny Bush, then later Coppenbarger, manned the operation.

"When I got here from Tiger Stadium where the clubhouse was real small, I thought the clubhouse at the Vet was awesome," outfielder Glenn Wilson said. "I loved it because it was my second home."

"In the 1970s, the clubhouse was state-of-the-art," added Del Unser. "It was big and lengthy, and it had everything you needed."

The most distinguishing feature of the main clubhouse over the years was an area at the back of one end. Especially prominent in 1993 when the Phillies went to the World Series, it was called "Macho Row." With lockers side by side, its residents were the team's loudest and brashest members, including Dykstra, John Kruk, Dave Hollins, Pete Incaviglia, and Mitch Williams. Darren Daulton, the Phils' unchallenged team leader, presided over the group from a lounge chair stuffed into his locker.

Around the room, nearly every player's locker had a personal touch. Family pictures adorned some lockers. Single players occasionally dis-played a shot of a pinup. Others hung baseball cards. New Englander Steve Bedrosian's locker used to contain a basketball autographed by the Boston Celtics. Luzinski had a set of bull horns hanging on his. In latter years, small television sets were replaced by boom boxes that often blasted loud music through the room.

Juan Samuel always kept his bats in his locker instead of storing them in the usual racks. "I like to keep my eye on them because some people, mostly pitchers, like to borrow them for batting practice," he said. "I like to protect them."

Tony Taylor claimed that when he played, the clubhouse had a special appeal for him. "Because of it, you enjoyed coming to the stadium every day," he said. "Although you didn't have to be there until 3:30, I used to come in at 2 o'clock every day. You wanted to come early and sit and relax, and get ready for the game. It was a nice way to do it."

There were, of course, flaws. One wasn't the clubhouse itself, but the tunnel that led from it to the dugout. That was the area that had prompted Mike Schmidt to complain about the "cat stink," and that Williams said had a smell that "was not very attractive."

"I thought it always smelled of hot dogs and beer," recalled Jim Eisenreich. "I didn't mind that. It sort of gave the place a ballpark flavor."

To some players, the condition of the clubhouse was far less important than just being in the big leagues. They would have happily dressed in a broom closet.

"The locker room was fine," said Mickey Morandini. "I wasn't picky. I just wanted to play ball. There really wasn't much else I was concerned with. I was happy to be in the big leagues, and I just wanted do to my best on the field."

A special appendage of the main clubhouse was the exercise room where for 17 years strength and conditioning guru Gus Hoefling put his minions through hellaciously grueling programs. Used through-out the year by some players, it was a large room filled with exercise machines of every conceivable kind and that worked on every conceiv-able part of the body. Weights, machines for stretching, for building mus-cles, and for rehabilitation peppered the room, which contained 23 work stations.

The room's most famous occupant was Carlton, who did leg and arm exercises in a 4-by-13-foot pit filled with rice. The Hall of Fame hurler spent many long hours in the room, sometimes as many as one to two hours *after* pitching a game. On occasion, Carlton was known to have worked out into the wee hours of the morning.

"In the 1970s and early 1980s, nearly the entire team worked out in there," said Hoefling, who spent until 1992 with the Phillies. "Larry Bowa, Bob Boone, John Denny, Don Carman, Darren Daulton, Kevin Gross, and Shane Rawley were some of the ones who worked out the most."

Off-limits to the prying eyes of writers and others, the room was where players did stretching and muscle-enhancement workouts on alternate days. Along with the machines, they also used a 13-foot iron bar, punching bags, training tables, and various other devices, some developed over the years by Hoefling, a practitioner of martial arts. They also spent many hours doing floor exercises.

"It was one of the best-equipped conditioning rooms in sports," said Hoefling, who originally came to Philadelphia in 1973 to work for the Eagles.

Another vital part of Hoefling's den was a closet-like enclosure that he designed and called a "behavior modification room." Called a "mood room" by others, it shut off all distractions. Players—one of the most frequent users being Carlton—could sit in the room and listen to subliminal messages delivered in soft, soothing voices that were designed to stress positive thoughts and enhance their performances on the field. Some players also listened to relaxing music prior to a game.

Some messages were also designed to build confidence or to get players to relax. Others addressed smoking or drinking problems. All lasted about 20 minutes and, coupled with the movement of the chair and variations in lighting, put the user in a kind of semi-hypnotic state. The enclosure was built at a cost of $15,000.

Video production manager Dan Stephenson helped pitcher Fred Toliver review his performance in a room filled with electronic equipment.

Just off the main clubhouse, conditioning guru Gus Hoefling put players through a variety of drills.

Lenny Dykstra (left) and John Vukovich shared some thoughts in the Phillies dugout.

Between the Phillies and visiting team's clubhouses was another clubhouse that had a special place in every game at the Vet. It was the little room where umpires changed from their street clothes to their battle garb.

For nearly two decades, the room's attendant was Jimmy Higgins, a man who began his connection with the Phillies in 1951 as an usher at Connie Mack Stadium. It was Higgins's job to serve as a valet for the umps, helping them with their clothes, packing and unpacking their travel trunks, cleaning their spikes, and keeping the room stocked with food and drink. One umpire always liked to have two hoagies on hand. Another's special taste leaned toward roast beef sandwiches.

Higgins was also in charge of removing the glossy finish of each baseball by rubbing it down with a special mud concoction that came from New Jersey. Usually, he prepared six to seven dozen baseballs for each game.

Higgins was one of many long-term Phillies employees who worked in the subterranean level of the Vet. Bush served as clubhouse manager for the first 18 years of the Vet. Coppenbarger was clubhouse and equipment manager for the stadium's last 15 years. Pete Cera was assistant to both men for many years.

Cooper served at the Vet as Phillies trainer for 23 years, the longest stint of an athletic trainer in the history of Philadelphia sports. Mark Andersen was assistant trainer for 18 years. Stephenson was the Phillies manager of video productions for 22 years. Kevin Steinhour, manager of the visiting clubhouse; Phil Sheridan, assistant manager of the home team clubhouse; Jeff Wright and Jody Boon of the grounds crew; and batting practice pitchers Steve Toler and Connie Newman all worked at the Vet for a number of years.

Many became good friends of the uniformed personnel. "The club-house guys, the groundskeepers, and many of the others," former manager Terry Francona said. "You're with them day and night, and you can't help but build good friendships. And that's what gives me some of my best memories of the Vet."

ROOTING FOR THE HOME TEAMS

There's no fan like a Philly sports fan

In most parts of the country, Philadelphia sports fans have a special reputation. It is not entirely flattering.

Philly sports fans—both the Phillies and Eagles varieties—can be loyal, enthusiastic, knowledgeable, and dedicated. They can also be demanding, critical, impatient, loud, uncouth, unruly, and sometimes prone to too many encounters with beverages stronger than milk shakes.

When Philadelphia sports fans like someone, that person knows it. When they don't like someone, he knows it, too. Philly fans are legendary in

Above: Fan favorite Tug McGraw always had a good time with the spectators.

their ability to demonstrate their disenchantment with whomever or whatever does not strike their fancy.

In most cases, the standard technique with which that is accomplished is with a vocal utterance called a "boo." Those who resort to that most unmelodious of sounds are called boobirds. And the term *boobirds* has become synonymous with the species known as a Philadelphia sports fan.

Noted comedian and former occasional catcher Bob Uecker once had this to say about Philadelphia sports fans: "They're so rough that they boo kids who come up empty handed in the Easter egg hunt. They'd boo unwed mothers on Mother's Day. I've even seen people standing on street corners booing each other."

"If you play in Philadelphia long enough," the eminent philosopher Larry Bowa once said, "you get used to it."

The condition is not new. Long ago at Baker Bowl, Phillies fans used to boo and otherwise show their displeasure by throwing seat cushions on the field. At Shibe Park/Connie Mack Stadium, boobirds hit their peak, booing pillars of the home team such as Del Ennis, Gus Zernial, and Dick Allen—just to name a few—and once even booing so loud and long (while also throwing debris on the field) that a game had to be forfeited to the opposing team.

Even though fans at Veterans Stadium booed Mike Schmidt in his early years, as well as others, the demeanor of the clientele changed somewhat after the Phillies left Connie Mack Stadium. "The fans there were mostly male and there were some pretty crusty ones," said Phils president David Montgomery, who went to the park at 21st and Lehigh as a youth. "The Vet was much more fan-friendly, so we attracted more of a family audience."

"The fans were younger at the Vet," said Tony Taylor, who played at both stadiums. "I think a lot of older people from Connie Mack Stadium never came to the Vet. But, at both places, the fans were the greatest in baseball. They knew the game and when a guy gives 100 percent; they supported a player when he tried hard."

No matter what age they were, Mitch Williams was one of many players who appreciated the Vet fans. "There's a different kind of fan here than other places," he said. "They're knowledgeable. They're demanding. But I would rather play in front of a crowd that demands the best than play in front of a crowd that just goes to a game because it's a social event. In Philadelphia it's not a social event. It's life or death to a lot of fans."

Williams was one of many players from the Vet who did not escape the fans' displeasure, especially after the 1993 World Series, when he and his family were subjected to various kinds of crude abuse by mindless idiots. Relief pitcher Jose Mesa was another. So was catcher Lance Parrish, who after coming to the Phillies with a big free agent contract, was loudly booed by fans following a long lack of productivity. Fans also heckled his wife when she came to games.

Parrish arrived with high hopes that he would be the catalyst that would drive the club to a pennant. But when the ex-Detroit Tiger didn't deliver as expected, fans treated him roughly. And they were not exactly models of gentility toward his wife when she would sit in the stands.

"Well, I deserved it," Parrish said many years later. "The fans had high expectations, although they were no higher than the ones I had for myself. My coming to Philadelphia had a lot of people thinking we would become a contender, but I wasn't too good, and I deserved everything I got. It was unfortunate because I had been pretty consistent up to that point."

Philly fans always knew how to give visiting players the raspberry, too. "When Pete Rose was with Cincinnati," remembered pitcher Larry Christenson, "the fans behind the third base dugout would really get on him. Pete would foul balls into the stands at them."

"They'd get on you," said pitcher Greg Maddux. "They could even be a little vulgar. But they'd support their team. They'd let them know when they're winning, and they'd let them know when they're not. They cared what happened. Players respect that. So we enjoyed coming to the Vet in that kind of atmosphere."

Phillies players enjoyed the atmosphere even more. And most of them were highly complimentary about the fans who came to the Vet to cheer them on.

"It was a great atmosphere to play in," said Bowa. "The crowds were always very enthusiastic. They were all baseball."

Catcher Darren Daulton said he had some moments over the years when fans heckled him. "But when you got them on your side," he said, "it was enjoyable to play in front of them. It became like a family—the fans, the press, the ushers. It became very comfortable."

"The fans were great," said Jay Johnstone. "They would get on the other team, and they could really make it unbearable. But they made the Vet a great place to play."

Glenn Wilson had similar views. "I can't think of a bad thing to say about them, other than my first season in 1984," he said. "I didn't have a good season, and the fans let me know about it. But they made me a better player.

"I'm remembered mainly for my arm and that I could throw people out from right field," he added. "I remember the build up when there was a base hit to right and there was a runner on second. I could actually hear the roar coming from the stands. It would just build and build as I was coming up to make a throw."

According to Gary Matthews, they made him a better player, too. "It was good playing at the Vet because of the people," he said. "It wasn't the stadium that made it good, it was the people. They electrified you as a player and made you perform better. They were into the game, knew the game and the kind of effort you were giving. It's not always statistics with the people in Philly. And that's the way it should be. Of course, if you're not playing well, they'd come out to boo you."

A classic example of the effect Vet fans had on players came in the 1977 NLCS when they booed a Los Angeles Dodgers pitcher (Burt Hooton)

Right fielder Glenn Wilson said the fans made him a better player.

off the mound (see Chapter 5). "That's the one thing that really sticks out in my mind about Philly fans," said Dallas Green, who pitched in front of fans at Connie Mack Stadium and managed before them at the Vet. "They made so much noise that he got so rattled he couldn't finish the inning. The fans ran him right out of the game. That's what home field advantage is all about. Philadelphia sports fans have been maligned a lot of times, but we have great fans and they love baseball."

Demonstrating that premise, Vet fans came out in large numbers. During the 33 years of the stadium, 66,728,403 fans attended 2,617 regular season games, and 1,522,493 fans watched 25 post-season outings. More than two million fans attended Vet games in each of 14 seasons, reaching a high of 3,137,674 in 1993. The low was 1,343,329 in 1972. Average yearly attendance over the 33 years was 2,022,728. (The Phils drew more than one million fans only six times—1946, 1950, 1957, 1964, 1965, 1966—prior to coming to the Vet.)

During the life of the Vet, the Phillies averaged 26,498 fans per game. "You can't ask for anything better than playing before 20 or 30,000 people every night," said Von Hayes.

The Phillies attracted crowds of more than 50,000 some 99 times. The club record for most crowds above 50,000 in a single season was 16 set in 1993. Another record was set that year when the Phillies drew 40,000 or more, 20 games in a row. The Phils also had a record eight sellouts in 1993, the last year they won a National League pennant at the Vet.

The largest single-game attendance was 67,064 on October 16, 1983, for the fifth and final game of the World Series, which the Baltimore Orioles won, 5–0. One day earlier, Game Four of that Series, which the Orioles won, 5–4, drew 66,947 for the second largest Vet crowd. The legendary sixth game of the 1980 Series on October 21 pulled the third highest crowd (65,838).

The largest regular-season crowd was the 63,816 that attended a July 3, 1984, fireworks night in which the Cincinnati Reds beat the Phillies, 6–5. Another fireworks night on July 5, 1982, when the Phillies lost to the San Francisco Giants, 3–1, attracted the second-largest regular-season audience (63,501).

On the bottom side, crowds of 10,000 or less appeared 61 times. The lowest crowd was 4,149 for a May 6, 1974, game between the Phils and the San Diego Padres, in which four future Hall of Famers—Schmidt, Steve Carlton, Dave Winfield, and Willie McCovey—appeared, the Padres winning, 7–6. The second-lowest crowd (4,288) showed up the next day to see the Padres again beat the Phils, 5–3, in 13 innings.

With an average crowd, fans consumed 9,700 hot dogs, 10,000 cups of soda, 9,000 cups of beer, 2,300 pretzels, and 1,000 orders of french fries. Some 260 people worked each game for various food concessionaires over the years, including vendors and people working the catering and restaurant areas. Altogether, including ushers, ticket-takers, security guards, vendors, and others, some 500 people worked each game.

Naturally, for the men in red pinstripes, playing before a large crowd had a substantial advantage over performing in front of crowds so small that hot dog vendors were nearly as plentiful as fans.

"When you play in front of 40,000 people, you really get pumped up and ready to play," said second baseman Mickey Morandini. "There's all the noise. You get a buzz when you come out on the field."

"You always try harder when you play in front of a big crowd," claimed Taylor. "They make you feel better."

Pitcher Randy Wolf agreed. "It's hard to play when there are 30,000 empty seats," he said. "But I remember in my rookie year, I pitched on fireworks night and there were 58,000 people in the stands. It was unbelievable pitching in front of that many fans."

Over the years, the Phillies, who sponsored many fan programs, including ones for youth and tours of the stadium, had a strong base of season-ticket holders. According to vice president for ticket sales Richard Deats, the number was around 5,000 in the early years of the Vet, then increased to about 8,000 after the Phils became a contender in the mid-1970s. Following the World Series victory in 1980, the number of season-ticket holders (both full and partial plans) ballooned to 13,000 in 1981. The highest total was 21,000 in 1994, the year after the team won another pennant.

About 30 fans held season tickets throughout the Vet's 33 years. A few were holdovers from Connie Mack Stadium.

On a good day, a walkup crowd averaged 6,000–7,000, the highest totals being during the summer months. Some of the biggest walkup crowds occurred in 1972, whenever Carlton pitched. The newly acquired hurler, who won 15 straight games that year and 27 of the team's total of 59, often attracted a walkup crowd as high as 15,000.

A typical ticket price in 1971 was from $3.25 to $4.25 for a seat in the 300 level. In 2003, the price of a similar seat had risen to $26.

Fans in the rows closest to the field often interacted with the players. "They were so close, you could hear every word they said," claimed catcher Ozzie Virgil. "And they could hear the players. That made it kind of fun."

There were times, though, when it wasn't fun for a player. "I never liked having to walk through a mob of fans on the way in or out," said shortstop Kevin Stocker. "Especially if they wanted an autograph, they were a little pushy. They'd keep on you until they'd get it."

The fans were active in other ways, too. In the latter years of the Vet, fan clubs became common. First, there was the Wolf Pack, a group of young men who wore wolf masks and stood high in the left field bleachers cheering on their favorite pitcher. Subsequent groups included ones with names such as Padilla's Flotilla, Millwood's Militia, Thome's Homeys, Burrell's Girls, Person's People, and Lake Placido.

Some fans sent cakes, pies, or various other delicacies to the broadcast booth. Some, usually attractive young women, danced on the home team's dugout roof with the Phillie Phanatic. And some hung around the players' entrance after games, seeking autographs.

Pitcher John Denny told a story about a fan who sat on Sunday afternoons behind the third base dugout. He had a loud voice, and he frequently badgered Schmidt.

"One Sunday, I'm looking in to get my sign," Denny said, "and all of the sudden the umpire calls time. I look around, first to one side, then to the other, then out to center field, but I don't see anything and I can't figure out what's going on. Then I look over to third base, and here comes Schmidt casually walking toward the mound.

"He took off his glove, put it under his arm, walked up on the dirt part of the mound, picked up the rosin bag, then put it down. He still hadn't said anything. Finally, he said, 'Johnny, I'm really sorry for breaking your concentration, but that guy over by the third base dugout has been on me all day, and I just want to get away from him for a second.' "

Children often attracted the attention of players. Over the years, many of them were taken by their fathers to the Vet to see their first Phillies games. For that reason, those children when they became adults held fond memories of the Vet. Many never knew any other stadium.

Neighborhood children also grew up with close ties to the stadium. "We had a lot of interaction with the kids from the neighborhood," recalled Christenson. "They were always there. We'd stop and talk with them and sign autographs."

One of those neighborhood kids was Frank Miceli, who grew up just four blocks from the Vet. "As a kid, I went to about 40 games a year," he said. "In the early days, the Phillies offered tickets to kids to the 700 level for 50 cents. Later, I had a courtesy pass. After the game, we'd always wait for autographs at the press entrance where the visiting players' bus parked. The best one I got was from Roberto Clemente who signed it 'To Frank.' "

Food vendors such as Cheryl Spielvogel did a brisk business in the stands.

Micelli said that neighborhood residents always knew what was happening during a game at the Vet. "We'd hear the crowd roar, and know something was happening. You'd yell, 'yo, what are the Phillies doing?' and somebody would give the score. When the fireworks went off, we knew a Phillie had hit a home run."

Another advantage of living close to the Vet, Micelli said, "was that you could plan in two minutes to go to a game. That was a great option to have every day. You couldn't do that if you lived in Roxborough or some place like that."

Micelli remembered when the Phillies won the 1980 LCS in Houston. "An impromptu party erupted on Broad Street," he said. "People drove up and down, honking horns, kissing and hugging each other, giving high fives. Then when the Phillies won the World Series at the Vet, it was pandemonium afterward. People in the neighborhood were handing out drinks. Some people climbed up light poles. It was insane."

Another neighborhood resident who later made sports his livelihood was Arizona Diamondbacks relief pitcher Mike Koplove. "I lived directly across the street from the Vet," he said. "It was kind of strange living that close, but I loved growing up in the neighborhood. The neighborhood was very close-knit. It was the best place on earth for a kid.

"Two of the greatest memories I have as a kid," Koplove added, "were when my dad and I snuck in for the last few innings of Terry Mulholland's no-hitter in 1990 and when I was here for the last game of the 1993 LCS when the Phillies beat the Braves."

There were times when misfortune occurred at the Vet. Such was the case when a fan fell out of the upper deck and was killed. Another time a maintenance worker driving a cart in the upper deck crashed through a guard rail and plunged 42 feet to his death. Various other fans have died from heart attacks. A young boy from the neighborhood was struck and killed by a truck while riding his bicycle in the Vet parking lot. Once, a woman succumbed after a piece of pretzel lodged in her windpipe.

Heat prostration, injuries (especially those resulting from people falling or getting knocked down), lacerations, and eye ailments that came mostly from material blowing into people's eyes have each been treated by the Vet's first aid unit thousands of times. "One time, a squirrel jumped on a man. Dug its claws right into his skin," said Rita Lyons, the dispensary's chief administrator for nearly three decades. "He rushed in here with the squirrel."

Fans that needed treatment also had encounters with flying bats (the mammal kind), flying bats (the wooden variety), cats, sickness, foul balls, and scores of other maladies. Sometimes, the injuries came from somebody else's fist.

"Our job was not only medical," Lyons said in an article in *Phillies Report*. "It's also important to be a psychologist and a public relations person. Most people come in here scared. Or angry. Or both."

Young fans could test their batting skills in one of the many activities on the Vet concourse.

Or drunk. Philly sports fans have never been shy about their familiarity with beverages that have a kick. Phillies personnel were trained to spot such people and deal with them. Starting in 1993, they also had to watch for smokers. Smoking was banned that year in all areas except the concourses.

Although fans were never permitted to bring booze (or soda) into the Vet, many tried. One trick was to remove the contents of a hoagie and stuff the roll with beer cans. Another was to pass cans or bottles to fans already inside the stadium. Once, some fans on the 500 level dropped a rope to their buddies outside with the idea of hoisting some suds.

"Guys in wheelchairs would sometimes try to smuggle in beer under a blanket," recalled Michael Casasanto, a Vet ticket-taker (the designation was later changed to "greeter," just as the name "usher" was switched to "hostess") for 26 years. "Sometimes, fans would bring kids wearing heavy jackets and they'd try to stuff beer cans into their pockets. We also had people with false-bottom coolers with beer underneath. No matter how good or efficient we were, sometimes, they'd get through. But usually the staff caught them."

If a fan carried any kind of bag, it was automatically searched for alcoholic beverages. Once, a fan obviously a few clowns short of a full circus brought a paper bag with a snapping turtle inside. Fortunately, an alert ticket-taker figured out the dastardly stunt before getting his fingers munched. "He told the guy," remembered fellow ticket-taker and later security guard Mort Stein, "'No pets allowed in here.' The guy said, 'Oh, okay,' and walked away."

Another pet story occurred at the Vet while long-time Phillies employee Pat Cassidy, who went back to the Connie Mack Stadium days, was the Phils' director of stadium operations. Cassidy was making his rounds of the stadium when he came across a blind fellow, who was obviously in need of some assistance. Cassidy asked the man if he needed help. "He said that he needed someone to help him find a pole because his dog had to go to the bathroom real bad," said Cassidy some years ago. "What could I do? I found him a pole."

A favorite trick of some fans was trying to sneak in to the stadium without a ticket. "Somebody was always trying to do that," said Ed Smith, who spent 22 years at the Vet, first as a security guard and later as the gate director.

According to usher and ticket-taker Don Newman, one fan tried to get in by offering to trade a 1915 World Series ticket. Sometimes, a would-be gate-crasher would try to use a counterfeit ticket. Once in a while, a fan tried to scale a part of the wall or fence in an attempt to get inside. And then there was the time a fan without a ticket tried to bribe his way into a game by giving a ticket-taker a $100 bill. In a hurry and not looking to see what it was, the ticket-taker ripped the bill in half, as was done with legitimate tickets.

Not all fans, of course, liked the Vet. In fact, many grumbled about it during its lifetime. "I loved Connie Mack Stadium," said Bob Schmeirer. "I grew up there, then suddenly to go to this concrete palace in South Philadelphia was such a contrast. I hated the Vet. The worst part was the artificial turf. But you couldn't see well from some seats. The parking lot deteriorated over the years. In August and September, you could still see the football lines when you went to a baseball game. It got to the point where I'd rather stay home and watch the game on television."

Most times, the Phillies, unlike many other local sports teams, did not ignore the complaints of their fans. They listened patiently and tried to solve problems. For a while, Bill Giles asked Joel Ralph to select the fans with the biggest complaints, and invite them to dinner with the two executives.

The Phillies also tried hard to make the fans happy by regularly holding giveaway days. Each year, too, the team held a photo day in which players paraded before fans who took their pictures. Players often signed autographs before games and threw balls into the stands during games.

Security at the Vet tightened considerably after September 11, 2001. Backpacks, women's pocketbooks, and all other kinds of carrying devices were checked. And fans were closely scrutinized with magnetic wands. During games, anywhere from 75 to 90 security guards worked at the Vet, plus a contingent of Philadelphia policemen.

Bat days were among the most popular giveaway promotions.

A lot of times, they had plenty to do. Such was the case when a fan who was part of a group occupying a 400-level luxury box couldn't find a bathroom and relieved himself over the front of the box onto the fans below. Shortly afterward, he was arrested. Another time, security guards were called to a super box, where they found 22 nude males and several female strippers celebrating someone's bachelor party. An occasional streaker or someone demonstrating some other form of mindlessness ran onto the field. Once a drunk clamored into the Phillies' dugout asking for a ball for his son. And then there was the now-famous incident when a male and female fan, all alone in the upper deck in the outfield, were carrying the art of love-making to the extreme.

These, of course, are just a few of the thousands of examples of less than acceptable behavior that Vet customers exhibited over the years. These and some of their other stunts did not exactly endear them to players from visiting teams.

Fans took pictures of the players, including (from left) Bruce Ruffin, Darren Daulton, Don Carman, and Wally Ritchie, on the highly popular photo days.

"I think the fans at the Vet are the worst," said Atlanta Braves outfielder Andruw Jones. "They talk trash to you. They throw things at you. You try to ignore what they're saying, but you hear it."

Phillies fans were at their worst when J. D. Drew came to town. In his first trip to the Vet, a couple of fans threw batteries at the outfielder, who had refused to sign with the club after it made him their first draft choice in 1997. In subsequent years, he was always booed loudly when he came to bat, as was third baseman Scott Rolen after his unpopular departure from Philadelphia.

As Newman said, though, most Phillies fans were anything but troublemakers. "I think they get a bad rap," he claimed. "They put out 100 percent all day at their jobs, and they just expected the players to do likewise."

And they compared favorably with the ones the Eagles attracted. Booze, fights, uncouth language, rowdyism, and all kinds of other forms of misbehavior were staples of the species. "There were always a lot of incidents," said Chuck Hund, a Philadelphia policeman assigned to the Vet for various games. "Crowd control was always an important part of our job."

"Phillies fans were a piece of cake compared to Eagles fans," said Joel Ralph, the stadium manager from 1973 to 1987. "They were two completely different kinds of crowds. Eagles fans were very rambunctious. Security was always heavier for Eagles games."

Eagles fans, who booed the choice of quarterback Donovan McNabb when he was chosen as the first selection of the Eagles in 1999, displayed excessive levels of midconduct so frequently that in later years a court was established inside the stadium. Offenders were tried and prosecuted right on the spot by a seasoned local judge named Seamus McCafferty.

According to Jimmy Gallagher, who served with the Eagles, mostly as director of public relations, from 1949 to 1995, the unruly condition of the fans became acute only after the team moved to the Vet. Gallagher said that only a small group of rowdy fans existed when the team played at Franklin Field. The Vet gave birth to the new breed of fan.

"Winning magnifies everything, and losing magnifies everything," said former Eagles coach Dick Vermeil. "When we were losing, the fans were very critical."

Offensive lineman Brian Baldinger had another characterization of Eagles fans. "They were like a racehorse," he said. "They'd been in the gate all week long, and were just waiting to start. Then the bell would ring and you could hear the noise, and it would get us all stirred up. The fans' ability to energize us was amazing."

Put another way, "they were almost like parents," said safety Randy Logan. "They'd scold you when you needed to be and encourage you when you needed that. They were tough, and they'd always watch you closely. And if you didn't perform or they felt you blew it, they'd let you hear about it."

Fans of visiting teams who came to the Vet wearing hats or jerseys from their teams were fair game. Muggings of such people were common. "I was always concerned for their safety," said Ralph.

Drinking was a major problem. Fans arrived early, tailgated in the parking lots, and were well on their way to inebriation long before the opening kickoff. That was an invitation to fights, which occurred almost as often as first downs.

"As players, we were aware of what was going on in the stands," said Bill Bergey, "even when you were on the field. If there was a timeout and you'd see a fight break out, someone would say, 'Hey, look up there in section 706. There's real good one going on.' You'd watch and see how many people were involved. There was always a show going on. And if there was some poor son-of-a-gun wearing an opponent's jersey, that person was harassed beyond words."

The fans with the worst reputations were those who sat in the 700 level. "They're a bunch of lunatics having one helluva good time," said Chuck Dunn, who sat every Sunday in the 700 level after first going to the Vet in the early 1970s with his father.

Women flashing was a common malady at Eagles games. Dunn remembered seeing a woman in the stands take her top off. A security guard came to take her away, and the fans tried to mug him. Another time, a fan fell over the row in front of him, and fans in each lower row pushed him down to the next one.

Fans, especially those in the 700 level, frequently broke seats. That was easy to do because the seats sat out in the sun all year and became somewhat fragile. The fans were also prone to cursing loudly, with or without women and children around, and demonstrating various hand signals when events on the field didn't go the Eagles' way. Once, a fan left a game without his clothes. He called the Vet the next day to ask if anyone had found them.

But the fans had other outrageous tendencies. They booed Santa Claus. They booed Ed Rendell when he was mayor of Philadelphia. They booed the Dallas Cowboys' Michael Irvin as he lay injured on the field. And to take matters well beyond the levels of booing, they once threw snowballs at Cowboys' coach Jimmy Johnson and golf balls at referee Jim Tunney when he left the field at halftime (and they were only range balls, at that). Another time, they heaved batteries at the opposing team. And these are only a couple of the legions of examples of indecent behavior.

Joseph (Chubby) Imburgia, who once gained a measure of distinction when his pants caught fire after he stood too close to a sideline heater during an especially cold game, served for one dozen years at the Vet as a member of the "chain gang" that measured first downs on the sidelines. Even the people in the lower seats could get rather crude, he remembered. "When we were standing in front of them, they'd yell for us to get out of the way," said Imburgia, his crew's drive-pole guy. "Some of the things they'd yell were not very kind."

Eagles fans never endeared themselves to the neighbors living in the 300 houses that bordered the north side of the stadium. "They would relieve themselves in people's yards," said Ralph. "They'd park in the driveways behind the houses, and when they were told to move, they'd start a fight. They'd throw their cans and bottles in the streets."

One resident called game days on his street "sheer murder." The situation became so bad and the neighbors became so upset that Ralph launched a group called the Veterans Stadium Neighbors' Association, which dealt with the problems caused by fans. The city also sent police to patrol the streets and cleanup crews to pick up the debris after games. Neighbors were issued special parking stickers for their cars, and signs that said other cars would be towed away were installed. And, in the interest of maintaining good relations, the Eagles—as well as the Phillies—held "good neighbor days" at the stadium.

The flawed conduct, of course, was not typical of all Eagles fans. Many were law-abiding. And all were extremely avid.

"They were really great fans," said Ralph. "Some, especially the ones in the 700 level, got pretty souped up before they came in. But they rooted hard for their team."

And they had a sense of humor. "I remember in the early 1970s when we weren't doing too well," said Bergey, "if we won the coin flip, we got a standing ovation because we'd at least won something."

"The one thing that always amazed me," said Mike Evans, who was with the Eagles when they began at the Vet, "was the way they sold out the stadium every game. The fans always came out. And they wouldn't hesitate to boo you. At most places, they don't boo anybody."

Whether it was Eagles fans or Phillies fans, most players were grateful for the support they were given.

"I never had a problem with fans," said Stocker. "The fans and I got along great. They're honest fans, so I appreciated that."

Juan Samuel said he couldn't think of any complaints about the fans. "They always let you know when things weren't going well," he said, "but they pay your salary, so you can't really complain."

Former security guard Ed Sickles had a theory about Phillies fans. "All they want is a winner," he said. "They have very high expectations and they want their teams to be successful. Give them that, and they're great fans."

No one enjoyed the support of fans more than Hall of Fame broadcaster Harry Kalas. From the time he arrived in 1971 until the Vet closed 33 years later, Kalas was a fan favorite. And the admiration was mutual.

"Philadelphia fans are very passionate," Kalas said. "They love their teams. They stand by their teams. They're very, very loyal. Sure, they get down on their teams once in a while, but for the most part they're great fans. I appreciate the fact that they're so supportive. None of us would be here without the support of the fans."

"They were very good fans," added Steve Bedrosian. "They were tough on me when I was traded here for Virgil, an All-Star catcher. They let me know it. But they demand good performances. When you're doing well, they love you, and when you're not doing so well, they let you know it. That's the way it should be."

Of all the players who walked onto the field at the Vet, none was exposed to the passion of the fans any more than Schmidt. And he saw it from every direction. Jeered in his early days, cheered later on, the Hall of Famer extracted virtually every emotion out of Phillies fans.

"There were good times, and there were bad times," he said. "That's part of the deal in Philadelphia. It's the greatest place in the world to play if you're a championship team and you're playing well, and it might be the toughest place in the world to play if you're not playing well. You have to take the good with the bad while you're in Philadelphia. If you want to play somewhere where they don't care the whole year about anything, go out to California. In Philadelphia, they care."

BEST SEAT IN THE HOUSE

The press box had both assets and liabilities

There was no better place to watch a game at Veterans Stadium than from the press box. Many called it the "best seat in the house."

Located on the 400 level between the upper and lower decks, the press box offered an excellent view of the playing field. It was high enough

Above: Many considered Ralph Bernstein the "Father of the Press Box."

In the "old days" residents of the press box wrote with typewriters.

to give its occupants a panoramic view of the entire field. They could look down at the action and have the perspective of viewing a play and all its accompanying parts. Yet, it was low enough to give a viewer the feeling of being reasonably close to the action.

Compared with the press boxes at some of Philadelphia's former ballparks, this one had just about everything that they lacked.

In addition to a good view, there was more than an ample number of seats for the flowers of the literary and broadcasting worlds who populated the place. There was room to move around. And there was heat as well as windows that could be slid shut when it was cold.

"It was a great place to cover a game," said Bob Kenney, who not only wrote about baseball for the Camden *Courier-Post* for more than three decades, but who was official scorer at the Vet for some 1,800 games. "I think it rates right at the top."

As official scorer and the man who succeeded Allen Lewis of the Philadelphia *Inquirer* in that post, Kenney had one of *the* best seats in the house. It was directly behind home plate. To his right was the rest of the baseball press box, and beyond that the public address and video booths.

The broadcasting team of Chris Wheeler, Harry Kalas, Andy Musser, and Richie Ashburn worked in booths on the press box level.

To his left were a few writers, and then the broadcast booths and television cameras. Also in that area were several boxes that housed Phillies executives.

Up to 97 people could be seated in the two rows of the baseball press box. Local writers from the city and suburban dailies sat in the front row with a smattering of radio and, on rare occasions, TV people. Out-of-town writers, Phillies staff members, representatives of the visiting team, and various others occupied the second row. In extreme cases, a temporary third row could be set up that would accommodate another 40 people.

For football, the setup was somewhat different. Two press boxes, located well to the right of the baseball press box, that looked out toward midfield were used by local writers. An auxiliary area farther down (at about the location of baseball's right field foul pole) was reserved for out-of-town writers. Additional members of the media sat in the baseball press box. In the case of the Eagles, a normal game might attract some 200 people from the media. But for big games, by adding extra seats, the various press boxes could accommodate as many as 300 people.

Even those numbers were dwarfed by the legions descending for a World Series or a baseball or football playoff game.

"For World Series games, we'd get people from all over the world," said Phillies vice president and director of public relations Larry Shenk. "Between 600 and 700 media credentials were issued. We not only used the regular press box, but the two football press boxes, the Stadium Club, and a press box in left field. It got a little crazy sometimes."

The huge crews working for network television during big games also added to the confusion, as would their big trucks and tons of equipment they lugged with them. ABC typically brought upwards of 50 people for Monday night football games. Post-season baseball games attracted a crew of 80 with 11 cameras deployed throughout the stadium. Network producers often called the Vet one of the better stadiums in the country from which to televise games because there was a minimum of problems.

Except for post-season games, the Phillies never had an overcrowded press box. In a way, though, fewer media made covering a baseball game a lot easier.

"There was plenty of space," said Paul Hagen, long-time baseball writer for the Philadelphia *Daily News*. "That was an advantage. The sight lines were pretty good, too. The proximity to the field was also good."

"I always thought it was a great facility to work from," said Harry Kalas, who came to the Vet in its first year and broadcast Phillies games during the entire life of the stadium. "I really enjoyed working there, especially my 28 years with the late, great Richie Ashburn."

So, too, did Merrill Reese, the voice of the Eagles from 1977 through the team's departure from the Vet after the 2002 season. Reese, who called the plays from a booth slightly to the left side of the 50-yard line, said that his spot compared favorably with those at most of the other NFL stadiums, including many of the newer ones.

"It was excellent," he said while noting that he always worked with the window open—no matter what kind of weather prevailed—so the crowd noises could be heard on the air. "It was among the best of its time. Even today, it would rank better than the ones at a lot of the new stadiums. It was spacious, the location was in an ideal position, the sightlines were great, the view was perfect. As a broadcaster, what more can you want?"

The positive aspects of the press box could largely be credited to Ralph Bernstein, a veteran sportswriter who covered Philadelphia teams for the *Associated Press* for more than 50 years.

When plans were being made to build the stadium, Philadelphia-area sportswriters were anxious to make sure that the section from which they would cover games would be suitable and not a replica of the nearly unworkable quarters that existed at most of the city's other sports venues. Bernstein, whose strong will and feisty reputation were legendary, was selected as the scribes' representative to the city. He was in charge of making sure the press box met the desired standards.

Merrill Reese began calling
Eagles games at the Vet in 1977.

Bernstein formed a committee that included Stan Hochman of the *Daily News*, Fred Byrod of the Philadelphia *Inquirer*, and Ed Hogan of the Eagles. The group then put together a 25 page report that Bernstein said, "showed how to build a press box, even down to the height of the tables, the chairs, and where to put an elevator.

"We thought we covered every angle," Bernstein said. "Then we went to the first meeting with the architect, Mayor Jim Tate's representative, and some TV executives—no working TV people took part in the planning. The plans [for baseball] had TV and radio areas going from first base to home plate and from third base to home plate with first base to right field and third base to left field for the writers. It was an absolute monstrosity."

Never one to back away from a battle, Bernstein blew his stack. "I screamed and hollered," he said. "We told them where they could put it, and then we walked out of the meeting."

The writers group then redid its original design, placing the radio and TV people from home plate to third base and the print media from home plate to first base. Then, the group took its plans directly to Tate.

"He said to his liaison to tell the architect to build the press box the way Ralph wants it built," Bernstein recalled. "He said, 'This is their office. This is where they do their jobs.' He wanted to be fair and equitable. And he was. The press box was built the way it should have been. We were very satisfied. The working stiffs were happy. But it didn't happen without one helluva fight."

Later, the writers gave Ralph a plaque that pictured him standing on top of City Hall. Underneath, were the words "Battling Bernstein."

The press box remained mostly unchanged over the years. And even though media people came and went, assessments of the facility also changed little.

"It always felt like a press box," said Jim Salisbury, the baseball writer at the *Inquirer* during the Vet's final decade. "In the press boxes at a lot of the other parks, you feel more like you're in a luxury box with all the bells and whistles. You wouldn't throw peanut shells or other stuff on the floor in them. You didn't get that feeling at the Vet."

But, said Ed Hilt of the Atlantic City *Press*, "it was adequate. You could cover a game there, and not have any serious problems."

Unless it rained. And if was raining hard enough, water could pour through open windows, forcing writers to grab their scorebooks and their typewriters—or later their laptops—and flee either to the second row or into the press dining room located behind the press box. Rare was the reporter who covered a game at the Vet who didn't at some time or another have an unfortunate encounter with water from the sky.

Hagen was one of them. "When it rained, and you were sitting in the front row, you got wet," he said. "I've seen some pretty deep water on the floor, too. One time, it was raining so hard that I came into the press [dining] room to do my story. The rain came through the roof onto my computer, and completely ruined it."

Tom Maloney, who covered Phillies games for several decades for KYW News, once had a similar situation. "One hot summer night, a thunderstorm came up," he recalled, "and the rain came down over the top of the press box. It was just a wall of water. It got all over my equipment, and it took about a month for it to dry out."

Reporters weren't the only ones affected by rain. The men who broadcast the games had their battles with it, too.

"The broadcast booth was frequently flooded," recalled Andy Musser, who called Phillies games for 25 years. "Three or four times a season, they had to come in with a vacuum and suck up the water. Drainage was very poor. Fans above us in the upper deck would frequently drop hot dog rolls or cups into drains, and they would get clogged. Then the rain would come right into our booth. One time 30 minutes before a game, the water in the booth was up to our knees. We had to leave and go to the press box to do the first few innings of the game."

Sitting on the third base side of home plate, the radio broadcast booth had some other flaws. "Sometimes, it got very uncomfortable, weatherwise," said Musser. "The temperature was inconsistent, and we suffered with the elements in the early and late parts of the season. The booth was always colder than anyplace else, and warmer than anyplace else, although the latter was partly because of the equipment."

The Eagles' radio booth also had a few problems over the years. One of the more inopportune ones occurred when something leaked out of a pipe overhead and dripped onto color analyst Mike Quick's head.

The baseball radio booth also had a visual problem. Its occupants couldn't see foul balls in the left field corner.

"We were a little offset," said Chris Wheeler, who began broadcasting Phillies games in 1977. "The writers had the choice seats. The TV booth was right behind home plate, so that was okay. But there was a blind spot in the radio booth. Otherwise, it was a great location. It was one of the best. I never heard anyone come into the place and complain about not being able to do a game."

Among writers, though, there was one virtually universal complaint: the chairs in the baseball press box.

"About the worst thing in the press box were the chairs," said Frank Dolson, sports columnist at the *Inquirer* for four decades. "They were very difficult to move in and out of. They were hard, too."

On the plus side, Dolson pointed out, was the better than average size of the baseball press box and the convenience of "getting down to the clubhouse." The media merely had to walk about 10 yards from the press box to an elevator that took them to the subterranean-level, where the clubhouses were located.

Going down after a game was not usually a problem, although on a number of occasions the elevator broke down, the most notable time following an Eagles game when the press was stuck in the elevator for 41 minutes after a malfunction in the equipment. Going up before a game, however, was another story.

"The elevator was supposed to be for the press only, and they did a good job limiting it strictly to the press after a game" said Bernstein. "But before a game, everybody rode it. Fans, ushers, vendors, you name it. Sometimes, you had to wait. People crowded on who had no right to be on."

On several occasions, the intrusions went beyond the discontented grumbling of the media. One such instance resulted in a nasty fistfight between a prominent member of the press, who took issue with a city employee who had hitched a ride.

Although uncommon, fistfights in the press box happened occasionally. Several times over the years, writers staged brief bouts with each other. Once, a TV executive engaged in a tussle with a member of the print media. There were a few other skirmishes, none too serious. And, of course, there were other unforgettable moments such as the time one of the more cantankerous press box habituates bellowed "get that witch off the field" while a female entertainer performed before a game.

Another diversion occurred when people who didn't belong there tried to enter the press box. It wasn't a regular occurrence, but when it happened, it was usually because the person was either lost or brazen—or stupid enough to think he or she could pull it off without getting stopped.

The chief ejector of the unaccredited in those cases was Art Cassidy, who served as a press box attendant during the entire life of the Vet. Cassidy had begun working for the Phillies back in the days when the team played at Connie Mack Stadium.

Three others who served lengthy terms in the press box and who went back to the Connie Mack Stadium era were Charlie McCormack, who was in charge of videotapes of the game, and Charlie Rowan and Carl Newman, both press box stewards for many years. While in his mid 70s, Newman once decked a whacko twice his size, who was attempting to invade the press sanctuary.

Over the years, there were gigantic changes in the press box constituency. Where once major league sports were covered mostly by a handful of grizzled veterans, they had during much of the life of the Vet been replaced by a mostly younger, more inexperienced crowd. Women also began covering games in the late 1970s.

Beginning at about the same time, an increasing number of radio stations as well as newspapers from outlying areas, including ones not only from the suburbs but also from places such as Lancaster, Reading, Allentown, Wilmington, Atlantic City, and Trenton, were sending people to the games on a regular basis. On a normal day, they increased the press box population three to four times what it had been when just three Philadelphia dailies, two wire services, and a few radio stations covered games.

Along with the changes in those reporting the games came other press box changes at the Vet. The media dressed more casually. Writers who grabbed foul balls hit into the press box threw them back out into the stands below. Portable typewriters gave way to laptop computers. Notebooks were replaced by tape recorders. Press notes that provided an endless supply of information on teams and players, plus every conceivable statistic, were made available before and after each game. Frequent announcements regarding matters of significance kept the media informed. A separate dining room with full-course meals stood ready to feed the ever-hungry denizens of the press.

Hanging on a wall just outside the dining room were plaques that paid tribute to members of the Philadelphia media who had been inducted into the Baseball Hall of Fame. Writers Lewis of the *Inquirer*, Bus Saidt of the Trenton *Times*, and Ray Kelly of the *Evening Bulletin* and broadcasters By Saam and Kalas comprised that special group.

Game coverage was always enhanced by a number of TV monitors located in the press box, usable for viewing replays. "That was often very useful," said Maloney. "Overall, I liked covering games at the Vet," he added. "The location [of the press box] was good and, except for the right field corner, you had a good view of all the action."

The press room behind the press box was often used for press conferences, such as the one when Steve Bedrosian's Cy Young Award was announced.

Covering football games by the print media, on the other hand, was no easy task, according to Ray Didinger, who has covered the Eagles for more than three decades. "The press box had all the limitations of a multi-purpose stadium," he said. "Even though you sat at the 50-yard line, you were farther away from the field. I never thought the view was very good. Then when they'd put up the tinted glass in the windows in the winter you literally couldn't see because the glass was always scratched and foggy."

Sometimes, somebody on the front row would open a window by sliding over his pane of tinted glass in front of the person next to him. The double pane made visibility almost impossible.

"There was always a lot of bickering about the drafts, too," Didinger said. "If you were in the front row, you were always cold when the temperatures dropped. There were heating vents down near the floor, but they only kept your feet warm. They were very hot, though. Once, I sat my bag on the floor in front of a vent, and when I picked up the bag after the game, all my pens had melted."

Over the years, many marvelous stories were written, and many wondrous pronouncements were broadcast from the Vet press box. Among those with especially lasting acclaim were the proclamations of Kalas, most notably his now-legendary "outta here" call that foretold of a home run. How did that come about?

"In the early 1970s, we were standing around the cage during batting practice, and Greg Luzinski hit one about nine miles," Kalas remembered. "Larry Bowa was standing there. He said, 'Wow, that's way outta here.' I thought, that's got a kind of neat ring to it. So that's how I started using 'outta here.'"

There were other trademark calls by Kalas and by Reese, just as there were truckloads of classic prose penned by the likes of Sandy Grady, Bill Lyon, Bill Conlin, and many other veteran scribes, including the ones cited earlier in this chapter. And there were the endearing remarks of Ashburn, plus the comments of a variety of other long-term broadcasters such as Scott Graham, Larry Andersen, and Kent Tekulve with the Phillies and color men Al Pollard, Stan Walters, and Quick with the Eagles as well as Charley Swift, who handled the play-by-play of Eagles games at the Vet from 1971 to 1977.

Yet, whether it was the seasoned veterans or the platoon of Johnny-come-latelies, the Veterans Stadium press box was the second home for a generation of media people. And, despite its flaws, it fit and it was comfortable.

"When we moved into the Vet in 1971, we thought the press box was beautiful," recalled Jimmy Gallagher, public relations director for the Eagles from the 1960s to the 1990s. "It was so nice. And so big. For all the years I was there, I always thought it was a great place to work."

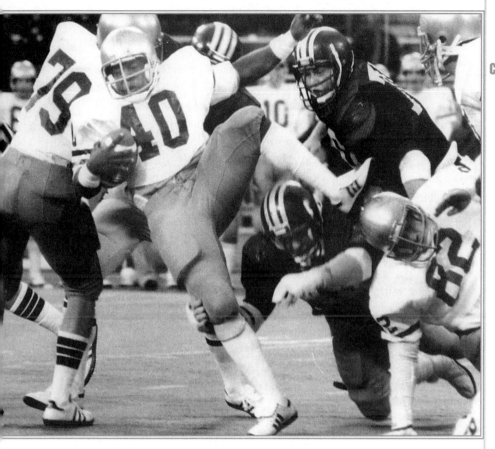

MULTIPLE USES

The Vet had Army-Navy games
and many other events

Throughout its life, Veterans Stadium was called a "multi-purpose" stadium. That was a label affixed to most municipal stadiums built in the same era as the Vet.

As the designation suggests, the Vet was designed to accommodate a variety of events. The intention was to have a stadium that would serve as a venue not only for different sports, but also for nonsports activities.

While that tended to produce a product that was not perfect for either baseball or football—or for any other sport—it had its advantages, not the least of which was economic. For the price of one stadium, a city could have a facility that could hold every kind of outdoor sport that required a playing field.

Above: Navy's Eddie Meyers from Pemberton, New Jersey, was upended by Army during the game in 1980.

Although that was in a way a contradictory premise, Alex Ewing, head of a local architectural firm that was hired in the 1960s by the Phillies to help with the design of the stadium, said it worked at the Vet. "The basic design was very good, despite what some of the critics said," he stated. "That was not true of some of the other multi-purpose stadiums such as Atlanta, Pittsburgh, and Cincinnati. They were basically unable to satisfy the requirements of baseball, football, and other sports."

The Vet, though, never wavered from the original plan. A variety of sports were held on its turf, as were scores of nonsporting functions.

Numerous football and baseball games played by teams other than the Eagles and Phillies were held at the Vet. Also held there were soccer games, softball games, concerts, religious gatherings, and a miscellaneous collection of other events.

The most frequent activity at the Vet was football. The Army-Navy game, the Philadelphia Stars, Temple University, and an assortment of other college and high school games all appeared at the Vet. The most prominent of these was the Army-Navy game.

The Army-Navy game was first held in Philadelphia in 1899. Over the next 104 years, it was held in the city 77 times. Between 1936 and 1979, it was played at Municipal (later JFK) Stadium every year but three.

In 1980, the game was moved to the Vet, despite the objections of officials from the Naval Academy, who wanted the game to remain at JFK. "I like the grass field. There are fewer injuries on natural turf," said Navy athletic director J. O. (Bo) Coppedge in an article in the *Evening Bulletin*. "I like the idea of playing in a bigger stadium. I like the tradition there. The game has been held there for a long time."

With Army strongly supporting the move, and the advantages of having better sightlines and more amenities, the switch to the Vet prevailed. The switch automatically decreased the potential size of the crowd because of the smaller seating capacity at the Vet, but in many respects, by then the game was less of an attraction than it used to be anyway.

In the first game, played November 29, 1980, Navy took the series lead for the first time in 58 years with a 33–6 whipping of Army. The Middies' Eddie Meyers rushed for 144 yards, and Steve Fehr kicked four field goals, including a then-series record 50-yarder.

One year later, the teams engaged in a much different kind of game. For the first time since 1934, neither team scored a touchdown. The result was a 3–3 tie, with Fehr booting a 42-yard field goal in the second quarter and Dave Aucoin matching it with a 27-yard kick in the third period. Aucoin missed a 55-yard attempt as time ran out in the fourth quarter.

In the ensuing years, all but six games were played at the Vet through 2002. There were many memorable battles, including one in 1985 when stellar running back Napoleon McCallum, playing in his last game at Navy, rushed for 217 yards on 41 carries to lead his team to a 17–7 victory. The following year, Army scored on five of its first eight possessions to capture a 27–7 victory.

Navy won its only game of the season with a 24–3 triumph in 1991. In the next meeting, Army overcame a 24–7 third quarter Navy lead to capture a 25–24 win with Patmon Malcolm kicking a 49-yard field goal with 12 seconds left in the game. In 1994, Army quarterback Jim Kubiak threw for 361 yards and two touchdowns, but it took Kurt Heiss's 52-yard field goal with 6:19 left to play to give the Cadets a 22–20 decision.

Another thrilling game took place in 1995 when late in the fourth quarter, Navy gambled and went for a touchdown on a fourth and goal situation at the Army one-yard line. The Middies failed, and Army then launched a 99-yard drive that culminated with John Conroy's one-yard touchdown with 1:03 remaining. It gave Army the game, 14–13.

More heroics occurred in 1996 when Army stopped Navy eight times inside the 10-yard line during the final four minutes of the game to preserve a 28–24 win. With President Bill Clinton as a spectator, the game marked the last time a U.S. chief executive was in attendance. Two years later, in the highest-scoring game in the history of the rivalry, Army took a 34–30 verdict as Ty Amey ran 70 yards for the game-winning touchdown three plays after Navy had lost a fumble on a first and goal at the Cadets' four-yard line.

In the 100th battle between the service academies in 1999, Army's Brian Madden passed for 177 yards and one touchdown, and Tim Shubzda tied a record with four field goals to sink Navy, 19–9. The last game at the Vet was played in 2001 before a crowd of 69,708. Army rolled to a 26–17 victory, sending Navy back to Annapolis with a 0–10 record, the worst in the Middies history.

In 17 games at the Vet, Army won the series, 11–5–1. It had been a memorable run, one that never lacked for excitement no matter what the team's records were.

"There's no comparison to an Army-Navy game," said Nick Trainer, a Delaware County native and a leading collegiate referee who worked two games in the 1990s between the service academies as well as Rose Bowl and Orange Bowl games. "The atmosphere is electric. It's the only college football game in which the whole country has an interest.

"For me, coming out on the field, and looking up in the stands, there was just so much excitement. And there was so much intensity on the field. Your adrenaline really surges. You realize, this is why you referee."

The game was not without some problems. Such was the case in 1998, when a railing collapsed in the Army student section and nine cadets plummeted 12 feet to the ground. There were several serious injuries, one cadet suffering a broken neck for which he later received a $1.5 million settlement. The mishap attracted nationwide attention and brought considerable embarrassment to the city.

"The Army-Navy game was always a tough event," said Joel Ralph, the director of operations at the Vet from 1973 to 1987. "We had all the generals and admirals and their aides, and they needed this, they needed that. And it was very hard logistically. We had to do a lot of alterations such as taking the railings out and building steps to get the corps—about 1000 each—on and off the field and into the stands. They had to get up in the stands fast because the game started very quickly after the parade."

Twice, Ralph said, peace activist Father Daniel Berrigan staged protests by pouring blood onto the field. He was arrested and levied a small fine.

Navy's appearances at the Vet weren't confined to its meetings with Army. The Middies met Notre Dame there three times, losing 42–23 in 1972, 14–6 in 1974, and 58–27 in 1993. Notre Dame's 58 points tied for the third highest point total ever allowed by a Navy football team.

Numerous other college games were played at the Vet, not the least of which were those involving Temple University. The Owls called the Vet home from 1974 through 2002. During those 29 seasons, Temple won 44 and lost 63 at Broad and Pattison.

As they upgraded their schedule, the Owls had moved to the Vet after playing most of their home games at Temple Stadium since 1927. The old stadium, located in West Oak Lane, was too small to accommodate the larger crowds that Temple's new big-time opponents were expected to attract, and the Vet was seen as an ideal place to call home.

"Veterans Stadium was a very good place for our situation," said Wayne Hardin, who had come from Navy to coach the Owls starting in 1970 and who had pushed for the switch in venues. "The facility was great, the location was great, it was very functional. I had no quarrel with the place, except maybe for the hard turf. But we practiced at the Vet, and we got to know the rough spots, which we hoped our opposition didn't learn."

Temple won its first game at the Vet, beating Delaware, 21–17, on October 26, 1974. It lost its last game there on November 23, 2003, to Boston College, 36–14.

In between, the Owls had games at the Vet with teams such as Army, Navy, California, Penn State, Syracuse, and Virginia Tech. They lost seven out of seven to Penn State, including a 1988 rout in which the Nittany Lions rolled to a 45–9 decision before a packed house of 66,592. That was the largest crowd ever to watch a Temple game at the Vet.

Probably Temple's most memorable game at the Vet was a titanic battle with Penn State in 1976. After trailing 24–17 at the end of the third quarter, the Owls outscored the Nittany Lions, 13–7, in the fourth period, only to lose, 31–30. Temple quarterback Terry Gregory passed for four touchdowns and 290 yards, while Ken Williams caught two TD passes.

That same year at the stadium, the Owls beat Grambling, also by a 31–30 score. Williams also grabbed a pair of TD aerials in that game.

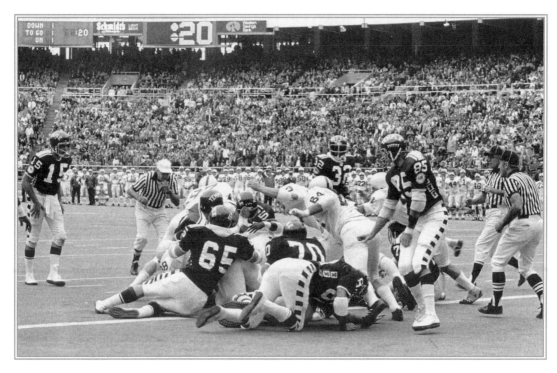

Temple made a goal line stand against Penn State in a legendary game in 1976 at the Vet.

Temple trailed, 30–21, after the third quarter before coming back to win with 10 points in the final session.

In 1978, the Owls lost another memorable game to Penn State in front of another packed house at the Vet. The Nittany Lions scored the go-ahead touchdown on the last drive of the game to win, 10–7. One year later, Temple overcame an early 14–0 deficit to beat Syracuse, 49–17, in what was Hardin's 100th career win.

Temple won three out of four games at the Vet with Villanova, including a 41–3 rout in 1975, and split 2–2 with Delaware. In one of its rare appearances in the North, Alabama walloped the Owls, 37–0, in 1988.

Many standout players wore Temple uniforms during the Owls' residency at the Vet. Among them were future pros of long standing such as Randy Grossman, Joe Klecko, Steve Watson, Paul Palmer, Joe Rinestra, Tre Johnson, Kevin Ross, Todd McNair, Zack Dixon, Nick Mike-Mayer, Lance Johnstone, Stacey Mack, and Tim Terry. Johnson, Klecko, Ross, and Watson were Pro Bowl participants, while Grossman earned four NFL championship rings with the Pittsburgh Steelers.

Temple coaches when the Owls played at the Vet included Hardin, Bruce Arians, Jerry Berndt, Ron Dickerson, and Bobby Wallace.

At most Temple games over the years, empty seats outnumbered the occupied ones by a three-or-four-to-one margin. A few games—particularly ones with Syracuse, Pitt, and Virginia Tech—drew crowds in the 34,000 to 40,000 range. But the typical attendance at most games was nearer to 10,000 or 12,000. Usually outclassed by stronger opponents and posting losing records—the Owls have had two winning seasons since 1980—Temple struggled to be a major attraction on the local sports calendar.

"Not being able to fill the stadium was a major disappointment," said Hardin, the winningest coach in Temple history and the Owls' mentor through the 1982 season. "We had thought the Vet would be an ideal location for students because they could get there so easily. But that never quite happened.

"Nevertheless," he added, "people tend to lose sight of the fact that our attendance did increase dramatically over what it had been at Temple Stadium. Twenty thousand didn't look like much at the Vet, but it was a lot more than we drew at Temple Stadium. And we never could have played Penn State or some of the other schools there."

Another football resident of the Vet were the Philadelphia Stars, a member of the short-lived United States Football League (USFL), which played its games in the spring and early summer months. Originally consisting of 12 teams, the USFL made its debut in 1983.

The Stars, reputed to be one of the best and most financially sound organizations in the league, were owned by local businessman Myles Tannenbaum. Carl Peterson, a former Eagles aid under Dick Vermeil, was the president and general manager, and Jim Mora was the head coach. The team had its offices on the concourse level of the Vet.

"It was a particularly entertaining brand of football, and was extremely well-received," said Bob Moore, now public relations director of the Kansas City Chiefs but then the Stars' public relations director and the first person hired by the team. "We had to work our schedule around the Phillies, but we had a good relationship with both them and the Eagles."

The Stars had plenty of stars. Running back Kelvin Bryant, quarterback Chuck Fusina, receivers Scott Fitzkee and Willie Collier, offensive lineman Brad Oates, defensive lineman Sam Mills, and punter Sean Landeta—a future Eagle—led the team to a 15–3 record in 1983. In their first game at the Vet, the Stars defeated the New York Generals led by Heisman Trophy winner Herschel Walker, 25–0, before a club record crowd of 38,205.

Although the team started strongly at the gate at the Vet, the Stars wound up averaging 18,650 at their nine home games, eight of which they won. In probably their most memorable game at the Vet, the Stars came from 21 points down to beat the Chicago Blitz, coached by George Allen, 44–38 in overtime in the division playoffs with Bryant scoring the winning touchdown. They then concluded the season with a 24–22 loss to the Michigan Panthers in the championship game at Denver, Colorado.

In 1984, the Stars' fortunes increased immeasurably. With an outstanding team and an ever-increasing following, the team's average attendance at the Vet soared to 28,668.

The Stars racked up a 16–2 record, including another 8–1 mark at home. And, after wins of 28–7 over the Generals and 20–10 over the Birmingham Stallions in the playoffs, they entered their second straight championship game and defeated the Arizona Wrangler's, 23–3, at Tampa, Florida.

Despite their growing fan base, the Stars were forced to leave Philadelphia the following season after the league announced plans to switch to a fall schedule. The Stars moved south where, unable to use the recently vacated Memorial Stadium in Baltimore, they had to play at Byrd Stadium at the University of Maryland. The Stars repeated as league champions, but after the season, the USFL folded under the weight of debts totaling more than $160 million.

Lasting a little longer at Veterans Stadium were the Philadelphia Atoms. Members of the North American Soccer League (NASL), the Atoms played three seasons at the Vet, which was considered a terrible place to watch a soccer game.

Under head coach Al Miller, a former All-American at East Stroudsburg and ex-coach at Hartwick College, the Atoms made their debut in 1973. The team's goalie was Bob Rigby from Ridley Township, who was not only the league's first draft pick but later became the first soccer player ever to appear on the cover of *Sports Illustrated.*

In their first game, preceded by a parade of some 3,000 local children in soccer uniforms, the Atoms drew 21,700 for a 0–0 tie with Dallas at the Vet. The average crowd during the season totaled 11,382, almost two times larger than the league average. After finishing with a 9–2–8 record during the regular season, the Atoms defeated the Toronto Metros, 3–0, in the playoffs before a crowd of 18,766 at the Vet to advance to the finals. With Rigby blanking the opposition, the Atoms captured a 2–0 decision at Dallas to win the first championship of the NASL.

A record crowd of 24,093 watched the Atoms drop the Denver Dynamos, 1–0, on a goal by Jim Fryatt in the 1974 inaugural at the Vet. Average home attendance that year increased slightly to 11,784, but with an 8–11–1 record, the Atoms failed to make the playoffs.

In 1975, the Atoms, picking first in the league draft, chose Chris Bahr, a Neshaminy High School and Penn State standout and son of Walt Bahr, one of the top soccer players ever to perform in Philadelphia. Chris Bahr, who later became an NFL placekicker, led the NASL in scoring and was named Rookie of the Year.

In their home opener that year, the Atoms faced the New York Cosmos and the legendary Pele, making his NASL debut. Bahr's goal gave the Atoms a 1–0 win with 20,124 watching. But with a 10–12 record, the team missed the playoffs again, and with the average attendance having tumbled to 6,849, the season became the Atoms' last at the Vet. The following year, the team moved to Franklin Field, where it played its final season before disbanding.

In a 1973 game at the Vet, Philadelphia Atoms' Bob Smith worked the ball as teammates Jim Fryatt (Left) and Chris Dunleavy (right) arrived to help.

Soccer, however, was not dead at the Vet. In 1978, a new team called the Philadelphia Fury joined the NASL. Owned in part by entertainers Peter Frampton, Rick Wakeman, and Paul Simon, the Fury got the league's first draft pick and selected Rick Reice, also from Neshaminy and Penn State. A number of other local players dotted the roster, including Brooks Cryder of

A kick by Pat Byrne (left) of the Philadelphia Fury was blocked in a 1978 skirmish by New England's Keith Weller as the Fury's Peter Osgood (right) watched.

Roxborough and Philadelphia Textile, Pat Fidelia of Rancocas High School and Mt. Holly, New Jersey, and later Rigby.

Wearing designer uniforms, the Fury got off to a rousing start when they drew 18,191 to their home opener, a 3–0 loss to the Washington Diplomats. The home crowd, however, dwindled to an average of 8,279 for the season as the Fury finished last in the Eastern Division with a 12–18 record.

Only 6,152 appeared at the Fury's 3–0 win over the Rochester Lancers at the team's home opener in 1979. Average Vet crowds during the season totaled 5,624. The Fury reached the playoffs, but because the Phillies had a home stand at the Vet, games were transferred to Franklin Field. A 1–0 loss to the Tampa Bay Rowdies in the quarterfinals ended the Fury's season.

In 1980, the Fury drew 9,574 for its home opener and an average of 4,778 during the season. A 10–22 record helped to keep the crowds down, and after the season, the team was sold and moved to Montreal.

Even that didn't end soccer's use of the Vet. In 1991 there, the U.S. Men's National Team defeated a team from Sheffield, England, 2–0.

Another game that was played at the Vet was softball. A team called the Philadelphia Patriots appeared briefly in a fast-pitch league there. The Philadelphia A's, a member of the American Professional Slow-Pitch League, also performed at the Vet in 1978.

The A's, the only team in the league to use a major league ballpark, played a 60-game schedule with Friday, Saturday, and Sunday doubleheaders each weekend during the season. A snow fence extending across the regular outfield was installed, and giveways and contests were featured before nearly every game. Wet t-shirt and string bikini contests helped the team develop a following.

The team was managed by former Phillies outfielder Johnny Callison. Its lineup included pro football star Billy (White Shoes) Johnson, newspaper columnist Ray Didinger, home run slugger Larry (Boom Boom) Hutchinson, and pitcher-shortstop Pete Simonelli. Other teams in the league, where pitches were thrown with a six-to-10-foot arc, also featured recognizable names, including former major league baseball players Joe Pepitone, Norm Cash, and Jim Northrup.

Toward the end of the season, a weekend series in Chicago was rained out, forcing the teams to play four games each on Saturday and Sunday at the Vet. The A's, who wound up second in the Eastern Division with a 29–35 record, won all eight games and went on to reach the league playoffs before losing two games to one to the Cleveland Jaybirds. The following season, the A's moved to Claymont, Delaware, where they played one season, then relocated to Berlin, New Jersey, for one more season before the league disbanded in 1980.

Over the years, a variety of other games were held at the Vet. Delaware State played football games there twice, dropping a 25–18 decision to Florida A & M in 1994 before a crowd of about 26,000 and losing 49–24 to Bethune-Cookman College in 2001 with a small group of less than 2,000 in attendance.

Howard University played football once at Veterans Stadium. Southern High School also played there, and the Catholic League football playoffs as well as Public League baseball playoffs were held at the Vet. And once the Catholic League staged a baseball tripleheader with six different high school teams participating.

For many years, the Vet was the home of the Liberty Bell Classic, an annual baseball tournament featuring eight Division I teams, including those from the Big Five, Drexel, and other area colleges. Another baseball tournament held at the Vet was the Carpenter Cup, which for some 20 years pitted 16 All-Star teams from high school leagues throughout the Delaware

Valley. The Vet was also the site of the Bill Giles Classic, which in its three years there pitted four Division II college baseball teams.

"The first time I played at the Vet," said native son and major league catcher Ben Davis, "was in the Carpenter Cup. It was a tremendous thrill playing on the same field that big leaguers played on."

Another local resident, Arizona Diamondbacks relief pitcher Mike Koplove, also fondly remembered his days as an amateur player at the Vet. "I played at the Vet in city tournaments and it was always exciting," he said. "Then to come back and do it as a pro was really awesome."

The Vet was also the site of numerous concerts, the first of which was a sold-out appearance by Bruce Springsteen in 1985. Madonna, the Rolling Stones, Billy Joel, Elton John, the Grateful Dead, David Bowie, The Who, U2, the Beach Boys, Pink Floyd, Paul McCartney & Wings, and Metallica were among the many individuals and groups that performed at the stadium, the last of which was Bon Jovi in 2003. For such events, the Vet was either filled or nearly filled to capacity

"That," said Ralph, "was where the real money was. You make in one concert what you make for a whole Eagles season. They were always sold out. The city could make $4 million on one concert."

Other events at the Vet included an annual convention held by Jehovah's Witnesses, plus other religious meetings such as ones by the Eucharistic Congress and the Billy Graham Crusade. The Policemen/ Firemen Hero Scholarship Thrill Show was also held at the Vet. In 1983, when the 76ers won the NBA championship, a huge parade that began at City Hall ended at the Vet, where a celebratory ceremony was held. And there were swap meets, antique shows, truck and tractor pulls, closed-circuit TV boxing matches, and pro wrestling matches.

Overall, the Vet provided the setting for thousands of games and events. That, of course, was what a multi-purpose stadium was meant to do.

THE FINAL YEAR

A memorable era comes to an end

Veterans Stadium began and ended the final year of its life with a bang. In between, it showed itself as a true field of memories.

The last season got off to a noisy start with a sell-out crowd on opening day. Nearly one year later, the old stadium crashed to the ground, the result of dynamite planted in its columns. You could say that the Vet went out in a blaze of glory.

Above: Slugger Jim Thome hit the last home run at Veterans Stadium.

With a huge crowd watching, the life of Veterans Stadium ended after 33 years.

In its final year, the Vet stood with class and dignity as its 33 years were celebrated throughout the season with special tributes and the recollections of the many memorable events that had taken place in its presence. Hundreds of thousands came to ride the sentimental journey that was tastefully created by the Phillies.

The last game was followed by a solemn yet upbeat hour-long salute with nearly 100 current and former players participating. Then, soon after, the Vet was carved up, some of its parts offered for sale and later at an auction. Finally, an implosion reduced the stadium that many said had outlived its usefulness to rubble.

It had been an extraordinary year. Emotions ran high throughout. And although the Vet, having clearly outlived its usefulness and been declared obsolete in accordance with modern stadium standards, had borne the brunt of countless slurs and abuses during its life, most of those were forgotten, replaced in the final year by tributes—often glowing ones.

"It was a big place in my life," said Mike Schmidt. "My whole baseball career was there. It was my home stadium. Carl Yastrzemski's was Fenway Park. Steve Garvey's was Dodger Stadium. Mine was Veterans Stadium. It was good to me."

Von Hayes had a similar view. "I spent basically my whole career here," he said. "Almost every home at-bat in my big league career was in this stadium. A lot of guys come and go, but this was it for me. It's going to be very sad not to be able to come back and look around."

"It was always home to me. Always a haven," said Darren Daulton. "I loved it and I hated it because I blew out a knee running the damn carpet. But I couldn't wait to get here. No matter what was going on outside, once I got in the Vet, I felt like I was home. It was comfortable."

The Vet's final season began auspiciously. With construction of the new Citizens Bank Park occurring a stone's throw from the Vet and even taking over space in some of the old ballpark's parking lot, the Phillies' home opener was scheduled for April 4 against the Pittsburgh Pirates. Tickets went on sale in January. Shortly afterward, the game was sold out. It was the Phils' first opening day sellout since 1994 and only the fifth (also 1971, 1992, 1993) at the Vet.

Many of the 59,269 fans were anxious to see newly acquired Jim Thome make his Phillies debut. They came early, caused a mammoth traffic jam on Broad Street, and loudly applauded Thome before the game. The soon-to-be enormously popular first baseman waved shyly to the crowd.

As would be their custom throughout the season, the Phillies invited former players back to the Vet for the weekend. The first group consisted of players from the 1971 team. Some greeted fans at the gates. One, Rick Wise, became the first person to change the number hanging on the right field wall that indicated how many home games were left to play at the Vet. The practice would continue throughout the season with a different person each game removing the number.

The Phillies wore 1971-style uniforms; the Pirates were clad in late-1970s yellow uniforms. The game looked like a return to those years as the Pirates clubbed the Phils, 9–1, with the latter managing just three hits. Jeff Suppan got the win in the final Vet opener, while Joe Roa took the loss.

The season had begun for the Phillies with great expectations. Those hopes seemed to be materializing as the team won 16 of its first 28 games—one being a no-hitter by Kevin Millwood at the Vet—then by June had captured the lead for the wild-card berth in the National League playoffs. By the All-Star break, the Phils were in hot pursuit of the division-leading Atlanta Braves, but an August slump dropped them back. Ultimately, the Phillies were passed by the Florida Marlins, who went on to win the wild-card spot and eventually the World Series. In their last season at the Vet, the Phils finished a distant third, 15 games behind the Braves.

By the end, all that was left was the final weekend of the season. After a year-long series of special events, the last three days of memory-laden nostalgia were billed the "Final Innings" weekend. The Phillies had worked on plans for the weekend for one and-one-half years.

The last night game at the Vet was Friday, September 26, with the Phillies losing to the Braves, 6–0. In a post-game ceremony, the stadium lights were turned off for the last time, and the final aerial fireworks show was staged. The following day, the U.S. Navy Leap Frogs parachuted into the

The implosion reduced the Vet to a pile of rubble.

stadium for their sixth and final time, and the Phillies All-Veterans Stadium team as selected by fans was introduced.

It included Greg Luzinski, lf, Garry Maddox, cf, Bobby Abreu, rf, John Kruk, 1b, Juan Samuel, 2b, Mike Schmidt, 3b, Larry Bowa, ss, Darren Daulton, c, Curt Schilling, rhp, Steve Carlton, lhp, Tug McGraw, rp, and Dallas Green, manager.

Jim Thome hit two home runs—the last one being the final four-bagger to be hit at the Vet—to clinch the National League home run title with 47. The Phillies won their final game, 7–6 in 10 innings, with Rheal Cormier getting the win in relief.

The biggest day was the last one, Sunday, September 28. It was the last of 11,859 days that the Vet was open, and it would turn into one of the most memorable days in the 33 year history of the stadium.

Tickets for the final game had also gone on sale in January. More than 30,000 tickets were purchased in less than nine hours, making the game a sellout more than nine months before it was held. The crowd for the game would eventually total 58,554.

Before the game, broadcaster Harry Kalas changed the final number to zero. "There was some sadness when I did it," he said later. "I thought, wow, this is going to be it for the Vet. I had a lot of good years there, and all kinds of memories. Thirty-three years is a long time to work in one place."

The final lineup card was presented by managers Larry Bowa, Dallas Green, and Danny Ozark. Shag Crawford, the home plate umpire for the Vet's first game, stood with his son Jerry, home plate umpire for the last game. Ceremonial first pitches were thrown by Jim Bunning, the Vet's first winning pitcher, and Frank Mastrogiovanni, a double-amputee veteran of Vietnam who had thrown out the first ball in 1971.

The game itself was insignificant. The Phillies lost, 5–2, with future Hall of Fame pitcher Greg Maddux getting the win for the Braves. Ironically, it had been a future Hall of Fame hurler—Bunning—who had won the first game at the Vet. Pat Burrell got the last hit, Chipper Jones scored the last run, and the last losing pitcher was Millwood, who angrily fired his hat into the stands as he left the field to a chorus of boos.

Despite the loss, the Phillies closed out their season with 20 wins in their final 29 games at the Vet. Over 33 years and 2,617 regular season games at the Vet, the Phils had a 1,415–1,199–3 record. There were 45,750 innings played, 24,123 hits, 23,106 runs, and 4,356 home runs. The Phillies hit 2,211 home runs to their opponents' 2,145. Total attendance was 66,700,288.

In addition, 1,522,493 fans attended 25 post-season games at the Vet with the Phillies posting an 11–14 record.

Following the final game, a marvelous hour-long tribute to the Vet took place. A video showed the great moments at the Vet, the Phillie Phanatic performed his last dance, and a parade consisting of nearly 100 past and present players, coaches, and managers was held. Members of the Phillies' office staff carried flags representing each year, followed by uniformed players who performed in those years. Ultimately, players from the present team's starting lineup went to their positions, each one accompanied by two former players at that position.

"I was really touched by the way our athletes, both past and present, approached that final event," said team president and CEO David Montgomery. "They showed some real respect for the place. So, of course, did our fans."

Schmidt, Thome, and Carlton got the loudest ovations. Burrell, who had been mired in a season-long slump, was cheered loudly. Larry Christenson wore a burgundy uniform. Players reacted in different ways. Hayes collected some dirt from the home plate area and stuck it in his pocket. Steve Bedrosian lay on the mound flapping his arms and legs. Carlton made an imaginary pitch. Bowa jumped on home plate. Dick Allen blew kisses to the fans.

The most poignant moment of the day came when McGraw, the last player to be introduced, arrived at home plate in a limousine. A thunderous cheer went up from the stands as he walked to the mound and threw an imaginary pitch, then repeated the leap he made after getting the last out of the 1980 World Series.

Another loud ovation by fans—who stood throughout the ceremony—came when Paul Owens was introduced as he appeared in the company of

Green and Ed Wade. Sadly, within a little more than three months, the lives of both McGraw and Owens would end. McGraw's ashes would be spread over the pitching mound.

One other special moment occurred when Schmidt hit an imaginary home run and circled the bases. As he arrived at home plate, Thome, in a spontaneous gesture, stepped out of the assembled crowd and hugged Schmidt. The two then held each other's arms aloft in a kind of touching tribute between the past and present.

As the ceremony closed, the players paraded down the third base line, where each touched home plate. Bob Dernier dove across the plate in a repeat of his memorable game-winning, inside-the-park home run. Many of the players greeted the members of the ground crew, each of whom wore a tuxedo.

"It was like seeing my life unfold right in front of me," said Jeff Miller, a Phillies season-ticket holder since the 1970s. "It was absolutely great."

No one seemed to want to leave. Players lingered. Fans remained. One held a sign that said: "Don't cry because it's over. Smile because it happened." Nearly everyone had special memories. Even many members of the media stood in the press box, gazing out over the field. One of them, *Inquirer* sports writer Sam Carchidi, scattered some of the ashes of his late father, Al Sattin, on the area at home plate.

"I have nothing but great memories," said Rico Brogna. "I had my best years here, and I had my longest tenure with any team, so I feel like it was very special to me. When I think of the Vet, I will remember that's where I had the best years of my professional life. And I enjoyed it so much."

Facility management director Mike DiMuzio said he would be especially sad to see the Vet go. "I'm one of the very few people who don't want to leave," he claimed. "I know the reason we have to go to a new ballpark, but I've grown up with this stadium. There are so many memories. Thirty-three years is a long time. I met an awful lot of people. I can look around, and say, 'that's where I did that.' When this place is not going to be here, it's going to be very difficult."

"This is where we won the National League pennant," Kruk said. "Most of the friends I have now were made at Veterans Stadium. It was home."

Said Bedrosian: "It was a special place. I have some special memories. You can't keep concrete and steel, but you can keep the memories. You take them with you. And you remember the guys you played with, the camaraderie you had. You can't tear that down."

New York Mets catcher Mike Piazza, a local guy who went away to play with other National League teams and who wound up hitting .363 with 16 home runs in 62 games at the Vet, grew up at the old ballpark. "As a kid, I dreamed about playing here," he said. "I didn't really think it would happen, but I'm glad it did. Not a lot of guys can say they played in the ballpark where they went as a kid. But I've enjoyed every game I've played here. It's been a great experience. I loved it here."

Even Thome, despite only a brief encounter with the old ballpark, felt a tinge of regret. "I only got to play here for one year," he said. "I wish I could've known it a little better."

Unlike the final game at Connie Mack Stadium in 1970, the Vet came to an orderly end. Although a few ripped out seats, fans did not tear up the place. The field was not overrun with people looking for souvenirs. As evening fell and the lights were dimmed, the old stadium that *Inquirer* columnist Bill Lyon had described as having "grimy, bent-nosed, cauliflower-eared, scabbed-knuckles character and perverse charm," stood intact.

Ironically, while the Phillies closed the Vet with a classy, touching farewell, the Eagles had barely acknowledged their years at the Vet at their last game early in 2003. The only admission that the team was leaving the scene of some of its greatest moments was a mock handoff from quarterback Ron Jaworski to running back Wilbert Montgomery in a recreation of the touchdown play in the 1980 NFL title game that helped send the Eagles to their first Super Bowl.

The Eagles lost their final game at the Vet on January 19, 2003, to the Tampa Bay Buccaneers, 27–10, in the NFC championship game. The team's final record in 32 years at the Vet was 144–111–2 during the regular season and 7–4 in playoffs.

Despite the team's lame exit, some people from the Eagles had strong feelings about the Vet. One was Bill Bergey.

"Am I sad?" he asked. "Absolutely. It was my home, my way of life. I'll drop a tear when it goes down because I had a lot of memories there. I don't know if I want to see it go because there might be a little bit of hurt for me. I was part of more losing teams than winning ones there, so you might say, yeah, blow the thing up. But that's not the case at all. I have a trophy room, and I'd like to put a chunk of stone from the Vet in there."

It was announced that the Vet would be imploded sometime early in 2004. Eventually, its space would be used as a parking lot for fans coming to the new Citizens Bank Park.

First, though, there was other work. The seats were removed and eventually sold in pairs for $280. Business was brisk with fans—and a number of players—purchasing more than 13,000 pairs by the time the sale ended on October 31.

Bit by bit, other parts of the stadium were removed. The small scoreboards came down, the turf was pulled up, the lights, the sound system, elevators, escalators, doors, kitchen equipment, turnstiles, everything that could be removed was removed.

Some of it was donated to colleges and other organizations. Widener University got the sound system. Various Little League teams received pitching machines, batting practice equipment, the tarpaulins used for rain delays, and some of the lights. Furniture and other equipment went to the School District of Philadelphia, the city Department of Recreation, the city Police Department, the Philadelphia Zoo, and assorted local schools. Other fixtures were set aside in the hopes of being sold to businesses. Some remnants, of the Vet were given to the Philadelphia Sports Hall of Fame with the hope that they would be displayed in the organization's planned museum. And some of it was saved so it could be used in a forthcoming auction.

As the last tenants, the Phillies had been given the job by the city of dismantling the stadium. It was agreed that the income from the Vet's contents would be applied to the cost of demolition. Through the fall and into the winter, the massive removal effort continued.

The statues outside the stadium were uprooted and placed in storage until they could be reinstalled at the new ballpark. A time capsule that had been buried near the Connie Mack statue on May 1, 1983, to commemorate the Phillies' 100th anniversary was excavated. The 4,000-pound Liberty Bell was removed. More than two dozen cats that lived at the Vet were removed, some given homes, some transferred to Citizens Park where they would resume their duties of keeping the rodent population down. And fences were erected around the stadium to keep out the ever-growing mob of souvenir hunters.

On January 8, 2004, the Phillies closed their offices at the Vet for the last time.

"The last game for me wasn't as sad as was January 8," Montgomery said. "To work in the same office [the one previously used by John Quinn and Owens] for 20 years was hard to leave. It was a very emotional day. It took me a while to get everything out. I didn't leave before midnight."

Jo-Anne Levy-Lamoreaux, the Phillies' manager of advertising and internet services, was in charge of coordinating the removal of the stadium contents that would be used in the new ballpark. That meant relocating items such as desks, chairs, filling cabinets, office equipment, and mountains of books and other paper goods. It was a monumental job that was not without its share of surprises.

"You'd walk around and look in corners and open doors, and you'd find stuff that was hidden and hadn't been seen in 30 years," she said. "Sometimes there'd be doors behind doors that nobody remembered were there."

Levy-Lamoreaux continued to handle the project in the week after all other staff members had moved out of the Vet. "By then, the heat and the hot water had been shut down, and pipes were starting to burst," she said. "For someone who had worked there as long as I had [more than 30 years] and to see the stadium in that condition, it was very depressing."

Naturally, it was not possible to move everything. Some paper products, pieces of furniture, even items such as sunflower seeds from the baseball clubhouses, ushers' uniforms, parts of whirlpool baths from the Eagles' locker room, and various odds and ends that nobody either wanted or had a place for were left behind.

Souvenir hunters tried to gather pieces of the Vet.

One month after the Phillies moved out, the team held a public auction at the Wachovia Center. At the day-long event, hundreds of items went on sale. Some 6,000 small boxes with pieces of turf were sold, as were 2,500 bottles of infield dirt, and 2,000 boxes of pieces of the outfield wall, each for $10 apiece. One thousand deluxe box seats were bought at $100 apiece. Other small souvenirs, such as hats and items left over from giveaways, were also sold over the counter.

The big-ticket items were reserved for the auction for which there was a registration fee of $50. More than 200 items from the Vet were put up for bid. The highest price—$10,100—went for the Richie Ashburn banner with his retired number 1 that hung on the outfield wall.

The adjacent lockers of Pete Rose and Tony Perez went for $6,400. Mike Schmidt's banner with the retired number 20 drew a price of $6,100. The high bid for Schmidt's locker was $5,900. The price for the wooden bat rack from the Phillies dugout was $5,600. Desk and office furniture used by Bob Carpenter and Bill Giles went for $3,700. The money flowed freely. Other high bids included $2,000 for the first base bag used in the ninth inning of the last game (bases were changed after each inning), $900 for the door between the Phillies' clubhouse and the runway to the dugout, $700 for a Bobby Abreu batting helmet, $600 for the seat of an upper deck Greg Luzinski home run blast, and $500 for a set of six Phillies accounting ledgers from the early 1970s.

Although it rained heavily all day, 8,000 fans attended the event. Gross proceeds for the day were $700,000, which was earmarked for Phillies Charities Inc.

The day was not without incident. While the Phillie Phanatic took a break, his headpiece was stolen from an unlocked dressing room. A promotions-minded local radio station offered a $5,000 reward for the return of the head. After a search lasting more than one week and involving the Philadelphia police, a radio caller said he had found the head. When he brought it to the station, the police had enough evidence to charge him with burglary, theft, and related offenses.

Later, the Phanatic, otherwise known as Tom Burgoyne, offered his feelings about the demise of the Vet. "It's very sad," he said. "There are so many memories here. The Phanatic knew all the nooks and crannies and how to get from here to there. It had become like an old pair of shoes that you've broken in and they're nice and comfortable."

General manager Ed Wade had a special reason to lament the passing of the Vet. "I met my wife [Roxanne] here," he said. "She was an usherette when I was a public relations intern in 1977. We met in the stands and got married four years later. I'm not sure I would've met anybody anywhere else because I was always at the ballpark."

Former manager Danny Ozark had his reasons for lamenting the demise of the Vet. "So many good things, so much action happened there," he said. "We broke a lot of attendance records there. We had great players. Great fans. A lot of things are going to be missed."

Throughout the winter, the actual structure of the Vet had been coming down. The Phillies had hired Brandenburg Industrial Service Company, of Bethlehem, Pennsylvania, the nation's largest demolition contractor, to take apart the stadium. That included removal with conventional equipment of the ramps, portions of the seating area, the Phanavision scoreboard, roof, and otherwise stripping the Vet to prepare it for implosion. One of the more delicate jobs was the removal of the 4,000-pound Liberty Bell, which stood atop the center field roof.

The date of the implosion was scheduled for March 21. The Vet would meet the same kind of ending as two of its closely related cousins, Three Rivers Stadium in Pittsburgh and Cinergy (formerly Riverfront) Field in Cincinnati. The job would be done under the direction of a subcontractor, Demolition Dynamics.

"When they told me they were blowing up the Vet," said Glenn Wilson, "I was very moved. The other ballparks I played in—Detroit, Seattle, Houston, Pittsburgh—are all gone. Now the Vet. Although I only played there for four years, to me it was my home. The most disappointing thing in my career was when I was traded. I guess now, though, I can really feel that baseball for me is finally over because my home stadium is not going to be there anymore."

Leading up to the implosion, there were numerous issues about the effects it would have. Particularly concerned were residents of nearby homes.

Dust, debris, rats, cracked roads, sidewalks and sewer pipes, and damage to their properties were especially worrisome. They were assured that their concerns were being addressed, that sewers were being cleared of rats, and that they would be reimbursed for any damage to their homes. The city had taken out a $61 million insurance policy.

In preparation for the implosion, it was announced that the area surrounding the Vet as well as parts of I-95 and the Schuylkill Expressway that ran past the stadium would be closed, as would the Walt Whitman Bridge and the Broad Street subway. Airplanes would be diverted away from the Vet. Some neighboring residents would be taken to a nearby hotel during the explosion. And all surrounding streets would be closed two hours before the event.

Over a six-week period, Demolition Dynamics had drilled 2,800 holes in the Vet's 103 columns (one column had previously been removed). Shortly before March 21, some 3,000 pounds of dynamite were packed into those holes, all connected by a detonation cord 22,000 linear-feet long. All that was left was the actual implosion itself.

As dawn arrived on the final day, an estimated crowd of 8,000 crammed into streets and on rooftops several blocks from the Vet. Some lined the banks of the Delaware River in New Jersey. An additional 2,500 VIPs and 248 representatives of the media got spots closest to the stadium along Packer Avenue. And nearby hotels, their rates inflated for the day, were filled to capacity.

A few current Phillies awoke early in Clearwater to watch the implosion on television. Meanwhile, more fans kept showing up at the Vet. At one point, some one thousand of them broke through barriers and with a loud cheer stormed across I-76, only to be chased back to the other side by Philadelphia police.

The Phillies arranged the final events, and numerous club officials and several former players attended. Conversely, almost nobody came from the Eagles. "We're not paying tribute to the Vet," an Eagles official had said. "We hate the place."

It was in part a festive, upbeat atmosphere and in part a somber one. To their credit, the Phillies rejected the suggestion that someone play taps as the final moment came.

"I think the Vet is still a beautiful stadium," said Larry Christenson. "People are looking at it and saying what a shame it has to come down. It still works."

"I loved the Vet," added Mitch Williams. "It was a place that had the good, the bad, and the ugly, but it was a great place to play ball. Only in Philadelphia could there be a place like this."

A Mummers band played. People sipped beverages stronger than coffee. The Phillie Phanatic cavorted. And master of ceremonies Dan Baker, dressed in a tuxedo, led the crowd through a pre-implosion program that included a trivia quiz and introduction of dignitaries in attendance.

One, Bill Giles, had come from Florida to watch the final moments of the stadium where he had been such a major figure. "They asked me if I wanted to push the button that would blow up the place," he said. "I said, no, the place has too many memories.

"The first 20 years," Giles continued, "I would get goose bumps driving to work and walking into the place. It was a great place. Then we started to study the economics; our lease versus other team's leases. I saw how we weren't going to compete financially unless we did something about changing our lease. All we wanted to do was change the revenue and expenses so we could put a competitive team on the field. We talked a lot about changing the Vet, building suites, a new club level. I didn't think at the time that we needed a new ballpark.

"Then in 1992 I went down to Camden Yards in Baltimore, and saw how great it was compared to the Vet. It changed my whole philosophy. I said, it's stupid to try to make a deal with the city when in the long term we need a real ballpark. We don't need a two-team facility."

At 6:59:50 A.M., 50 seconds after a "final warning siren" was given, Mayor John Street began a countdown. Luzinski, producing a "final Bull blast," pushed an imaginary plunger that ignited the explosion. The first stick of dynamite went off at 7 A.M.

As dynamite charges exploded clockwise around its perimeter, the shell of what was once Veterans Stadium dropped inward like a stack of dominoes. While an elevator column lingered briefly before falling, the sections fell one at a time until the whole stadium had crashed to the ground. As it did, pigeons flew from the remains of the structure. It took just 62 seconds for the entire stadium to fall.

Surprisingly, there was not a thunderous noise. And the ground had no strong vibrations. A huge cloud of dust wafted from the implosion and— in a final touch of irony—blew across the new Citizens Park, almost as though the old stadium was symbolically leaving some of itself on its fancy new replacement.

While the Vet fell, some cheered, perhaps dazzled by the spectacle and by the precision of the technology that had just taken place. Some watched the event in silence. Many had tears streaming down their faces. Only the hardest of hearts watched the implosion without some emotion.

Joel Ralph, a man who had spent so much time at the Vet, had a special reason to feel sorrow. The implosion occurred on his birthday. "It was not a very good birthday present," he said. "I loved that building. It was my life. It was a great building, and it served the citizens well."

"There's a lot of my life in there," Luzinski said. "A lot of great players played there, and a lot of great games were held there."

Public relations director Larry Shenk, one of only a handful of Phillies people who worked at the Vet throughout the life of the stadium, said he was "in awe" of the implosion. "Everything the demolition company said would happen, happened just as they described it," he said. "I was a little emotional watching it come down—we're losing a good friend—but it didn't really hit me until later that night."

Mayor Street joined in the salute to the old stadium while pointing out that it was time to move on and "embrace" the new ballpark. "When it was built, the Vet was a symbol of some real progress in this city," he said. "And we will always respect the memories and the great things that happened there.

"As I was riding to the stadium today," Street added, "I was thinking about two things. One was that technology is a wonderful thing. In the past, it would've taken forever to remove the Vet. And I was thinking about Tug McGraw and the role he played in elevating the Phillies and sports in this city. I rode all the way down here thinking about Tug and the excitement and enthusiasm he had for the game. This is a bit of a tribute to that enthusiasm and that excitement."

After the implosion, the crowd seemed reluctant to leave. Many lingered, taking a final look at the stadium's remains as they lay in a massive pile of broken concrete and twisted steel. That night, the media circus that had been so conspicuous in the morning materialized in the form of repeated recaps of the implosion, on both local and network television. One radio station had even provided live coverage of the event. Newspapers the next day were filled with stories and pictures.

"It was sad to see it go down," said Rosemary Ferraro, for many years an assistant gate director at the Vet. She, too, had met her husband there and had made many other lasting friendships. She stood during the implosion with a woman whose wedding reception had been held at the stadium.

Workers were quickly back on the job. As city workers cleaned streets with flusher trucks and power washers, construction personnel were stationed among the remains of the Vet to begin the long process of separating the concrete from metal material, which was sent to a facility for recycling.

The day after the implosion, several thousand people flocked to the area to take pictures and to pan for souvenir pieces of the stadium, much of it through 15 holes cut in the fences surrounding the rubble. Many came away with chunks of concrete or whatever else they could find that would in years to come remind them of the old ballpark. Within a few days, some of it showed up for sale on the Internet. For weeks thereafter, hundreds more flocked to the rubble in search of anything they could keep or sell.

The tons of concrete were eventually crushed into 70,000 cubic yards that were used as part of the 400,000 cubic yards needed to fill the hole where the Vet once stood and where parking for 5,500 cars would eventually take its place.

A few parts of the Vet were moved to Citizens Park. Among them, were some office furniture and pieces of turf, which would be used as the floor in the new ballpark's indoor batting cages.

The Phillies painted a field on the parking lot. It was a replica of the field once used at a storied ballpark named Veterans Stadium.

Veterans Stadium, 1971–2004. Truly a field of memories.

ONE LAST LOOK

*First, lasts, and a few other
facts and figures*

Because records play an important role in the life of any ballpark, this final chapter deals with significant facts and figures connected with Veterans Stadium. Particular attention is given to the Phillies as the primary resident.

Phillies Firsts

Game – Phillies 4, Montreal Expos 1
Date – April 10, 1971
Winning pitcher – Jim Bunning, Phillies
Losing pitcher – Bill Stoneman, Expos
Save – Joe Hoerner, Phillies
Batter – Boots Day, Expos
Hit – Larry Bowa, Phillies
Run – Ron Hunt, Expos
Double – Ron Hunt, Expos

Triple – Larry Bowa, Phillies
Home run – Don Money, Phillies
RBI – Bob Bailey, Expos
Walk – Ron Hunt, Expos
Stolen base – Ron Hunt, Expos
Putout – Deron Johnson, Phillies
Assist – Jim Bunning, Phillies
Error – Mack Jones, Expos
Home plate umpire – Shag Crawford

Above: Fans gather for a last look at the Vet moments before demolition on March 21, 2004.

Phillies Lasts

Game – Atlanta Braves 5, Phillies 2
Date – September 28, 2003
Winning pitcher – Greg Maddux, Braves
Losing pitcher – Kevin Millwood, Phillies
Save – Jason Marquis, Braves
Batter – Chase Utley, Phillies
Hit – Pat Burrell, Phillies
Run – Chipper Jones. Braves
Double – Jason Michaels, Phillies

Triple – Jesse Garcia, Braves
Home run – Jim Thome, Phillies
RBI – Robert Fick, Braves
Walk – Chase Utley, Phillies
Stolen base – Marlon Byrd, Phillies
Putout – Robert Fick, Braves
Assist – Marcus Giles, Braves
Error – Mike Lieberthal, Phillies
Home plate umpire – Jerry Crawford

Phillies Records at the Vet

Games	Mike Schmidt	1,202
At-bats	Mike Schmidt	4,020
Runs	Mike Schmidt	784
Hits	Mike Schmidt	1,094
Doubles	Mike Schmidt	220
Triples	Larry Bowa	49
Home runs	Mike Schmidt	265
RBI	Mike Schmidt	825
Stolen bases	Larry Bowa	149
Highest batting average (min. 200 AB)	Lonnie Smith	.368
Games pitched	Steve Carlton	242
Innings pitched	Steve Carlton	1,887.2
Strikeouts	Steve Carlton	1,614
Wins	Steve Carlton	138
Losses	Steve Carlton	62
Saves	Jose Mesa	58
Lowest ERA (min. 200 IP)	Tug McGraw	2.73

Phillies Opponents' Records at the Vet

Games	Andre Dawson	146
At-bats	Andre Dawson	547
Runs	Barry Bonds	87
Hits	Andre Dawson	148
Doubles	Ted Simmons	32
Triples	Tim Raines	7
Home runs	Barry Bonds	27
RBI	Barry Bonds	80
Stolen bases	Vince Coleman	42
Highest batting average (min. 50 AB)	Manny Mota	.415
Games pitched	John Franco	48
Innings pitched	Bob Forsch	198
Strikeouts	Greg Maddux	149
Wins	Bob Forsch	15
Losses	Jerry Reuss	12
Saves	John Franco	22
Lowest ERA (min. 25 IP)	Gene Garber	0.75

First Game at Veterans Stadium

Montreal	AB	R	H	RBI
Day, cf	4	0	0	0
Raymond, p	0	0	0	0
Reed, p	0	0	0	0
Brand, ph	1	0	0	0
Hunt, 2b	3	1	1	0
Staub, rf	4	0	1	0
Bailey, 3b	4	0	1	1
Fairly, lf	2	0	1	0
Jones, lf	4	0	0	0
Bateman, c	4	0	2	0
Wine, ss	1	0	0	0
Fairey, ph	1	0	0	0
Laboy, ph	1	0	0	0
Stoneman, p	2	0	0	0
O'Donoghue, p	0	0	0	0
Marshall, p	0	0	0	0
Sutherland, ph	0	0	0	0
Totals	31	1	6	1

Phillies	AB	R	H	RBI
Bowa, ss	4	1	2	0
Money, 3b	3	1	1	2
Montanez, cf	2	1	1	0
Johnson, 1b	3	1	1	0
Briggs, lf	3	0	0	0
Freed, rf	3	0	2	1
McCarver, c	3	0	1	1
Doyle, 2b	2	0	0	0
Taylor, ph-2b	2	0	0	0
Bunning, p	2	0	0	0
Hoerner, p	0	0	0	0
Totals	27	4	8	4

```
Montreal    0 0 0 0 0 1 0 0 0 - 1
Phillies    0 0 0 0 0 3 1 0 x - 4
```

Errors: Jones, Money. Double plays: Bunning, Bowa, and Johnson; Wine and Fairly. Left on base: Montreal 10, Phillies 7. Two-base hits: Hunt, Bailey. Three-base hit: Bowa. Home run: Money. Stolen bases: Hunt, Bowa. Sacrifice: Bunning. Sacrifice flies: McCarver, Money.

	IP	H	R	ER	BB	SO
Stoneman (L, 0–1)	5	7	3	3	3	1
O'Donoghue	1/3	0	0	0	0	0
Marshall	1/3	0	0	0	0	0
Raymond	2/3	1	1	1	2	1
Reed	$1\frac{1}{3}$	0	0	0	0	1
Bunning (W, 1–0)	$7\frac{1}{3}$	6	1	1	3	4
Hoerner	$1\frac{1}{3}$	0	0	0	1	2

Save: Hoerner (1). Hit by pitch: by Bunning (Hunt). Time: 2:43. Attendance: 55,352.

Last Game at Veterans Stadium

Atlanta	AB	R	H	RBI
Furcal, ss	4	0	0	1
Giles, 2b	4	0	0	0
Sheffield, rf	5	0	2	1
Marquis, p	0	0	0	0
C. Jones, lf	3	2	2	0
Langerhans, lf-cf	2	0	0	0
A. Jones, cf	3	0	2	0
Bragg, pr-cf-lf-rf	1	0	0	0
Lopez, c	4	1	2	0
Wright, p	0	0	0	0
Hernandez, p	0	0	0	0
Hessman, lf	0	0	0	0
Fick, 1b	3	1	2	2
DeRosa, 3b	1	0	1	0
Garcia, ph-3b	3	1	1	1
Maddux, p	2	0	0	0
Cunnane, p	0	0	0	0
Estrada, c	1	0	1	0
Totals	36	5	13	5

Phillies	AB	R	H	RBI
Byrd, cf	4	2	2	0
Rollins, ss	4	0	0	0
Abreu, rf	2	0	1	2
Michaels, rf	2	0	1	0
Thome, 1b	4	0	0	0
Punto, 3b	0	0	0	0
Lieberthal, c	4	0	1	0
Burrell, lf	4	0	2	0
Utley, 2b	3	0	0	0
Perez, 3b-1b	3	0	1	0
Millwood, p	1	0	0	0
Wendell, p	0	0	0	0

Phillies	AB	R	H	RBI
Stinnett, ph	1	0	0	0
Hancock, p	0	0	0	0
Ledee, ph	1	0	0	0
Williams, p	0	0	0	0
Plesac, p	0	0	0	0
Totals	33	2	8	2

```
Atlanta     0 1 0 3 1 0 0 0 0 - 5
Phillies    1 0 1 0 0 0 0 0 0 - 2
```

Error: Lieberthal. Double play: Atlanta 1. Left on base: Atlanta 8, Phillies 5. Two-base hits: Burrell, Lopez, C. Jones, Fick, Lieberthal, Michaels. Stolen base: Byrd. Sacrifice flies: Fick, Furcal.

	IP	H	R	ER	BB	SO
Maddux (W, 16–11)	5	4	2	2	0	2
Cunnane	1	0	0	0	0	1
Wright	1	2	0	0	1	1
Hernandez	1	1	0	0	0	0
Marquis (S)	1	1	0	0	0	0
Millwood (L, 14–12)	4	11	5	5	1	3
Wendell	1	1	0	0	0	1
Hancock	2	0	0	0	0	3
Williams	$1^2/_3$	1	0	0	0	0
Plesac	1/3	0	0	0	0	1

Millwood pitched to two batters in the fifth. Wild pitches: Maddux, Wright. Time: 2:51. Attendance: 58,554.

Eagles' First Game
September 26, 1971—lost 7–42 to Dallas

Eagles' Last Game
January 19, 2003—lost 10–27 to Tampa Bay (NFC championship)

Temple's First Game
October 26, 1974—won 21–17 over Delaware

Temple's Last Game
November 23, 2002—lost 14–36 to Boston College

Army-Navy Scores

November 29, 1980 – Navy 33, Army 6
November 28, 1981 – Navy 3, Army 3
December 4, 1982 – Navy 24, Army 7
December 1, 1984 – Army 28, Navy 11
December 7, 1985 – Navy 17, Army 7
December 6, 1986 – Army 27, Navy 7
December 5, 1987 – Army 17, Navy 3
December 2, 1988 – Army 20, Navy 15
December 8, 1990 – Army 30, Navy 20
December 7, 1991 – Navy 24, Army 3
December 5, 1992 – Army 25, Navy 24
December 3, 1994 – Army 22, Navy 20
December 2, 1995 – Army 14, Navy 13
December 7, 1996 – Army 28, Navy 24
December 5, 1998 – Army 34, Navy 30
December 4, 1999 – Navy 19, Army 9
December 1, 2001 – Army 26, Navy 17

Team Records

Phillies – 1,414–1,199–3
Eagles – 144–111–2

Temple – 44–63
Army (vs. Navy) – 11–5–1

Phillies Managers at the Vet

Frank Lucchesi, 1971–72
Paul Owens, 1972, 1983–84
Danny Ozark, 1973–79
Dallas Green, 1979–81
Pat Corrales, 1982–83
John Felske, 1985–87

Lee Elia, 1987–88
John Vukovich, 1988
Nick Leyva, 1989–91
Jim Fregosi, 1991–96
Terry Francona, 1997–2000
Larry Bowa, 2001–03

Eagles Coaches at the Vet

Jerry Williams, 1971
Ed Khayat, 1971–72
Mike McCormack, 1973–75
Dick Vermeil, 1976–82
Marion Campbell, 1983–85

Fred Bruney, 1985
Buddy Ryan, 1986–90
Rich Kotite, 1991–94
Ray Rhodes, 1995–98
Andy Reid, 1999–2002

Temple Coaches at the Vet

Wayne Hardin, 1971–82
Bruce Arians, 1983–88
Jerry Berndt, 1989–92

Ron Dickerson, 1993–97
Bobby Wallace, 1998–2002

Phillies Annual Vet Attendance

1971 – 1,511,233	1982 – 2,376,394	1993 – 3,137,674
1972 – 1,343,329	1983 – 2,128,932	1994 – 2,290,971
1973 – 1,475,934	1984 – 2,062,696	1995 – 2,043,588
1974 – 1,808,648	1985 – 1,830,350	1996 – 1,801,677
1975 – 1,909,233	1986 – 1,933,355	1997 – 1,490,638
1976 – 2,480,150	1987 – 2,100,110	1998 – 1,715,702
1977 – 2,700,070	1988 – 1,990,041	1999 – 1,825,337
1978 – 2,583,389	1989 – 1,861,985	2000 – 1,612,769
1979 – 2,775,011	1990 – 1,992,484	2001 – 1,782,054
1980 – 2,651,650	1991 – 2,050,012	2002 – 1,618,230
1981 – 1,638,932	1992 – 1,927,448	2003 – 2,259,948

Phillies Attendance Records at the Vet
(regular season only)

Largest crowd	63,816	July 3, 1984 vs. Cincinnati
Smallest crowd	4,149	May 6, 1974 vs. San Diego
Largest home opener	60,985	April 9, 1993 vs. Chicago
Largest season's average	39,221	1993

Eagles Annual Vet Attendance

1971 – 457,506	1982 – 297,635	1993 – 488,744
1972 – 460,040	1983 – 445,682	1994 – 518,691
1973 – 414,441	1984 – 458,997	1995 – 576,187
1974 – 420,210	1985 – 486,019	1996 – 514,003
1975 – 428,631	1986 – 466,659	1997 – 535,783
1976 – 377,094	1987 – 429,950	1998 – 527,990
1977 – 368,747	1988 – 510,776	1999 – 519,835
1978 – 501,956	1989 – 552,421	2000 – 589,344
1979 – 550,611	1990 – 585,645	2001 – 593,040
1980 – 696,455	1991 – 514,196	2002 – 656,700
1981 – 619,253	1992 – 521,369	

Eagles Attendance Records at the Vet
(regular season only)

| Largest crowd | 72,111 | November 1, 1981 vs. Dallas |
| Smallest crowd | 4,074 | October 4, 1987 vs. Chicago |

Name Index